My
iPad®

EIGHTH EDITION

Gary Rosenzweig

800 East 96th Street,
Indianapolis, Indiana 46240 USA

My iPad®, Eighth Edition

Copyright © 2016 by Pearson Education, Inc.

ISBN-13: 978-0-7897-5536-0
ISBN-10: 0-7897-5536-X

Costco Edition ISBN-13: 978-0-7897-5827-9
Costco Edition ISBN-10: 0-7897-5827-X

Library of Congress Control Number: 2015952356

Printed in the United States of America

First Printing: November 2015

Trademarks

Warning and Disclaimer

Special Sales

For information about buying this title in bulk quantities, or for special sales opportunities (which may include electronic versions; custom cover designs; and content particular to your business, training goals, marketing focus, or branding interests), please contact our corporate sales department at corpsales@pearsoned.com or (800) 382-3419.

For government sales inquiries, please contact governmentsales@pearsoned.com.

For questions about sales outside the U.S., please contact international@pearsoned.com.

Editor-in-Chief
Greg Wiegand

Senior Acquisitions Editor
Laura Norman

Development Editor
Todd Brakke

Marketing Manager
Dan Powell

Managing Editor
Kristy Hart

Senior Project Editor
Lori Lyons

Indexer
Erika Millen

Proofreader
Kathy Ruiz

Technical Editor
Greg Kettell

Cover Designer
Mark Shirar

Compositor
Bronkella Publishing

Graphics Technician
Tammy Graham

Manufacturing Buyer
Dan Uhrig

Contents at a Glance

Table of Contents

2 Customizing Your iPad 37

3 Networking and Syncing 61

7 Surfing the Web   153

17 Games and Entertainment   399

About the Author

Gary Rosenzweig is an Internet entrepreneur, software developer, and technology writer. He runs CleverMedia, Inc., which produces websites, computer games, apps, and podcasts.

CleverMedia's largest site, MacMost.com, features video tutorials for Apple enthusiasts. It includes many videos on using Macs, iPhones, and iPads.

Gary has written numerous computer books, including *ActionScript 3.0 Game Programming University*, *MacMost.com Guide to Switching to the Mac*, and *Special Edition Using Director MX*.

Gary lives in Denver, Colorado, with his wife, Debby, and daughter, Luna. He has a computer science degree from Drexel University and a master's degree in journalism from the University of North Carolina at Chapel Hill.

Website: http://garyrosenzweig.com

Twitter: http://twitter.com/rosenz

More iPad Tutorials and Book Updates: http://macmost.com/ipadguide/

Acknowledgments

Thanks, as always, to my wife, Debby, and my daughter, Luna. Also thanks to the rest of my family: Jacqueline Rosenzweig, Jerry Rosenzweig, Larry Rosenzweig, Tara Rosenzweig, Rebecca Jacob, Barbara Shifrin, Richard Shifrin, Barbara H. Shifrin, Tage Thomsen, Anne Thomsen, Andrea Thomsen, and Sami Balestri.

Thanks to all the people who watch the show and participate at the MacMost website.

Thanks to everyone at Pearson Education who worked on this book: Laura Norman, Lori Lyons, Kristy Hart, Tricia Bronkella, Kathy Ruiz, Mark Shirar, and Greg Wiegand.

We Want to Hear from You!

As the reader of this book, *you* are our most important critic and commentator. We value your opinion and want to know what we're doing right, what we could do better, what areas you'd like to see us publish in, and any other words of wisdom you're willing to pass our way.

We welcome your comments. You can email or write to let us know what you did or didn't like about this book—as well as what we can do to make our books better.

Please note that we cannot help you with technical problems related to the topic of this book.

When you write, please be sure to include this book's title and author as well as your name and email address. We will carefully review your comments and share them with the author and editors who worked on the book.

Email: feedback@quepublishing.com

Mail: Que Publishing
          ATTN: Reader Feedback
          800 East 96th Street
          Indianapolis, IN 46240 USA

Reader Services

Visit our website and register this book at quepublishing.com/register for convenient access to any updates, downloads, or errata that might be available for this book.

Learn to tap, swipe, flick,
and pinch to use your iPad.

Learn to use the iPad's
physical switches.

In this chapter, you learn how to perform specific tasks on your iPad to become familiar with the interface.

Getting Started

Before you learn how to perform specific tasks on your iPad, you should become familiar with some basic concepts. If you have used an iPhone or iPod touch before, you already know how to use a touch screen device. But if the iPad is your first such device, you need to take time to become accustomed to interacting with it.

Generations of iPads

The first thing you may want to do is identify which iPad you have and what features are available to you. There have been many versions of the iPad since the original appeared in 2010.

Identifying Your iPad

The following table shows the major differences between these iPads:

iPad Comparison Chart

Model	Released	Display (inches)	Retina Display	Processor	Connector
iPad	4/2010	9.7		A4	30-pin
iPad 2	3/2011	9.7		A5	30-pin
3rd Gen	3/2012	9.7	✔	A5X	30-pin
4th Gen	11/2012	9.7	✔	A6X	Lightning
iPad mini 1st Gen	11/2012	7.9		A5	Lightning
iPad Air	11/2013	9.7	✔	A7	Lightning
iPad mini 2	11/2013	7.9	✔	A7	Lightning
iPad Air 2	10/2014	9.7	✔	A8X	Lightning
iPad mini 3	10/2014	9.7	✔	A7	Lightning
iPad mini 4	9/2015	7.9	✔	A8	Lightning
iPad Pro	11/2015	12.9	✔	A9X	Lightning

iPad displays vary not only in size, with the iPad mini models being smaller than the other iPads, but also in pixel density. The retina display has four pixels for every one of a regular display. While a regular display is 768x1024 pixels, a retina display is 1536x2048 pixels. This means photographs and text are crisper and clearer. In fact, you can't even distinguish the individual pixels with your eye unless you hold the iPad very close. The iPad Pro has even more pixels at 2048x2732.

Another difference between iPad models is the camera. The original iPad had no camera at all. The 2nd and 3rd generations had cameras, but the more recent iPads also have a rear-facing camera that is capable of much higher resolution for both still photos and video.

Each iPad has also become a little more powerful with a faster processor at its heart. Other parts have picked up speed and power as well, processing graphics and accessing memory faster. Early models aren't powerful enough to use features like voice dictation and advanced 3D game graphics.

>>>*Go Further*

THE NEED FOR SPEED

With each generation of iPad, the processor changes. Each iPad is faster and more powerful than its predecessor. It is hard to quantify, but by some metrics the iPad Pro has more processing power than many desktop computers. This also helps apps to run smoother, games to display faster with more detailed graphics, and makes performing taxing tasks like editing video or flipping through hundreds of high-resolution photos work faster.

iOS 9

The primary piece of software on the iPad is the operating system, known as iOS. This is what you see when you flip through the screens of icons on your iPad and access default apps such as Mail, Safari, Photos, and iTunes.

This book covers iOS 9, the version released in September 2015. There have been eight generations of the software that runs iPhones and iPads. The original iPhone OS was developed for the first iPhone. The third version, iOS 3, worked on iPhones and the iPad. This latest version, iOS 9, works on the iPad 2 and newer. If you have an original iPad, you can only use up to iOS 5.

Many features and tasks in this book work the same in iOS 5, 6, 7, and 8, but you will not be able to use the latest features such as the new News app or Split View. To find out which version you are using and to learn how to update, you use the Settings app. In the Settings app, under the General settings, tap the About item. The About screen shows you information about your iPad, including its model number, serial number, version of iOS currently running, and available memory. You learn how to use the Settings app when you get to Chapter 2, "Customizing Your iPad."

Also keep in mind that the iPad 2, although it supports iOS 9, cannot use some of the features of iOS 9—most notably Siri. Some features, like Split View, only work on an iPad Air 2 or newer.

New to iOS 9

There are some changes in iOS 9 you will notice. For features that have changed significantly, or are completely new, we have added an indicator to the text and table of contents to help you easily locate them. When you see **New!**, be sure to check out those tasks to quickly get up to speed on what's new in iOS 9.

The iPad Buttons and Switches

The iPad features a Home button, a Wake/Sleep button, a volume control, and side switch.

The Home Button

The Home button is probably the most important physical control on the iPad and the one that you will use the most often. Pressing the Home button returns you to the Home screen of the iPad when you are inside an application, such as Safari or Mail, and you want to get back to your Home screen to launch another app. You can also double press the Home button to switch between apps. We'll look at this in the section titled "Viewing Currently Running Apps" in Chapter 15, "The World of Apps."

Wake/sleep button

Side switch (older models)

Volume control

Home button

Where's the Quit Button?

Few, if any, apps on the iPad have a way to quit. Instead, think of the Home button as the Quit button. It hides the current app and returns you to your Home screen. The app is actually still running, but hidden, in the background. It is usually unnecessary to truly "quit" an app. But if you really want to completely quit an app, see "Quitting Apps" in Chapter 15.

The Wake/Sleep Button

The primary function of the Wake/Sleep button (sometimes called the On/Off or Power button) at the top of your iPad is to quickly put it to sleep. Sleeping is different than shutting down. When your iPad is in sleep mode, you can instantly wake it to use it. You can wake up from sleep by pressing the Wake/Sleep button again or pressing the Home button.

Peek a Boo!
If you are using the Apple iPad Smart Cover, Smart Case, or the iPad Pro Smart Keyboard (see Chapter 18, "iPad Accessories"), your iPad will go to sleep when you close it and wake up when you open it, as long as you use the default settings. Many third-party cases and covers also do this.

The Wake/Sleep button can also be used to shut down your iPad, which you might want to do if you leave your iPad for a long time and want to preserve the battery life. Press and hold the Wake/Sleep button for a few seconds, and the iPad begins to shut down and turn off. Confirm your decision to shut down your iPad using the Slide to Power Off button on the screen.

To start up your iPad, press and hold the Wake/Sleep button for a few seconds until you see the Apple logo appear on the screen.

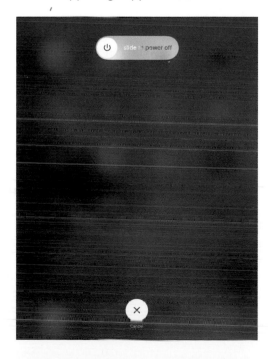

When Should I Turn Off My iPad?

It is normal to never turn off your iPad. In sleep mode, with the screen off, it uses little power. If you plug it in to power at night or during longer periods when you aren't carrying it with you, you don't need to ever shut it down.

The Volume Control

The volume control on the side of your iPad is actually two buttons: one to turn the volume up, and the other to turn it down.

Your iPad keeps two separate volume settings in memory: one for headphones and one for the internal speakers. If you turn down the volume when using headphones and then unplug the headphones, the volume changes to reflect the last settings used when the headphones were not plugged in, and vice versa. A bell icon and a series of rectangles appear on the screen to indicate the current level of volume.

The Side Switch

The side switch is a feature on older iPads. The switch can do one of two things: It can be set as a mute switch or an orientation lock. You can decide which function this button performs in your iPad's settings. See "Setting Side Switch Functionality" in Chapter 2.

If you choose to use this switch as a mute switch, it will mute all sound if switched to the off position. You will see a speaker icon appear briefly in the middle of the screen when you do this. A line through the icon means you just muted the sound; otherwise, you just unmuted your iPad. By default, the iPad comes with the switch configured to mute.

If you choose to use this switch as an orientation lock, it will do something else entirely. Your iPad has two primary screen modes: vertical and horizontal. You can use almost every default app in either orientation. For example, if you find that a web page is too wide to fit on the screen in vertical orientation, you can turn the iPad sideways and the view changes to a horizontal orientation.

When you don't want your iPad to react to its orientation, slide the iPad side switch so that you can see the orange dot, which prevents the orientation from changing. When you need to unlock it, just slide the lock off.

This comes in handy in many situations. For instance, if you are reading an eBook in bed or on a sofa while lying on your side, then you may want vertical orientation even though the iPad is lying sideways.

Newer model iPads don't have a side switch. The controls for orientation lock and mute appear in the Control Center, which we look at in the later task "Open Control Center."

Orientation and Movement

In addition to the physical switches you see on your iPad, the entire iPad is a physical control.

Your iPad knows which way it is oriented, and it knows if it is being moved. The simplest indication of this is that it knows whether you hold it vertically with the Home button at the bottom or horizontally with the Home button to one of the sides. Some apps, especially games, use the screen orientation of the iPad to guide screen elements and views.

Shake It Up!

One interesting physical gesture you might perform is the "shake." Because your iPad can sense movement, it can sense when you shake it. Many apps take advantage of this feature and use it to set off an action, such as shuffling songs in the Music app, erasing a drawing canvas, or as an "undo" function.

Screen Gestures

Who knew just a few years ago that we'd be controlling computing devices with taps, pinches, and flicks rather than drags, key presses, and clicks? Multi-touch devices such as the iPhone, iPod Touch, and the iPad have added a new vocabulary to human-computer interaction.

Tapping and Touching

Since there is no mouse, a touch screen has no cursor. When your finger is not on the screen, there is no arrow pointing to anything.

A single, quick touch on the screen is usually called a "tap" or a "touch." You usually tap an object on the screen to perform an action.

Occasionally you need to double-tap—two quick taps in the same location. For instance, double-tapping an image on a web page zooms in to the image. Another double-tap zooms back out.

Pinching

The screen on the iPad is a multitouch screen, which means it can detect more than one touch at the same time. This capability is used with the pinch gesture.

A pinch (or a pinch in) is when you touch the screen with both your thumb and index finger and move them toward each other in a pinching motion. You can also pinch in reverse, which is sometimes called an "unpinch" or "pinch out."

An example of when you would use a pinch/unpinch gesture would be to zoom in and out on a web page or photograph.

Dragging and Flicking

If you touch the screen and hold your finger down, you can drag it in any direction along the screen. This action often has the effect of moving the content on the screen.

For instance, if you are viewing a long web page and drag up or down, the page will scroll. Sometimes an app will let you drag content left and right as well.

What if you have a long web page or a list of items inside an app? Instead of dragging the length of the screen, lifting your finger up, and moving it to the bottom to drag again, you can "flick." Flicking is like dragging, but you move quickly and lift your finger off the screen at the last moment so that the content continues to scroll after you have lifted your finger. You can wait for it to stop scrolling or touch the screen to make it stop.

Jump Up
In certain apps, such as Settings, Mail, and Safari, you can quickly jump back to the top of a screen by tapping near where the time is shown at the top-middle of the screen.

Pull Down and Release to Update

A common gesture is to tap in a list of items, drag down, and release. For instance, you would do this in Mail to get new messages. With your email inbox on the left, tap and drag down in the list. A blank space appears above the first message, and a circle of lines appears to let you know more mail is being downloaded.

Many Apple and third-party apps use this gesture to let you signal that you want to update the list of items. So if you don't see an obvious "update now" button, try this gesture.

Four-Finger Gestures

You can perform one of three special functions by using four or five fingers at a time on the screen. If you put four or five fingers on the screen and pinch them all together, you will be taken out of your current app and back to the Home screen, similar to just pressing the Home button.

You can swipe left or right using four or more fingers to quickly page between running apps without going to the Home screen first. Swiping up with four fingers will bring you to the multitask switcher. See "Viewing Currently Running Apps" in Chapter 15.

Learning Your Way Around

When you pick up your iPad and touch either the Wake/Sleep button or the Home button to activate the screen, you see what is called the Lock Screen. From there, you would unlock your iPad and return to the last screen you were using—either the Home screen or an app's screen.

Let's look at the different types of screens you see every day on your iPad, and how to navigate between them,

The Lock Screen

The default state of your iPad when you are not using it is the lock screen. This is just your background wallpaper with the time at the top and the words Slide to Unlock at the bottom.

You can see the date under the time. The battery status is at the top right, and you can also see it under the time, alternating with the date, if the iPad is currently charging. There is also a small button at the bottom right for quick access to the camera app. The top and bottom of the screen show short bars to allow you to access the Notifications Center at the top and the Control Center at the bottom.

We look at customizing the lock screen in Chapter 2, as well as the Control Center and the Notifications Center later in this chapter.

By default, you see the lock screen when you wake up your iPad. Sliding your finger from left to right near the words Slide to Unlock takes you to the Home screen or to whichever app you were using when you put the iPad to sleep.

The Home Screen

Think of the Home screen as a single screen but with multiple pages that each features different app icons. At the bottom of the Home screen are app icons that do not change from page to page.

The number of pages on your Home screen depends on how many apps you have. The number of pages you have is indicated by the white dots near the bottom of the screen, just above the bottom icons. The brightest dot repre sents the page you are currently viewing. You can move between pages on your Home screen by dragging or flicking left or right.

We'll look at adding more apps to your iPad in the tasks found in Chapter 15.

An App Screen

When you tap on an app icon on the Home screen, you run that app just like you would run an application on your computer. The app takes over the entire screen.

At this point, your screen can look like anything. If you run Safari, for instance, a web page displays. If you run Mail, you see a list of your new email or a single incoming email message.

If you are on your Home screen looking at page one of your app icons, you can drag from the center of the screen downward to bring up a Spotlight Search field at the top and a keyboard at the bottom. This allows you to search your iPad for apps, contacts, events, and other information.

Home Screen Searching

You can type in anything to search for a contact, app, email message, photo, and so on. You don't have to define what type of thing you want to search for.

1. From the Home screen, tap in the center of the screen and drag down. Don't start at the very top of the screen, as that will bring up Notifications Center instead. This can be a bit tricky; so if you do accidentally open Notification Center, just swipe it back up out of the way and try again.

If you've been using your iPad for a while and have Siri enabled, you will see suggestions for apps, contacts, and other content on this screen even before you type a search term.

2. Type a search term using the on-screen keyboard.

3. You see a list of items on your iPad that match the search term. The search results show apps, calendar events, email messages, reminders, or even web search results.

4. Tap the Search button on the keyboard to dismiss the keyboard and complete the search.

5. Tap the X in the search field to clear the search and start again.

6. Tap any of the items to go to the appropriate app and view the content.

Virtual Buttons and Switches

Several interface elements are more complex than a simple button. In typical Apple style, these elements are often self-explanatory, but if you have never used an iPad before, you might find some that give you pause.

Switches

A switch is a simple button that allows you to turn something on or off. You need to only tap the switch to change it—no need to slide it. The background of a switch turns green when it is "on."

For example, two switches indicate whether the iCloud Music Library and Sound Check features of the Music app are on or off. Tapping on either switch changes the position of the switch.

Toolbars

Some apps have a set of controls in a toolbar at the top of the screen. Buttons shown there are sometimes nothing more than a word or two that you can tap on to trigger an action. The toolbar might disappear or the buttons might vary depending on the mode of the app. If a toolbar disappears, a tap on the screen brings it up again.

An example of a toolbar is in the iTunes app. When you are viewing the music section of the iTunes store, it has a button to access Genres, a title in the middle, a button that brings up more controls, and a search field. But, this toolbar can change. For instance, if you switch from viewing the Music screen to viewing Top Charts, you get a set of buttons that let you switch between Music, Movies, TV, or Audiobook charts.

Menus

Often tapping a single button in a toolbar brings up more buttons or a list of choices, which are like menus on your computer. The choices in the list are usually related. For example, a button in Safari gives you many different ways to share a web page.

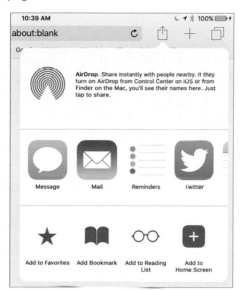

Tab Bars

Sometimes you see a row of buttons at the bottom of the screen that function similarly to toolbars, but each button represents a different mode for the app. For instance, at the bottom of the iTunes app, you see a Tab bar that you use to switch between various screens: Music, Movies, TV Shows, Audiobooks, Top Charts, Genius, and Purchased.

Entering Text

Entering text on your iPad means interacting with an on-screen keyboard or speaking to your iPad. Even if you are not a writer, you'll need to do this quite often to enter addresses in the web browser, or to compose messages and emails.

Using the On-Screen Keyboard

The on-screen element you might interact with the most is the keyboard. It pops up from the bottom of the screen automatically whenever you are doing something that requires entering some text.

Keyboard Modes

An on-screen keyboard can have many different modes. With the default keyboard, the first mode shows you letters and a few punctuation marks. There are two shift keys that enable you to enter uppercase letters. You also have a Backspace key and a Return key.

The standard on-screen keyboard

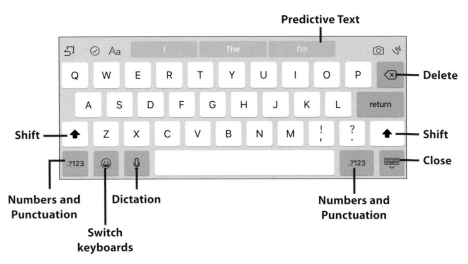

Is There a Quicker Way to Capitalize?

To capitalize a word, you tap the Shift key, and then type the letter, right? You can. But a faster way is to tap the Shift key; then, without letting your finger off the screen, drag it to the letter and release in a single tap, slide, release action.

You can do the same with numbers and punctuation by tapping the .?123 key and sliding and releasing over the key you want.

To enter numbers and some other punctuation, tap the .?123 key to switch your keyboard into a second mode for numbers and punctuation. In addition, this mode includes an Undo key for undoing your recent typing. To return to the letters, just tap the ABC key.

Numbers and punctuation mode

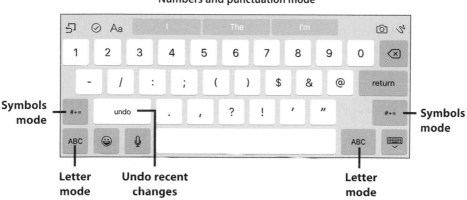

Symbols mode — Symbols mode

Letter mode   **Undo recent changes**   **Letter mode**

From the numbers and punctuation mode, you can tap the #+= key to go to a third keyboard mode that includes less frequently used punctuation and symbols. On this screen, the Undo button is now a Redo button that you can use in case you hit Undo by mistake.

Punctuation and symbols mode

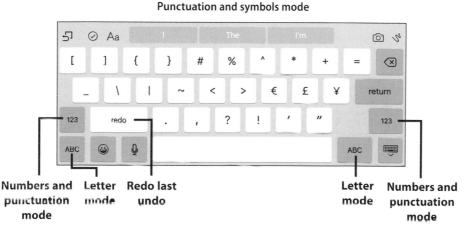

Numbers and punctuation mode   **Letter mode**   **Redo last undo**   **Letter mode**   **Numbers and punctuation mode**

There are other keyboard variations. For instance, in some cases if you type in a location that needs a web address, a keyboard that doesn't have a spacebar appears that instead has commonly used symbols such as colons, slashes, underscores, and even a .com button.

Not only are there other keyboard variations, there are completely different keyboards you can use. The iPad has many non-English language keyboards, and even a keyboard composed of little images (smiley faces and other pictures) called Emoji. Plus, you can add third-party keyboards from developers. We look at adding new keyboards in the task "Modifying Keyboard Settings" in Chapter 2.

Undocking and Splitting the Keyboard

You can also split the keyboard and/or move it up away from the bottom of the screen. This can make it easier for you to type if you are holding your iPad. Grasp it with your hands on either side of the iPad, and type with your thumbs.

1. To undock or split your keyboard, just tap and hold the keyboard button at the bottom-right corner.

2. Select Undock to simply move the keyboard up from the bottom of the screen and give you control of its vertical position.

3. Select Split to undock the keyboard, but also split it in half so you can reach all the keys from either side using your thumbs. You can also do this by tapping the keyboard button and dragging up.

Unpinch
Another way to activate the split keyboard, if it's undocked already, is to tap in the middle of the keyboard with two fingers and unpinch.

4. When the keyboard is undocked or split, you can tap and hold the keyboard button to drag it vertically to find the best position for you. If you tap and hold but do not drag, then you get the option to Merge, or Dock and Merge.

5. Tap Merge to merge the two halves of the keyboard back into one. You can also do this by tapping in the middle of the keyboard and pinching inward.

6. Tap Dock and Merge to merge the halves, and also lock the keyboard to the bottom of the screen. You can also do this by dragging the keyboard all the way back down to the bottom of the screen.

Using the Keyboard Shortcut Bar New!

Above the letter and number keys on the on-screen keyboard is the shortcut bar. This narrow horizontal strip can contain a variety of buttons and some predictive text shortcuts. We look at predictive text in the next section.

The buttons in the shortcut bar vary depending on which app you are using and even what type of text you are typing within the app.

If you don't see the shortcuts bar, but instead see a narrow line with a smaller white line in the center, then tap and drag that small white line up to reveal the shortcut bar.

So far, we've been looking at the keyboard as it appears in the Notes app. Let's take a tour of the shortcut bar as it appears when typing in Notes.

1. Tapping this button brings up undo and paste from the clipboard buttons. If you have text selected, it instead brings up cut, copy, and paste buttons.

2. This undoes the last insertion or edit.

3. This redoes the last undo.

4. You can paste text you may have previously copied into the clipboard. This is similar to using Command or Control+v on a desktop computer.

5. In Notes, you get a button to begin writing a checklist.

6. You can also choose from a variety of other text styles such as Title, Heading, Body, and so on.

7. You can tap this button to take a picture with your iPad's camera or insert a photo from your library.

8. Notes includes a special sketch function that lets you add a drawing to your note. We take a closer look at that in Chapter 6, "Organizing Your Life."

>>>*Go Further*

MORE KEYBOARD VARIATIONS

If you bring up the on-screen keyboard in the Mail app while composing a message, you get a slightly different set of buttons. Instead of the Undo, Redo, and Paste buttons being combined into one button on the left, you get each as its own button. In addition, you get a style button on the right that lets you choose bold, italic, or underline and an attach button that lets you choose a file to attach to your message.

Another example of a shortcut bar is the one you get when typing a URL or search term in the address field in the Safari web browser. Here, you only get Cut, Copy, and Paste buttons.

Using Predictive Text

You may have noticed that while you are typing, three buttons with words in them appear on top of the keyboard in the shortcut bar. This is the predictive text feature of the keyboard, also sometimes referred to by Apple as QuickType.

While typing, these three buttons enable you to complete a word with just one tap. For instance, you may be typing the word "Clever." As you type, the three buttons change to represent what comes closest to the letters you have typed so far. When you have typed "Cle," you might get "Clearer" and "Clear" as suggestions. But when you get to "Cleve," you will probably see "Clever" as one of the buttons. Simply tap that button and the word is completed without you needing to type "r." Notice that a space is automatically inserted as well. If the word you inserted was the end of your sentence, simply tap the space bar two times and a period is inserted and the app is ready to start a new sentence.

Predictive text is not just looking at the letters in the word you are typing, but also in the context of the whole sentence. For instance, If you type "pur," you might get "put" and "pure" as suggestions. But if you type "color pur," you will get "purple" as a suggestion.

Also note that the leftmost button of the three usually displays the text exactly as you have typed, but with quotes around it. This allows you to type a name or unusual word without having autocorrect get in the way.

Predictive text also looks at which app you are using and what the situation involves. For instance, it might suggest different words based on the person whom you are emailing, whether it is a work colleague or friend. When you respond to text messages in the Messages app, you might see "Yes" and "No" appear automatically when you are responding to a question. If someone messages you asking whether you want to meet at 6:00, 7:00, or 8:00, you will see those three options appear before you even type the first letter of your response.

Dictating Text

If you have a 3rd generation iPad or newer, any model of iPad mini, or iPad Pro, you can also dictate text using your voice rather than typing on the keyboard. Almost any time you see a keyboard, you should also see a small microphone button to the left of the spacebar. Tap that and you will be prompted to speak to your iPad. You will need to be connected to the Internet through a Wi-Fi or cellular connection for this to work.

1. Any time you see the default keyboard, there is a microphone button to the left of the spacebar. Tap it to begin dictating.

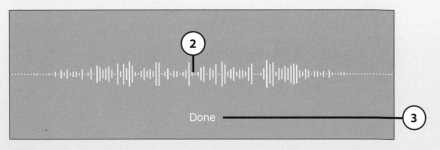

2. The keyboard is replaced with a waveform line that vibrates as you speak. Speak a few words or a sentence or two. As you speak, the text appears in your document or text field, though it may lag behind by a few seconds.

3. Tap Done when you are finished speaking. You can now edit the dictated text as needed before sending it.

Speak Clearly

Speak somewhat slowly and clearly, and in segments about the length of a sentence for best results. Of course, this feature isn't perfect. Pay careful attention to what is transcribed and correct any mistakes using the keyboard. Over time you will get better at speaking in a way that minimizes mistakes.

>>>Go Further

DICTATION TIPS

The dictation button appears any time a standard keyboard is present in any app. You can use it in Notes, Pages, or any writing app. You can use it in search fields and text entry fields on the web. You cannot use it when there are specialty keyboards, like the ones used to enter in email addresses, web URLs, and telephone numbers. So, for instance, you can use it in the Contacts app to speak a name or address, but not to enter an email address.

You need to be connected to the Internet for dictation to work. Your iPad sends the audio to Apple's servers, which handle the transcription and send the text back to your iPad. If you are not connected, it does not work.

Dictation works according to your language set in Settings, General, Language & Region. Not all languages are supported, but Apple is adding more all the time.

You can indicate the end of a sentence by saying "period" or "question mark." You can also speak other punctuation like "comma" or "quote."

You can speak commands like "new line," or "cap" to capitalize the next word. There is no official list of what the dictation feature supports, and since the transcription takes place on Apple's servers, they can change how it handles commands at any time.

Editing Text

Editing text has its challenges on a touch-screen device. Even though you can just touch any portion of your text on screen, your fingertip is too large for the level of precision you usually get with a computer mouse and cursor. To compensate, Apple developed an editing technique using a magnifying glass area of the screen that you get when you touch and hold over a piece of text.

For example, if you want to enter some text into a field in Safari, touch and hold on the field. A circle of magnification appears with a cursor placed at the exact location you selected.

EMAIL ADDRESS

YOUR NAME

e a ques

MESSAGE

Hello. I have a question.

SEND

When you find the exact location that you want to indicate, release your finger from the screen. A variety of options then display, depending on what kind of text you selected, such as Select, Select All, and Paste. You can ignore the options presented and start typing again to insert text at this location.

Copy and Paste

You can copy and paste text inside an app, and between apps, on your iPad. Here's how you might copy a piece of text from one place in a document to another in the Notes app.

1. Launch Notes. If you don't have any notes yet, create one by typing some sample text.

2. Touch and hold over a word in your note. The Select/Select All pop-up menu appears.

3. Choose Select.

4. Some text appears highlighted surrounded by dots connected to lines. Tap and drag the dots so the highlighted area is exactly what you want.

5. Tap Copy.

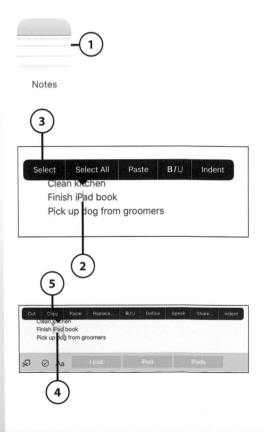

6. Alternatively, you can tap this icon on the keyboard shortcut bar to bring up Cut, Copy, and Paste icons, and then choose the Copy icon.

| Cut | Copy | Paste | Replace... | B I U | Define | Speak | Share... | Indent |

Clean kitchen
Finish iPad book
Pick up dog from groomers

6

Variations

In other apps, you may find the Cut, Copy, and Paste icons already visible on the keyboard shortcut bar; and in still other apps, you may not find this alternative at all.

8

7. Tap at the bottom of the document once to bring up a pop-up menu with the Paste command.

| Select | Select All | Paste | B I U | Indent |

Clean kitchen
Pick up dog from groomers

8. Tap Paste to insert the copied text. Alternatively, you can use the same method as in step 6 to paste.

7

>>>Go Further

YOUR KEYBOARD AS A TRACKPAD New!

A new feature in iOS 9 is the ability to more precisely position the text cursor in apps where you work with text such as Notes, Pages, Mail, and so on. With the on-screen keyboard visible, tap on it with two fingers and keep your fingers pressed to your iPad. Then drag your fingers around, and you can move the cursor as if you were using a trackpad or mouse on a computer. Notice that the keyboard letters disappear when you are doing this to indicate that you are in trackpad mode.

You can also tap quickly with two fingers to simply select the word that currently contains the text cursor. Two taps with two fingers selects the whole paragraph. Then you can tap and drag with two fingers to expand the selection.

This takes some getting used to. If you plan to use this feature, you may want to practice with a sample document first.

Talking to Your iPad with Siri

Siri is another way to communicate with your iPad. You can use your voice and speak commands to your iPad, and Siri will respond. It will either give you information or take action using one of the apps on the iPad.

To use Siri, you need to make sure you have Siri turned on in the Settings app under General settings. Then, you use the Home button to activate Siri. We look at how to work with the Settings app in Chapter 2.

Asking Siri Questions

1. Press and hold the Home button for about a second. The Siri interface pops up, showing a waveform line at the bottom of the screen that reacts to the sound of your voice.

   If you hesitate for a few seconds, you are shown a list of examples of things you can ask Siri.

2. Speak clearly at a normal pace and say, "What's the weather like today?" As you speak, the words appear near the top of the screen. When you stop speaking, Siri attempts to perform an action based on those words.

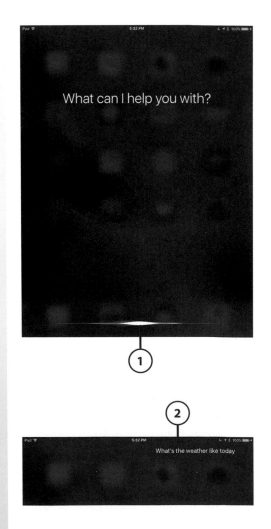

3. In this case, a short weather fore-
    cast appears.

4. Siri also responds with a state-
    ment and speaks it audibly.
    The text of the response typi-
    cally appears above the screen
    content.

5. You can ask Siri another question
    by tapping the microphone but-
    ton at the bottom of the screen.

6. If you wait for the list of sugges-
    tions to appear, you also see a
    question mark appear at the bot-
    tom left. Tap it to get a detailed
    list of apps that Siri can interact
    with, and things you can say for
    each app.

Siri Tips

To use Siri, you must have a connection to the Internet. It can be a Wi-Fi connection or a mobile connection. When you speak text, the audio is transmitted
to Apple's servers to convert it to text and interpret the command. The results
are sent back to your iPad.

It is best to speak clearly and to limit background noise. Using Siri in a quiet
room works better than in a crowded outdoor space or in a car with the radio
on, for instance.

Because Apple's servers control Siri, they can update Siri's capabilities at any
time. For example, originally Siri did not understand a request for local sports
scores, but after an update this functionality was added. Siri includes greatly
expanded functionality in iOS 9.

You can use Siri to perform many tasks on your iPad without typing. For example, you can search the Web, set reminders, send messages, and play music.
Throughout the rest of this book, look for the Siri icon for tips on how to use Siri
to perform a task related to that section of the book.

>>>Go Further
HEY SIRI!

You can activate Siri without pressing the home button. In the Settings app, just under the setting to turn on Siri, is a switch labeled Allow "Hey Siri." Turn that on and anytime you utter the words "Hey Siri" followed by a question, Siri will respond.

There's an initial setup sequence when you first turn it on. You need to speak a few phrases so Siri can distinguish your voice from other people and react only to you. Since this means your iPad needs to leave your microphone on and constantly monitor input, it only works when your iPad is plugged into AC power. Otherwise, it would drain your battery very quickly.

Using Notifications and Control Center

To move between pages on your Home screen, you swipe left and right. But you can also pull down and pull up two special screens from any Home screen, or just about any screen at all, even if you are in an app.

Open Notifications Center

Swiping from the very top of your screen downward pulls down the Notifications Center.

1. Swipe down from the top of the screen to pull down the Notifications Center. If you are having trouble, try placing your finger above the screen, outside of the actual screen area, and moving your finger down onto the screen, continuing all the way down.

2. In large type at the top of the screen, you will see today's date.

3. Under that, you may see a summary of today's weather, depending on your settings for the Notifications Center.

4. Under the weather, you usually find information about your next calendar event.

5. A preview of more calendar events for the day are shown. You can tap on an event to open the Calendar app and go right to it.

6. If you have any items set for today in the Reminders app, you will see them here. You can tap them to open the Reminders app. Or, tap on the circle to the left of the item to mark it as completed without going to the Reminders app at all.

7. If you have more information than can fit on the screen, you can swipe up to see it. This screen shows information about tomorrow as well as today.

8. Tap Notifications to see other notifications, such as incoming email, messages, and App Store updates. You can also swipe right to left to get to this screen.

9. Tap Edit to decide which items appear in the Today list. For instance, you could turn off Reminders but leave Calendar events.

10. Tap the flat arrow at the bottom of the screen and drag up to the top of the screen to close the Notifications Center. You can also just press the Home button at the bottom of your iPad.

Quickly Dismiss Notifications

While looking at Notifications in the Notifications Center, you can quickly dismiss items by swiping right to left to reveal a small X button. Tap that button to clear the item from the screen. In addition, each app heading in the notifications list has a small X button that you can tap twice to clear all the items for that app. The first time you tap, it turns into a "Clear" button; and then the second time you tap, it clears that section.

You can customize the Notifications Center in the Settings app, deciding exactly what appears in it. See "Modifying Notifications Settings" in Chapter 15.

Open Control Center

The Notifications Center comes down from the top of your iPad's screen, but the Control Center comes up from the bottom.

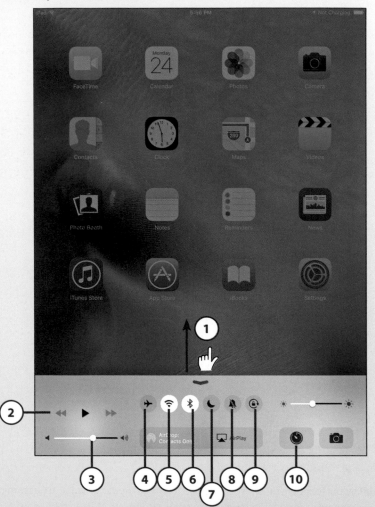

1. To bring up the Control Center, swipe up from the very bottom of the screen. If you are having trouble, try starting below the screen and swiping up onto the screen area all the way to the top.

2. The upper-left corner of the Control Center is a complete set of music playback controls. You see the name of the song playing and can pause or resume the song, and move the white line to jump around inside the song. You can also skip to the next or go back to the previous song.

3. Below the playback controls is a volume slider.

4. The first in a set of buttons in the middle of the Control Center is a switch that lets you quickly turn on Airplane mode. This shuts off all Wi-Fi, Bluetooth, and cellular data connections.

5. The next button lets you toggle on and off the Wi-Fi connection.

6. Likewise, you can toggle on and off the Bluetooth connection that you may be using with wireless headphones, a keyboard, or to connect to a wireless audio speaker.

7. You can quickly switch to Do Not Disturb mode, which silences all notifications such as incoming messages.

8. This button mutes your iPad. If you have an older iPad with a side switch, and you have set that side switch to act as a mute switch, then this button may not appear here.

9. This button locks your iPad's orientation. If you have an older iPad with a side switch, and you have set that side switch to act as an orientation lock, then this button may not appear here.

10. This is a shortcut to take you to the Clock app.

11. This is a shortcut to take you to the Camera app.

12. If you have an iPad that supports AirDrop, this button lets you turn AirDrop on or off. We'll look at AirDrop in Chapter 3.

13. The AirPlay button lets you choose a device to stream audio or video to, assuming you have such a device connected to your network. We look at AirPlay in Chapter 4.

14. The bottom-right corner of Control Center lets you adjust the brightness of the iPad's screen.

15. To dismiss Control Center, you can tap the flat arrow at the top and drag down. You can also tap the screen above Control Center or simply press the Home button.

There's not much that Control Center does that cannot be done in the Settings app or the Home screen. Control Center simply provides quick access to a variety of functions.

Customize how your iPad
looks and works through
the Settings app.

In this chapter, you learn how to change some of the settings on your iPad such as your background images, sounds, passcode, and how some apps behave.

→ Changing Your Wallpaper

→ Setting Alert Sounds

→ Password Protecting Your iPad

→ Make Access Easier with Touch ID

→ Setting Side Switch Functionality

→ Setting Your Date and Time

→ Modifying Keyboard Settings

→ Do Not Disturb Settings

→ Setting Parental Restrictions

→ Making Text Easier to Read

→ Controlling Automatic Downloads

→ Other Useful Settings

Customizing Your iPad

Like with any relationship, you fall in love with your iPad for what it is. And then, almost immediately, you try to change it.

It's easier, though, to customize your iPad than it is your significant other because you can modify various settings and controls in the Settings app. You can also move icons around on the Home screen and even change how the Home button works.

Changing Your Wallpaper

The wallpaper is the image behind the icons on the Home screen and on the lock screen. You'll see it often, so make sure it's something you like.

Settings

1. Tap the Settings icon on your Home screen.

Settings	Wallpaper
Q Settings	
	WALLPAPER
✈ Airplane Mode	Choose a New Wallpaper ──── ③
🛜 Wi-Fi CleverMedia	
✦ Bluetooth On	
VPN VPN Not Connected	
🔔 Notifications	
🎚 Control Center	
🌙 Do Not Disturb	
⚙ General	
AA Display & Brightness	
② ❋ Wallpaper	
◀ Sounds	
👆 Touch ID & Passcode	
🔋 Battery	
✋ Privacy	

2. Choose Wallpaper from the Settings app on the left side of the screen.

3. Tap Choose a New Wallpaper.

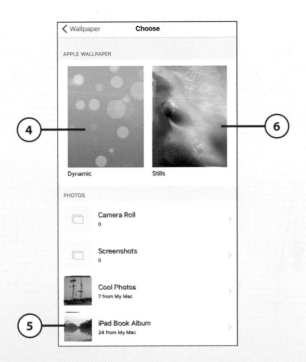

4. Now you have three choices. The first, Dynamic, is if you want to use one of Apple's dynamic wallpapers. Dynamic wallpapers have patterns that slowly animate.

5. A second choice is to use a photo from your photo library—either of a photo you took with your iPad or one you synced from your computer. Tap one of the groups of photos listed.

6. A third choice is Stills, which is a collection of Apple's default wallpaper images.

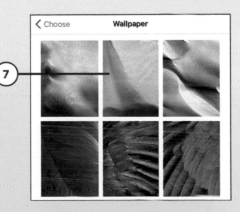

7. Choose an image from the category you selected in step 4, 5, or 6.

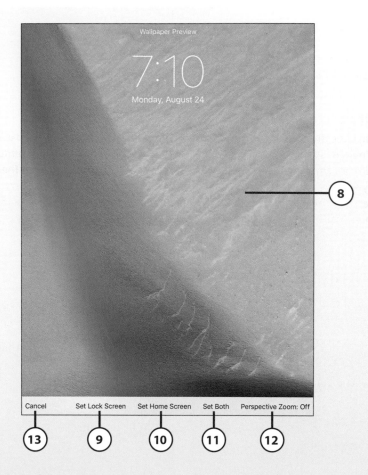

8. You'll see the full image in a preview covering the entire screen.

9. Choose Set Lock Screen to set this image as the background of your lock screen.

10. Choose Set Home Screen to set this image as the background for your Home screen.

11. Choose Set Both to make the image the background for both screens.

12. Perspective Zoom is an option that appears when you choose one of Apple's stills or your own photo. When it is on, the image is slightly enlarged and seems to sit in a 3D space below your lock screen text or home screen icons. As you move your iPad, you see the image move slightly behind the other elements. You can turn this off by tapping the Perspective Zoom: On button.

13. Tap Cancel at the bottom-left corner of the screen to go back to the wallpaper icons.

Adjusting the Wallpaper Image

You can touch and drag in a photo to move to other areas of the image so you can choose the part of the image you want as your wallpaper. You can also pinch to zoom in and out on your photographs.

If Lost, Call…

In later chapters, you find out about apps that allow you to create and edit images. Some apps make it easy to create an image that includes information like an emergency contact phone number on your iPad's lock screen. Then if you lose your iPad, someone could see the number on the lock screen and be able to contact you to return it. You can check out Sticky Notes by TapFactory in the App Store as one option for creating this type of image.

Setting Alert Sounds

Your iPad can be a noisy device with various events that trigger alert sounds. Just typing on the on-screen keyboard can produce a series of clicks. Here's how to adjust your iPad's sound settings.

1. Just as we did in the "Changing Your Wallpaper" task, tap the Settings icon on your Home screen to launch the Settings app. Then, tap Sounds from the list of settings on the left.

Settings	Sounds
✈ Airplane Mode ⬭	RINGER AND ALERTS
🛜 Wi-Fi CleverMedia	🔈 ———⬤——— 🔊
✳ Bluetooth On	Change with Buttons ⬭
VPN VPN Not Connected	The volume of the ringer and alerts will not be affected by the volume buttons.
	SOUNDS
🔲 Notifications	Ringtone Opening >
🎛 Control Center	Text Tone Note >
🌙 Do Not Disturb	New Mail Ding >
	Sent Mail Swoosh >
⚙ General	Tweet Tweet >
A🅰 Display & Brightness	Facebook Post Swish >
🌼 Wallpaper	Calendar Alerts Chord >
🔊 Sounds	Reminder Alerts Chord >
👆 Touch ID & Passcode	AirDrop Pulse >
🔋 Battery	
✋ Privacy	Lock Sounds ⬭
	Keyboard Clicks ⬭
☁ iCloud	

2. Adjust the volume of system sounds, like FaceTime ringtones and notification alerts. This does not affect the volume of music or video.

3. When this is turned on, the volume in step 2 can change by using the buttons on the side of the iPad. If you turn this off, you can still use the buttons to adjust the volume of music and video when those are playing; but otherwise, the side volume controls won't affect the system sound volume.

4. Tap any of these settings to set the sound that plays when an event occurs. You can choose ringtones, alert tones, or custom tones for any of the events. Ringtone refers to FaceTime calls and Text Tone refers to the Messages app.

5. Switch the Lock Sounds on or off. When this setting is on, a sound plays when you unlock the Lock screen.

6. Switch Keyboard Clicks on or off.

How About Custom Sounds?

Any sound event can play a ringtone rather than a plain alert sound. You will see a list of "Alert Tones" that are built into iOS, as well as a list of ringtones, which include the built-in ringtones and any custom ringtones. You can add your own custom ringtones in iTunes on your Mac or PC and then sync them with your iPad. After the sync, you will see them listed when selecting an alert sound. See "Syncing with iTunes" in Chapter 3. By obtaining or creating your own custom ringtones, you can set your alert sounds to anything you want.

Password Protecting Your iPad

Password protecting your iPad is very important. By using a passcode, you can make sure that someone else can't access your information or use your iPad. It is so important, in fact, that Apple includes setting up a passcode as part of the welcome screens you go through when you first use your new iPad. If you skipped that, you'll want to set it up now.

1. Open the Settings app and tap Touch ID & Passcode from the list of settings on the left. If you have previously set a passcode, you are required to enter it before moving into the Passcode settings. If you have an older iPad without Touch ID, the button on the left will read simply Passcode instead of Touch ID & Passcode. See the "Make Access Easier with Touch ID" section later in this chapter to learn more about Touch ID.

Even More Security

To lock your iPad automatically when you aren't using it, choose Auto-Lock from the General Settings and set your iPad to automatically lock at 2, 5, 10, or 15 minutes. You can also choose to never have it auto-lock. Of course, you can manually lock your iPad at any time by pressing the Wake/Sleep button at the top.

Settings	Touch ID & Passcode
Airplane Mode	USE TOUCH ID FOR:
Wi-Fi — CleverMedia	iPad Unlock
Bluetooth — On	Apple Pay
VPN — Not Connected	App and iTunes Stores
	Use your fingerprint instead of your Apple ID password when buying from the App and iTunes Stores.
Notifications	FINGERPRINTS
Control Center	Finger 1
Do Not Disturb	Finger 2
	Finger 3
General	Add a Fingerprint...
Display & Brightness	
Wallpaper	Turn Passcode On — ②
Sounds	Change Passcode
Touch ID & Passcode	
Battery	Require Passcode — Immediately ⑥
Privacy	ALLOW ACCESS WHEN LOCKED:
	Today
iCloud rosenz@mac.com	Notifications View ⑦
App and iTunes Stores	Siri
Wallet & Apple Pay	
	Erase Data ⑧
Mail, Contacts, Calendars	Erase all data on this iPad after 10 failed passcode attempts.

2. Tap Turn Passcode On to activate this feature. You then are prompted to enter a passcode. If you already had a passcode set and you want to change it now, tap Change Passcode.

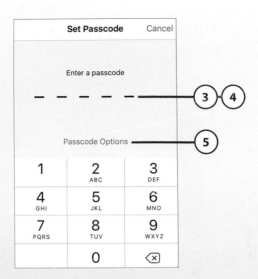

3. Type in a six-digit passcode that you can easily remember. Write it down and store it in a safe place—you can run into a lot of trouble if you forget it, most likely needing to erase your iPad and restore it from your last backup.

4. You are asked to re-enter your passcode.

5. Tap Passcode Options to switch from the default six digits to something else, like four digits or a longer alphanumeric passcode.

6. Tap the Require Passcode button and choose the delay before a passcode is required. If you choose anything other than Immediately, someone else using your iPad can work on it for that period of time before needing to enter the code.

7. Some features of your iPad's lock screen can be accessed even without a passcode. You can allow viewing of today's calendar events and reminders, notifications, and ask Siri questions without your passcode.

8. Turn on Erase Data if you want to erase the iPad data after 10 failed passcode attempts. This is a good idea from a security standpoint, but not so good if you think a mischievous child might grab your iPad and try guessing the passcode. If you use the Erase Data feature, be very sure you back up your iPad very often.

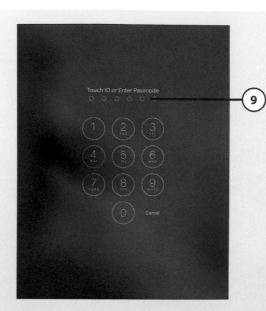

9. Press the Wake/Sleep button to confirm your new settings work. Then press the Home button and Slide to Unlock. The Enter Passcode screen displays.

Use a Real Password

Would you rather use a real password with letters and numbers instead of just a set of digits? If so, good for you! That's much more secure. And you can set one easily. Just follow steps 1 and 2 in the preceding task, and then in step 3 tap the Passcode Options button. You can set an alphanumeric code, a custom numeric code that can be as many digits as you like, or a four-digit numeric code that was the default option in iOS 8 and earlier.

It's Not All Good

You Forgot Your Passcode?

Well, it wouldn't be secure if there were a way to get around the passcode. So, you're out of luck until you can connect your iPad to your Mac or PC and use iTunes to restore it or erase the iPad using your Apple ID. Hopefully, this never happens to you. For the gory details on what to do in this dire situation, see http://support.apple.com/kb/ht1212. The one ray of hope is that if you have backed up your iPad recently, you'll be able to restore your data from that backup after you reset the iPad.

Make Access Easier with Touch ID

After you set a passcode for your iPad, you can make it easier to get access to your iPad by using Touch ID on newer iPads. Touch ID allows you to touch your fingertips to your Home button instead of typing the passcode.

1. Tap Touch ID & Passcode on the left side of the Settings app. If you only see Passcode instead of Touch ID & Passcode, then your iPad does not have a Touch ID sensor.

2. Tap Add a Fingerprint.

3. You are instructed by your iPad to repeatedly place and lift a finger on the Home button. Follow the instructions carefully as your iPad will continue to ask until it has enough information from your fingerprint. Remember to only use one finger while doing this. You will have the opportunity to add more fingers later.

4. When you are done, you will see your first fingerprint listed as Finger 1. You can tap here to change the name of this fingerprint or delete it.

5. You can now add more fingerprints. You may want to add both thumbs and both index fingers so you can use Touch ID while holding your iPad in different ways.

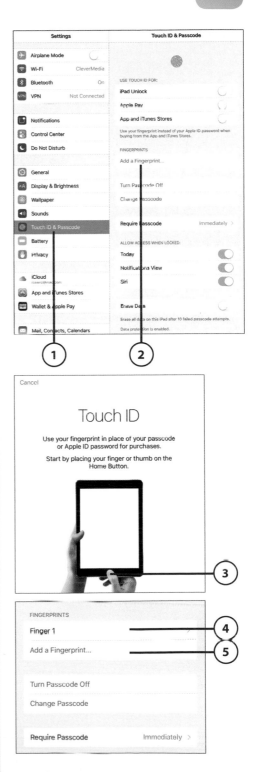

Buy with Touch ID

Touch ID not only makes it quicker and easier to unlock your iPad, but it also can be used by some third-party apps and in the iTunes store. Instead of needing to confirm your identity in those places, you may be asked to place your finger on the Home button to get access to data or purchase an item.

>>>Go Further

MAKING TOUCH ID WORK FOR YOU

If your iPad supports Touch ID, you are prompted to set it up while going through the welcome screens. You can always add more fingerprints, or redo the one you entered, in the Settings app. It can be useful to have both your thumbs and perhaps your index fingers recorded in the Touch ID settings. This makes it easier to unlock your iPad in different situations, depending on how you are holding it at the moment. Also, if it seems that Touch ID is often having trouble with one finger or another, you can erase that finger and re-record it.

Setting Side Switch Functionality

Most iPads, except the latest models, have a side switch. The switch on the side of your iPad can be used for one of two things: muting the sound or locking the screen orientation. Whichever one you choose for the switch, the other will then appear in the Control Center as a button. See "Using Notification and Control Center" in Chapter 1. So either way, you have fairly quick access to both functions.

1. Open the Settings app and tap General.

2. Tap Lock Rotation if you want your side switch to be an orientation lock switch.

3. Tap Mute if you want the side switch to mute the volume on the speakers and earphones.

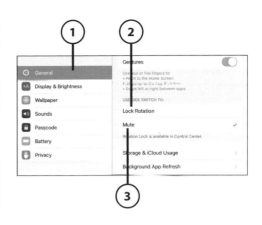

Setting Your Date and Time

You can set the date, time, and time zone for your iPad and even choose whether to display the time in 12- or 24-hour mode.

1. Launch the Settings app and tap General.

2. Scroll down to the bottom of the General Settings list and tap Date & Time.

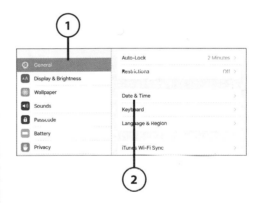

3. Turn the 24-Hour Time switch on to show the time in 24-hour format (military time). Turn it off to revert to 12-hour format.

4. Turning on Set Automatically syncs the date and time with the Wi-Fi network or cellular network that the iPad is connected to. In most cases, you can just stick with this. But if you find this isn't working for you, make sure Set Automatically is turned off and continue to step 5 to set it up manually.

5. Tap the Time Zone button and then enter the name of your city, or a nearby city, to set the zone.

6. To manually set the time, tap the date and time shown to bring up a set of controls underneath.

7. The controls are four "wheels" that you can spin by dragging up and down. You can set the day, hour, minute, and AM or PM.

Modifying Keyboard Settings

If you use your iPad for email or word processing, you will use the on-screen keyboard a lot. The keyboard does several things to make it easier for you to type, but some of these might get in the way of your typing style. Use the following steps to modify the keyboard settings to your preferences.

1. Open the Settings app and tap General.

2. Scroll down to the bottom of the General Settings list and tap Keyboard.

3. Use the Keyboards button to choose a different keyboard layout. In addition to keyboards commonly used in other countries, you can switch to a Dvorak keyboard or one of several other alternatives to the traditional QWERTY keyboard. You can also select a keyboard installed by a third-party app.

4. You can add your own shortcuts. For instance, you can set it so when you type "omw," it will instantly expand to "On my way!" Add your own shortcuts for things you commonly type.

5. Turn Auto-Capitalization on to automatically make the first character of a name or a sentence a capital letter.

6. Turn Auto-Correction on to have mistyped words automatically corrected.

7. Check Spelling underlines words in red that do not appear to be spelled correctly.

8. Turn Enable Caps Lock on. When Caps Lock is turned on, you can double-tap the shift key to lock it.

9. In Chapter 1, you learned about the shortcut bar. You can disable it with this switch if you prefer.

10. Turn on or off Predictive Text. See "Using Predictive Text" in Chapter 1 for more about this time-saving feature.

11. If you want to lock the keyboard so it can never be split and moved up vertically, then switch this to off. See "Using the On-Screen Keyboard" in Chapter 1 for more details on using a split keyboard.

12. Turn on the "." shortcut if you want a double-tap of the spacebar to insert a period followed by a space.

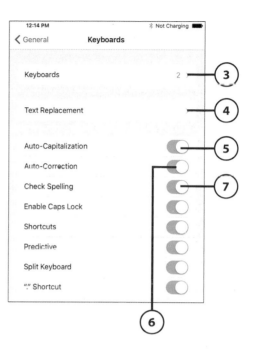

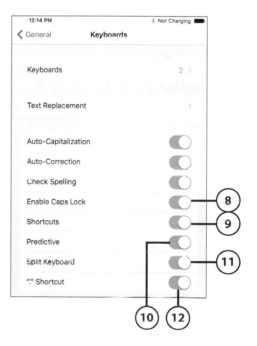

13. A shortcut to change keyboards is to use the key to the left of the spacebar that looks like a globe. Tap it to move to the next keyboard in your list, or tap and hold to get a list of keyboards to select one. You can also turn off Predictive Text and Shortcuts in this menu.

13

KEYBOARDS GALORE

You can add all sorts of keyboards created by third-party developers to your iPad. Doing this is just a matter of installing the developer's app on your iPad. Then you will see them appear in the list in step 3.

Some third-party keyboards allow you to type in different ways. For instance, the **Swype** and **TouchPal** apps give you keyboards that allow you to tap the first letter of a word, and then swipe with your finger across the keyboard to the other letters to form the word instead of tapping for each letter. The **TextExpander 3** app gives you advanced capabilities for creating shortcuts to type long pieces of text. See Chapter 15 to learn how to search for and install apps.

Do Not Disturb Settings

Your iPad is trying to get your attention. It beeps and rings with notifications, FaceTime calls, messages, and event alarms. In fact, it might be hard to have it nearby when you are trying to sleep or enjoying some time "offline."

Do Not Disturb is a mode where your iPad quiets down. Most audible alerts are silenced. You can set your iPad to enter this mode manually with the Do Not Disturb settings, or set a predefined block of time each day.

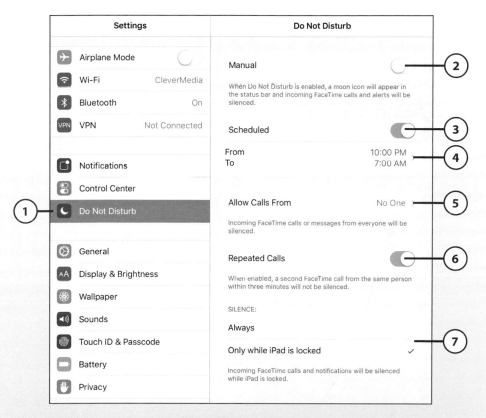

1. Launch the Settings app and tap Do Not Disturb.

2. You can turn on Do Not Disturb mode manually with this switch. (You can also turn Do Not Disturb on and off from the Control Center.)

3. Tap Scheduled for Do Not Disturb mode to automatically start and end at a specific time. For instance, you can set it to start at 10 p.m. and end at 7 a.m. so you aren't disturbed while sleeping.

4. Tap here to use time and date controls to set the start and end times.

5. Tap Allow Calls From to allow FaceTime calls and messages from specific people by selecting a group in your contacts list.

6. Turn on Repeated Calls so that someone can reach you in an emergency by calling twice within three minutes.

7. Do Not Disturb can work at all times, or only when you have your iPad locked. Tap the desired setting so that a blue checkmark appears next to it.

Setting Parental Restrictions

If you plan to let your kids or grandkids play with your iPad, you might want to set some restrictions on what they can do.

1. Open the Settings app and tap General.

2. Tap Restrictions.

3. Tap Enable Restrictions to turn restrictions on.

4. Type in a four-digit code, and then re-enter the code when prompted. It is important to remember this code, or you can't turn off or change restrictions later!

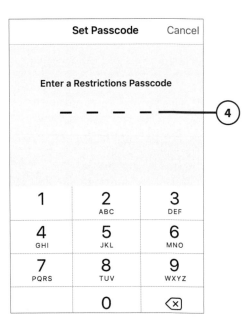

5. The Restrictions settings are a long list of apps and functions that you can allow or disallow. The switches you use depend on how much you want to restrict your iPad's use.

6. Continue to scroll down the list and review all the possible settings. Some settings, like the ones for movies, TV shows, books, and apps, allow you to set a maximum content rating. For instance, for apps you can set this to 4+, 9+, 12+, 17+, Allow All Apps, or Don't Allow Apps.

‹ General	Restrictions
ALLOW:	
Safari	
Camera	
Siri & Dictation	
FaceTime	
AirDrop	
iTunes Store	
Apple Music Connect	
iBooks Store	
Podcasts	
News	
Installing Apps	
Deleting Apps	
In-App Purchases	
ALLOWED CONTENT:	
Ratings For	United States ›
Music, Podcasts, News & iTunes U	Explicit ›
Movies	All ›
TV Shows	All ›
Books	All ›
Apps	All

It's Not All Good

Settings Not Remembered

It would be nice if you could just switch Restrictions on and off so that you could hand your iPad to Junior after quickly turning them on. But the settings are reset each time you switch Restrictions off. So you need to set the switches again each time after turning Restrictions back on. Once they are on, however, you can go back any time and adjust the individual settings.

Making Text Easier to Read

If you find that text in standard apps like Calendar, Reminders, and Notes is difficult to read because it is too small or the letters are too thin, you can change that in the Display & Brightness settings.

Settings	Display & Brightness
General	BRIGHTNESS
1 — Display & Brightness	☀ ——————⬤———— ☀
Wallpaper	Auto-Brightness ⬤
Sounds	
Touch ID & Passcode	Text Size — 3
Battery	Bold Text ○ — 2
Privacy	

1. Open the Settings app and tap Display & Brightness.

2. You can make the letters of standard text thicker and easier to read. Changing this setting requires your iPad to restart.

3. Tap Text Size to make the default text larger or smaller.

❮ Display & Brightness **Text Size**

Apps that support Dynamic Type will adjust to your preferred reading size below.

Drag the slider below

4 — A ——————⬤——— A

4. Tap and drag the dot along the line to change the size of text. Because the Settings app is one of the apps affected by this, you'll see the changes in most of the text on the screen as you drag.

Here, you can see the Calendar app in Week view with text size set to the default.

Here, the text size is set to maximum.

Note that text size doesn't affect all apps. It works on some of the Apple preinstalled apps, but even in those, it only works in some places. With the Calendar app, you can see the change in Week and Day view but not Month view.

Controlling Automatic Downloads

You iPad can automatically download app updates when they become available. This saves you from missing an update to your favorite apps. You can also set your iPad to download new content that you purchase from iTunes on another device.

1. Open the Settings app and tap iTunes & App Store on the left.

2. There are three switches that control automatic content downloads. Turn these on if you want your iPad to automatically get music, apps, or books when you purchase them on another device such as your computer or an iPhone.

3. Turn on Updates if you want updates to Apple and third-party apps to automatically download and install.

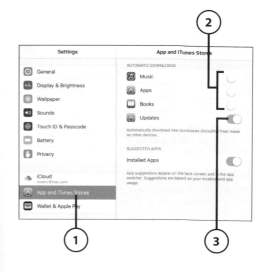

Cellular Data

Note that if you have an iPad with mobile wireless capability, you'll see another setting here for Use Cellular Data. Turn this off to prevent these automatic downloads from happening while you are away from a Wi-Fi connection.

Other Useful Settings

The Settings app contains too many controls to go into detail on each one. It is worth taking the time to explore each section of the Settings app to see what is possible. The item to tap on the left side of the Settings app screen is listed first in each of the following bullets, followed by the items you tap on the right side. For example, in the first bullet you open the Settings app, tap General on the left side, and then tap About on the right side. When the About settings appear, tap Available to see your available storage.

- **General, About, Available**: See the remaining amount of storage space you have on your iPad.

- **General, About, Version**: Quickly find out which version of iOS you are using.

- **General, About, Model**: Get the model number of your iPad. This could come in handy if you ever need to figure out if an accessory will work with your specific model.

- **Control Center, Access Within Apps**: If you find that you are accidentally bringing up the Control Center at the bottom of the screen while playing your favorite game, you can turn off Control Center inside apps. You can still access it by going to the Home screen first.

- **Wi-Fi, Ask to Join Networks**: Whether or not this switch is on, your iPad will look for and connect to any Wi-Fi network you have previously signed on to. If you switch this setting on, if it can't find any familiar network, it will pop up a dialog asking if you want to join the strongest network it can find. Since you don't want to join networks you don't know or trust, leave this off and simply go to the Wi-Fi settings to join a new network.

- **General, Spotlight Search**: Here you can turn on and off different types of content you see when you search the contents of your iPad. You can also set the order by dragging the items in the list up or down.

- **General, Lock/Unlock**: If you use an Apple Smart Cover, or some other case that can automatically put your iPad to sleep when it is closed, you can control whether or not this happens by changing this setting.

- **General, Reset**: Here is a set of potentially dangerous switches that allow you to erase your settings and content. If you ever decide that your iPad's home screens are too disorganized, you can use the Reset Home Screen Layout to move the Apple default apps back to their original positions and your other apps out of folders into alphabetical order starting on screen two. The other reset options should only be used if you understand their end result.

More Apps, More Settings

The Settings app adds new items as you add new apps to your iPad. Some apps have settings inside the app, while others have all their settings as an item along the left side of the Settings app. Still others put some settings in the app and some in Settings. It is a good idea to periodically check the Settings app to see what new items have appeared, and then look to see which settings are available for that app.

Put your favorite
photos on your iPad.

View your iCloud files.

Sync your music and other
content with your Mac or PC.

In this chapter, you find out how to connect your iPad to your local Wi-Fi network. You also see how to sync your iPad with your Mac or Windows computer and with Apple's iCloud service.

→ Setting Up Your Wi-Fi Network Connection

→ Setting Up Your Cellular Data Connection

→ Syncing with iCloud

→ Syncing with iTunes

→ Syncing Photos with iTunes

→ Keeping Your iPad Up-To-Date

→ Sharing with AirDrop

→ Viewing Your Mac's Files with iCloud Drive

Networking and Syncing

Your iPad connects you to the world. You can surf the web, view all sorts of information, communicate with friends, and share photos. But first, you must connect your iPad to the Internet. You can do that using a Wi-Fi connection. Some iPads also have the capability to connect to a cellular network.

Setting Up Your Wi-Fi Network Connection

One of the first things you need to do with your iPad is to establish an Internet connection.

Chances are that you did this when you started your iPad for the first time. It should have prompted you to choose from a list of nearby Wi-Fi networks. You might need to do this again if you first used your iPad away from home, or if you need to switch to use another Wi-Fi network.

To connect your iPad to a wireless network, follow these steps.

1. Tap the Settings icon on the Home screen.

Settings

2. Choose Wi-Fi from the list of settings on the left.

3. Make sure that Wi-Fi is turned on.

4. Tap the item that represents your network. (Tap on the blue-circled i button next to each network to customize your network settings.)

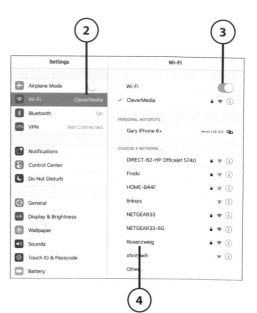

I Don't Have a Wireless Network

If you don't have a Wi-Fi network but do have high-speed Internet through a telephone or cable provider, you have several options. The first is to call your provider and ask for a new network modem that enables wireless connections. Some providers might upgrade your box for free or a small cost.

Another option is to keep your current box and add a wireless base station of your own, such as the Apple Airport Extreme base station.

5. If the network is protected by a password, you will be asked to enter the password.

6. Tap Join. Once you enter the password, your iPad will remember it. If you switch between two locations, like work and home, you will be asked to enter the password the first time you use that connection. From that point on, your iPad automatically logs on to each connection as you move around.

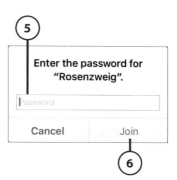

Enter the password for "Rosenzweig".

Password

Cancel   Join

>>>Go Further

SECURITY? YES!

Your wireless network at home should have security turned on. This means that you should see a padlock next to it in the list of Wi-Fi networks on your iPad. When you select it for the first time, you should be asked to supply a password.

If you don't require a password, seriously consider changing your Wi-Fi network box's settings to add security. The issue isn't simply about requiring a password to use your Internet connection. It is about the fact that a secure network will send encrypted data through the air. Otherwise, anyone can simply "sniff" your wireless connection and see what you are doing online— such as using credit cards and logging on to websites and services. See your network equipment's documentation to set up security.

Setting Up Your Cellular Data Connection

If you have an iPad with cellular data capabilities, you can set it up to use AT&T, Verizon, or any other compatible network. You can purchase a monthly data plan, or purchase service in shorter increments. If you have previously set up a plan, you cannot complete these steps again. You need to contact your service provider directly to change or cancel your plan.

1. Open the Settings app and tap Cellular Data on the left.

2. Turn on Cellular Data. In addition, turn on Enable LTE for a faster connection.

3. Tap View Account.

4. You have three options to set up an account with AT&T. (Other carriers may offer different options.) The first one is to set up a completely new account. If you choose this, skip to step 8.

5. Another option is to add your iPad's data plan as an additional service to your existing AT&T plan. Use this if you are already an AT&T customer. You will be prompted for your mobile phone number, zip code, passcode, and social security number to complete the setup.

6. The Transfer Service From Another iPad option is for those who already have an iPad data plan, and want to transfer it from an old iPad to a new one.

7. Choose a data plan that best fits your needs.

8. Tap and swipe up to scroll down. This screen consists of a long form that you need to fill out with your personal and payment information to complete the setup of your account. When you are done, you have to approve the service agreement and confirm your purchase. Still, it beats going to the mall and dealing with a salesperson at a mobile phone store, right?

It might take a few more minutes for your cellular data service to activate. After establishing service, you can return to this section of the Settings app to view your usage and modify your plan. Then you can see your pay details and status.

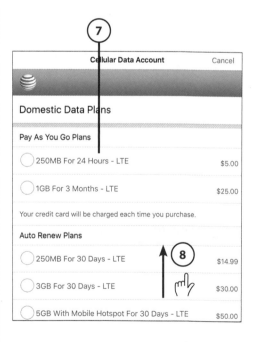

Working with Wi-Fi and Cellular Data

After you establish a cellular data plan, your iPad should still connect to your Wi-Fi networks when it is in range and use cellular data only when it cannot find a Wi-Fi network. You can also return to Settings and turn on or off Cellular Data to specifically prevent your iPad from using the cellular data network. This is handy when you are completely out of mobile data range but have local Wi-Fi; for instance, you might be on an airplane flight.

Looking at the top-left corner of your iPad's screen, you can tell which sort of connection you are currently using. You see the Wi-Fi symbol, a fan of four curves, when you are connected to Wi-Fi. If you have a cellular data plan, you see the name of your network next to it, such as "AT&T," plus a series of bars that show your connection strength. You are only using that connection if the characters "3G," "4G," or "LTE" are shown instead of the Wi-Fi symbol.

It's Not All Good

Watch for Data Roaming

In the Cellular Data settings, you can turn Data Roaming on or off. This is what enables your iPad to connect to wireless data networks that are outside of your data plan, such as networks in other countries. If you leave Data Roaming on and your iPad connects to such a network, you may find a surprise bill in the mail. You can avoid extra charges by leaving Data Roaming off or by purchasing a plan from AT&T for International data roaming.

Syncing with iCloud

When you think of your contacts, calendar events, and email messages, you might be tempted to think of that information as being "on your iPad" or "on your computer." But today this information is usually in both places, and more. This is referred to as "the cloud"—when the actual location of the information isn't important as long as it is where you need it, when you need it.

As an iPad user, you have access to several different cloud services, most notably Apple's system called iCloud. It is a free service that offers email, contacts, calendar, documents, and other types of data stored on Apple's servers and is automatically synced to your iPad and the other Apple devices you may own.

Or, you could choose to use other cloud services, such as Gmail or Yahoo!, for mail and calendar events. There's no reason to pick just one. For instance, you can use both iCloud and Gmail on your iPad.

When you use cloud services, you get automatic syncing as long as you have a connection to the Internet. For example, add a contact to your iPad and your iPhone automatically updates to show that new contact. Let's look at how to set up an iCloud account, or link to one you've already created.

Connecting to iCloud

1. Open the Settings app and tap iCloud on the left.

2. If you have never set up an account with Apple before, then tap Create a New Apple ID to set one up. Any account you have with Apple, such as an iTunes account, would be an Apple ID, and you should use that instead of starting a new account.

3. If you already have an Apple ID, even if you have never used iCloud before, enter your ID and password. Apple IDs can be any email address, not just an @iCloud.com email address.

4. Tap Sign In to access your account. If your account has only been used for things like iTunes in the past, you are prompted to set up the new iCloud part of your account.

5. If you think you have used an email address to log on to iTunes or some other Apple service before, but you can't remember the password, tap Forgot Apple ID or Password to reset your password.

It's Not All Good

Don't Confuse ID with Email

An Apple ID is a unique identifier that allows you to log in to your iCloud account. It can be an Apple email address, like myipadbook@icloud.com, but it can also be a non-Apple email address, like myipadbook@gmail.com. In the former case, the ID is the same as your iCloud email address. In the latter case, the ID is just an ID. Your email account would be a Gmail account and have nothing to do with your iCloud account.

6. You can manage your iCloud Drive storage by tapping the iCloud Drive setting. iCloud Drive is the file and documents storage part of iCloud. For example, your Pages, Numbers, and Keynote documents can be stored on your iCloud Drive. You can then access them on other iOS or OS X devices. Also see the section about iCloud Drive later in the chapter.

7. You can turn photo-related iCloud services such as Photo Stream and iCloud Photo Library on or off here. See Chapter 9 to learn about how photos are stored.

8. You can use your iCloud email on your iPad. This would typically be an @icloud.com email address. These addresses are part of the free iCloud service. If you happen to be using a non-Apple email address as an Apple ID, note that this setting has nothing to do with that email account.

9. If Contacts is on, iCloud stores all your contacts so they automatically sync with the iCloud servers and then to your other Apple devices.

Storage	3.9 GB Available >
iCloud Drive	On >
Photos	On >
Mail	
Contacts	
Calendars	
Reminders	
Safari	
Notes	
News	
Backup	On >
Keychain	>
Find My iPad	On >

10. Likewise, iCloud can store your calendar events when the Calendars switch is on.

11. Turn on Reminders to have the Reminders app use iCloud to store reminders and automatically sync them with your other devices.

12. Safari can sync over iCloud as well. Things like your bookmarks, tabs, and reading list would sync across devices when the Safari switch is on.

13. Turn the Notes switch on so that Notes can also sync over iCloud.

14. You can have your News app preferences sync across your devices. We look at the News app in Chapter 16.

15. iCloud Backup backs up your settings, documents, photos, and other data to iCloud wirelessly. If your iPad is lost or breaks, you are able to restore your data to a repaired or new iPad later. You should use iCloud Backup unless you prefer to back up to your computer via iTunes and do so on a regular basis.

16. iOS allows you to store passwords while using Safari so you don't need to enter them each time. Syncing these over iCloud means that you can also access these passwords on other Apple devices. Tap Keychain to configure this setting. See "Saving Time with AutoFill" in Chapter 7 for more details on working with the Keychain.

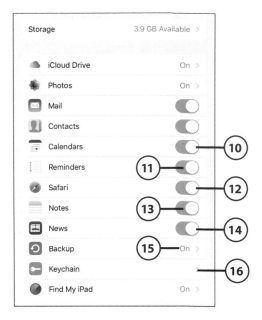

17. Find My iPad is an option that lets you locate your iPad on a map using another Apple device or the iCloud.com website. Be aware that if your Location Services are not on, this feature does not work. See "Using Find My iPad" in Chapter 19.

18. You can check to see how much storage space you have remaining in your iCloud account. As of late 2014, Apple provides each iPad user with 5GB of free space. You can purchase more if you find that you have a lot of documents or other data, and 5GB isn't going to be enough.

Storage	3.9 GB Available >	18
iCloud Drive	On >
Photos	On >
Mail	⬤
Contacts	⬤
Calendars	⬤
Reminders	⬤
Safari	⬤
Notes	⬤
News	⬤
Backup	On >
Keychain	>
Find My iPad	On > 17

>>>Go Further

iCLOUD.COM

In addition to syncing between devices, much of your iCloud information is available if you go to iCloud.com and log in using your Apple ID. You can do this on any computer. So even if you are using your iPad as your only computing device, there still is another way to get to your data when you need it.

Syncing with iTunes

With iCloud, the iPad can be a truly stand-alone device, no desktop computer needed. iCloud is also great for keeping your iPad and your Mac in sync, sharing settings, music, photos, and so on. An alternative is to use iTunes to sync your iPad and your Mac or Windows computer. There are several advantages to doing so:

- Each day you sync your iPad, iTunes stores a backup of its content. You can restore all your data from these backups if you lose your iPad. You can do the same with iCloud backup, but it can take a lot longer to restore an iPad because it has to transfer the data across the Internet.

- Syncing with a computer is a good way to get a large number of photos from your collection on your iPad if you aren't using iCloud Photo Library.

- Syncing is how you get your music stored on your computer onto your iPad if you aren't using iTunes Match or Apple Music. If you have a large collection of music, you can opt to copy only a selection of it to your iPad at any one time.

You might get a message asking if it is okay to sync your iPad to this computer the first time you connect your iPad and open iTunes. The message won't reappear after you have connected the iPad to the computer.

After connecting the first time, iTunes should automatically open when you connect your iPad. While connected to your computer, you can always click the Sync button in iTunes to re-sync and apply any changes to the iPad.

You can also choose Sync over Wi-Fi connection in your iPad's options in iTunes. This allows you to sync when your iPad isn't connected to the computer by the USB cable. It only needs to be on the same network as your Mac or PC that is running iTunes.

As we look at some of the syncing options for the iPad, the Mac version of iTunes is used as an example. The Windows version of iTunes is similar but not exactly the same.

Syncing Options

After your device is in sync, you can change some general options for your iPad from the Summary screen in iTunes. Most of the options are self-explanatory, such as Open iTunes When This iPad Is Connected.

1. Using iTunes 12.2 or newer, look for a button representing your iPad at the top of iTunes. After you select it, the items in the rest of the iTunes window will pertain to your iPad, with settings and content categories listed on the left.

2. You can configure your backups. iCloud backups are convenient for those without regular access to a computer, but it uses Internet bandwidth and can be a problem if you have a slow connection. Backing up to your computer is a good option if you regularly sync to your computer anyway.

3. You can set your iPad to connect via Wi-Fi. From then on, you only need to be on the same network as your computer to sync with iTunes.

4. A handy chart of your iPad's storage is shown.

5. Any changes you make on this screen, or any other iTunes sync screen, requires that you click Sync to re-sync with the new settings.

One option that dramatically changes how your iPad syncs is Manually Manage Music and Videos. This option turns off automatic syncing of music and videos and enables you to simply drag and drop songs and movies from your iTunes library onto the iPad icon on the left. (You might need to scroll down the Summary page to locate this checkbox if your screen size is too small to show the entire page at once.)

>>>Go Further
BACK IT UP!

Perhaps the most important part of syncing with your computer is backing up your data. Everything you create with apps, every preference you carefully set, and every photo you take could be gone in a second if you drop your iPad or someone swipes it. Even a hardware failure is possible—the iPad isn't perfect.

Choosing This Computer saves all your data on your computer in a backup file. Try to do it once per day. With a good backup, you can replace a lost iPad and restore all your data from the backup. It works incredibly well.

You can always plug your iPad into your Mac or PC, launch iTunes, and click the Back Up Now button in the Backup section. Backup also happens automatically, once per day, if you connect your iPad to your computer and click Sync.

Your other option is iCloud. This backs up your data wirelessly to iCloud. It is your only option if you are not going to sync your iPad with a computer. It does use up your data storage allotment in your iCloud account, so you might need to upgrade your iCloud account to allow for more data.

Even so, backing up to iCloud is a great alternative, especially if you travel often and use your iPad for critical tasks. You can always do both types of backups by selecting iCloud in step 2, but connecting your iPad to your computer on a regular basis and clicking the Back Up Now button in iTunes.

Syncing Music

The simple way to sync music is to select Entire Music Library in iTunes on your computer. If you have more music than can fit on your iPad, though, you must make some choices. Syncing Movies, TV Shows, Podcasts, Tones (ringtones for messaging and FaceTime), iTunes U, and Books all work in a similar way to syncing music, so you can apply what you learn in these steps to those items as well.

1. Select your iPad at the top of the iTunes window.

2. Click the Music button of your iPad's settings in iTunes.

3. Select Sync Music, if it isn't already turned on.

4. Click the Selected Playlists, Artists, Albums, and Genres button.

5. Check off any playlists in the Playlists section that you want to include.

6. Check off any artists for which you want to include every song by that artist.

7. Check off any genres to include in their entirety.

8. Check off any albums you want to include.

9. Use the search box to quickly find specific artists.

10. Click the Apply button if you want to apply the changes now.

One Copy Only

Note that songs are never duplicated on your iPad. For instance, if the same song appears in two playlists and is also by an artist that you have selected to sync, the song only has one copy on your iPad. But it appears in both playlists and under that artist, album, and alphabetical list of all songs.

>>>*Go Further*

MORE WAYS TO SYNC

iTunes Match is a service from Apple. For an annual fee, you can sync your music collection with Apple's servers. Then you can access all your music on your iPad by turning on iTunes Match in the Music settings in the Settings app. When you do this, you no longer need to sync your music. Instead, you see all your music on your iPad, and it will download from Apple's servers when you want to listen to a particular song.

Visit www.apple.com/itunes/itunes-match/ to find out more about Apple's iTunes Match service.

Apple Music is a service from Apple where you pay a monthly subscription fee in return for access to a huge library of music from iTunes. You can add any songs in the Apple Music catalog to your collection and they will appear on your iPad and other Apple devices for as long as you remain a subscriber. See "Having It All with Apple Music" in Chapter 4.

You can also sync your music and videos manually. This sounds like a lot of work, but it can be an easier way to sync your music for many people. If you check off Manually Manage Music and Videos on the iTunes Summary screen for your iPad, you can then drag and drop music from your iTunes music library on to your iPad. It requires a bit of knowledge about how the iTunes interface works, however. You'll need to choose View, Show Sidebar so you can see your iPad in the left sidebar. Then you can look at the Music item listed to see which songs are there. Switch to your iTunes Music library to see what songs you have on your computer and simply drag and drop songs, albums, or artists from the iTunes Music library to your iPad in the left sidebar.

Syncing Photos

The process for syncing photos from your computer to your iPad is very similar to how you move music, videos, and other data to your iPad. So let's use photos as an example. The steps here are very similar if you want to sync something else, like movies, to your iPad. You would just choose the Movies tab in iTunes instead of the Photos tab.

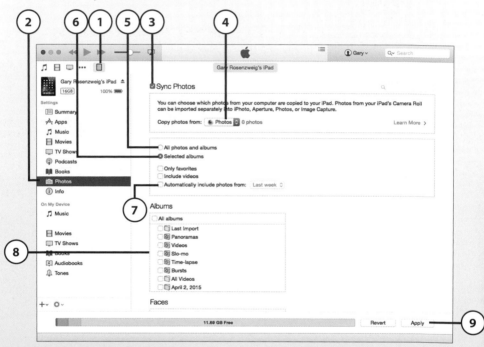

1. Select your iPad.

2. Choose Photos.

3. Click the checkbox to indicate that you want to sync photos.

4. You can choose from any applications that are compatible with iTunes and store photos. For instance, on Mac you can choose the new Photos app or the old iPhoto or Aperture apps, if you have them. You can also simply select a folder to use as the location for your photos. The rest of the steps here assume you are using iPhoto.

5. Click All photos and albums to sync all your photos. Only do this if you have a fairly small collection.

6. Choose Selected albums to select which albums to sync.

7. You can also have photos taken over a recent period of time automatically sync. For instance, you can have it sync all photos from the past 6 months.

8. Choose which albums you want to sync. Albums are collections of photos, like music playlists, that allow you to compile your favorite or related photos into a group.

9. When you are satisfied with your selections, click Apply to begin the transfer.

No Duplicates

Like with music, you get only one copy of each photo, no matter how many times the photo appears in albums, events, and faces. The photos appear in all the right places but take up only one spot in memory on your iPad.

It's Not All Good

One Direction

Syncing photos can be a confusing concept: You sync photos from your photo collection to your iPad using iTunes, but you sync photos from your iPad to your computer using iPhoto or a similar app.

Think of it this way. Syncing to your iPad works the same for music, videos, and photos. These are all media stored on your computer, and iTunes lets you copy them from your computer to your iPad. But when you take photos with your iPad, your iPad is acting just like a digital camera. You want to copy those to your photo-handling app on your computer as you would if you were using a digital camera.

When you sync photos from your computer to your iPad, the original is on your computer, and there is merely a copy on your iPad. Your iPad is just a viewing device for these photos. It is important that you maintain your real photo library on your computer and remember to back it up.

Syncing Everything Else

Music and photos are two out of many types of items you might want to sync between your computer and your iPad. In most cases, if you use iCloud for that type of item, there is no need to ever sync it via iTunes.

If you look in iTunes, you have the ability to sync Info, Apps, Tones, Music, Movies, TV Shows, Podcasts, Books, and Photos. Each has a similar screen to the Music and Photos syncing settings screens we have already examined. Let's take a look at each and see why you may or may not want to sync them using iTunes.

- **Info**: This means syncing Contacts and Calendars. If you use iCloud, this happens automatically as you make changes. There is no need to sync.

- **Apps**: Since your Mac or PC cannot run iOS apps, these settings in iTunes allow you to keep copies of your apps on your computer so you can restore them to your iPad in case of a problem. You can also use the iTunes interface to arrange the apps on your Home screens.

- **Tones**: This refers to ringtones and sounds used by Messages, FaceTime, and other things where your iPad sends you an audible alert. If you are creative and good with GarageBand on the Mac, you can create ringtones with it and use iTunes to sync these new ringtones to your iPad. You can also download iOS-compatible ringtones, which are .m4r files, and sync them this way.

- **Music**: If you are using Apple Music or iTunes Match, you don't need to use iTunes to sync your music. If you don't have much music, and want to save a few dollars, you can simply sync your music with iTunes on your computer.

- **Movies and TV Shows**: These two categories are used mainly to sync videos you have purchased in the iTunes Store. However, it also works for other videos you store in iTunes. Videos that are part of your photo collection are synced under Photos.

  One thing to keep in mind is that once you purchase a movie or TV show episode, you can always re-download it from Apple later. So if you buy 22 episodes of a TV season and watch them all, you don't need to keep them on either your iPad or your computer. You can remove those items from iTunes to save some storage space, and then download them again from Apple if you want to watch them again later.

- **Podcasts**: Thanks to the stand-alone Podcasts app that comes with your iPad, there's not much of a need to sync podcasts across from your computer to your iPad. You can simply download episodes directly to your iPad. See "Listening to Podcasts" in Chapter 4.

- **Books**: Books work in much the same way as Movies. When you buy a book from Apple, you can re-download it later. If a book is just text, it is a quick download. If you buy a book on your computer in iBooks, you can easily find it and download it in the iBooks app on your iPad, too. Syncing can also be useful for those who import other types of books into the iBooks library on a Mac, and then want to get it to their iPad later on.

- **Photos**: As noted earlier, the main reason to sync photos is if you aren't using iCloud Photo Library and you want to take some recent or favorite albums on your computer and put them on your iPad for viewing.

Sharing with AirDrop

A quick way to get files from your iPad to another iOS device or Mac is using AirDrop. This technique uses Wi-Fi, but instead of going through a Wi-Fi network, it uses your iPad's Wi-Fi hardware and goes directly from device to device. The devices don't need to be on the same network—they don't need to be on any Wi-Fi network at all. They just need to be nearby.

AirDrop requires the latest Wi-Fi hardware in your iPad, so it only works with the 4th generation iPad or newer, or an iPad mini. On a Mac, it requires a very recent model as well, running at least Mac OS X Yosemite. Using AirDrop is pretty straightforward.

Using AirDrop

To use AirDrop, follow these steps:

1. To use AirDrop, make sure you have turned it on. Do this by accessing Control Center. See "Using Notifications and Control Center" in Chapter 1. Make sure that it is set to Everyone. Another option is to set it to Contacts Only, which means you can only use AirDrop with devices that have Apple ID email addresses that are in your Contacts.

2. Let's use the Photos app as an example. You can use any app that can share items, such as the Notes app, Contacts app, and so on. Select a photo, and then tap the Share button. In Photos, the Share button is sometimes at the top, and sometimes at the bottom. It is always the same boxed arrow.

3. In addition to sharing options such as Message and Mail, you'll see a list of other AirDrop-compatible devices that are within range. You see whatever image the user has chosen as a user icon, plus their name. If you do not see your other device, it could be asleep, or have AirDrop disabled, or possibly is not a model that has AirDrop available.

4. After you tap the icon, you see a "Waiting" message below it. In the meantime, the recipient receives an alert asking them to accept the transfer. You can accept the cute picture of the puppy, or decline it. If the sender is in your contacts, however, you just get the photo without needing to confirm it.

Friends Share

The real power of AirDrop is sending between friends. For instance, if you are standing with your iPad next to a friend with an iPhone, you can send her a picture without both of you needing to share a common Wi-Fi network or exchanging email addresses. You just Share, select her for the AirDrop, and she accepts.

>>>Go Further

HANDOFF

Handoff is a feature of iOS and Mac OS X that allows you to put down one device and pick up another to continue what you are doing. There are no settings for this; it just works as long as both devices are signed into the same iCloud account, and they are nearby.

Suppose you start composing an email on an iPhone. Then you decide that it would be easier to type the message on your iPad. All you need to do is look at the Lock screen of your iPad. You'll see a little Mail app icon at the bottom left telling you that you can pick up your work on the iPad. Slide the icon up to unlock your iPad, instead of using the usual Slide to Unlock gesture. The result will be that the Mail app opens and your half-completed message appears, ready for you to finish. On your iPhone, the Mail app gracefully closes the composition screen.

There are a lot of things that need to be just right for Handoff to work. Both devices need to not only use the same iCloud account, but also need to see each other using Bluetooth and Wi-Fi systems. A little radio interference is all it takes for this to not work one time, but work other times.

Viewing Your Mac's Files with iCloud Drive New!

If you are a Mac user, you are probably already familiar with iCloud Drive. This special folder on your Mac enables you to store files in the cloud and access them on your other Macs. It is very useful if you have both a desktop and a laptop Mac.

You can also access your iCloud Drive files on your iPad in iOS 9. In iOS 8, you could access Pages, Numbers and Keynote files that were stored on your iCloud Drive in the appropriately named folders. You could only access these in the equivalent apps on your iPad.

With the new iCloud Drive app in iOS 9, you can see all your iCloud Drive files. In particular, it gives you access to text files, images, and PDFs, which can all be viewed inside the iCloud Drive app.

Accessing Your Files

Here is how to access your iCloud Drive files.

1. Open the Settings app and go to iCloud, iCloud Drive. You see a switch to turn on iCloud Drive access. It should be on by default.

2. Turn on Show on Home Screen. This shows the iCloud Drive app on your Home Screen. It may not be on the first page.

3. Find the iCloud Drive icon on your Home Screen and tap it.

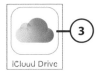

4. The iCloud Drive app shows your iCloud Drive folders. This should match what you see on your Mac in iCloud Drive. You see some special default folders, like the one for Pages.

5. You also see folders created by third-party Mac apps you may have that use iCloud Drive, such as the image editing app Pixelmator.

6. Some app-specific folders may be inactive and inaccessible. For instance, this folder is for Automator scripts, which can only be used on Macs.

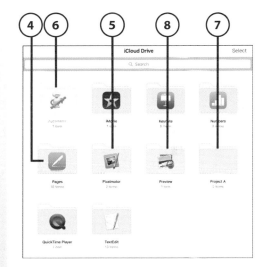

7. If you have created any general use folders on your iCloud Drive, you see those, too. You can tap them to dig down to the folders and files inside.

8. You also see folders for Mac apps, such as Preview and TextEdit, that have no iPad equivalent. But you can still access the files inside with the iCloud Drive app. As an example, suppose you have a Preview document. You would tap this folder to view the file.

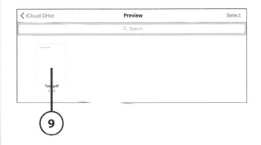

9. The next screen shows a list of files. In this case, there is only one: a PDF file. Tapping it opens the file, if it has a supported app for it.

10. Although the iCloud Drive app does not allow you to edit or do much else with PDF files like this one, you can at least view it.

11. You can also move the file to a new location inside your iCloud Drive. This change is reflected on other iOS devices and your Mac.

12. You can also delete the file. This deletes it from iCloud Drive, so it also disappears from your Mac.

13. The action button allows you to take the file outside the iCloud Drive app.

14. In this case, the only app installed that handles PDF files is iBooks. You can use this button to copy the file to your iBooks library. If you have other apps installed, such as Adobe's PDF Reader app, you see it here and are able to copy the file to it.

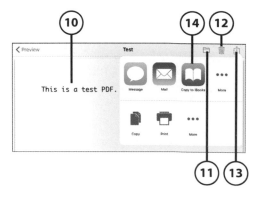

Opening Files

The iCloud Drive app acts as a simple viewer for files like PDFs, text files, Word docs, images, and so on. You can use steps 13 and 14 to open those files in appropriate apps, if you have them installed.

>>>Go Further

YOU STILL MAY NEED AN APP

Just because you can see the file in iCloud Drive doesn't mean you can work with it on your iPad. The iCloud Drive app acts as a simple viewer for many file types. But, just like with desktop computers, you need the right app to work with the file.

For instance, if you get a Photoshop file on your desktop computer, you wouldn't expect to edit it unless you had Photoshop installed. The same is true on the iPad. You need the right app to work with the file. Sometimes, the app doesn't exist as an iPad app and there is nothing you can do to work with the file.

Creating documents and then saving them to iCloud Drive also requires the appropriate app. An app developer needs to build iCloud Drive compatibility into the app to allow you to save the file to iCloud Drive.

Purchase music and
buy or rent videos.

Listen to podcasts.   Play your music.

In this chapter, you learn how to use the Music and Video apps to play music and watch video. You also learn how to use Apple Music and iTunes Radio.

→ Playing a Song

→ Building a Playlist

→ Making iTunes Purchases

→ Sharing Purchases with Your Family

→ Having It All with Apple Music

→ Listening to Podcasts

→ Playing Video

→ Using AirPlay to Play Music and Video on Other Devices

→ Home Sharing

→ Listening to iTunes Radio

Playing Music and Video

The iPad handles playing music as well as any iPod or iPhone ever has, plus it has a large, beautiful screen for you to use to browse your collection. In Chapter 3, you learned how to sync music to your iPad from your computer. That's one way to get music onto your iPad. You can also use the iTunes app to purchase music, or the iTunes Match service to sync all your music from iCloud. Families can share purchases using the Family Sharing feature. A new option to subscribe to Apple Music gives you unlimited access to nearly all the songs on iTunes.

No matter how you put music on your iPad, you play your music using the Music app. You can also listen to iTunes Radio, free streaming music from Apple.

Playing a Song

So let's start by simply selecting and playing a song with the Music app.

1. Tap the Music icon. It is located along the bottom of your Home screen, unless you've customized your toolbar and moved it elsewhere.

2. Tap My Music on the bottom, if it isn't already selected.

3. At the top of the screen, you see either Artists, Albums, Songs, Genres, or Composers. This indicates how your list is presented below. You can tap here to switch. Select Songs to see an alphabetical list of all your songs.

4. Tap the name of a song to start it. You can also tap and drag up and down on the screen to scroll through the list. If you have a lot of songs, the letters of the alphabet will appear on the right side, and you can use these to jump to a position in the list of songs.

5. At the bottom of the screen, the Play button changes to a Pause button. You can tap this button to pause the song.

6. Tap the name of the song.

7. Use the volume slider to adjust the volume, or use the physical volume controls on the side of your iPad.

8. Tap the Repeat button to choose whether to repeat this song over and over again, or repeat the playlist or album you are currently listening to. After you have turned on Repeat, you can tap here again to change the repeat range, or turn it off.

9. Tap the Shuffle button to make your iPad play the songs in the album or playlist in a random order.

10. Tap the down-pointing arrow button at the top left to return to the main Music app interface.

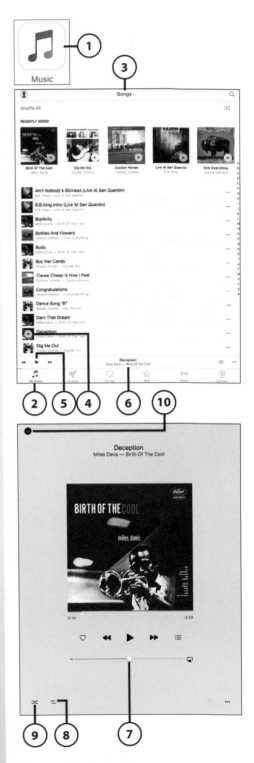

11. Tap the list option at the top of the screen and change it to Artists.

12. A list of artists is shown on the left. Tap on an artist to view the songs by album for that artist.

13. The list of albums and songs appears on the right. You can scroll up and down and tap on any song to play it.

14. Tap the Search button at the top of the list to search your songs. When you use search in the Music app, you are given two options: My Music and Apple Music. If you are not a subscriber to Apple Music, be sure to choose My Music or you will not be able to use any of the results.

Playing iTunes Match Music

If you are using iTunes Match, you will see all your music in the list—even songs not currently on your iPad. You can still tap the name of a song to start it. The song downloads and plays, assuming you are connected to the Internet. You can also tap the iTunes Match (cloud) icon for each song to simply download each song so it is ready to listen to later, even if you are not connected. You would want to do this for some songs if you are going to be away from your Internet connection and plan to listen to music.

Visit www.apple.com/itunes/itunes-match/ to find out more about Apple's iTunes Match service.

How Else Can I Listen to Music?

You can also listen to music using third-party apps. Some apps access your music collection on your iPad, but the most interesting ones play streaming music from over the Internet. We look at apps, such as Pandora and Spotify, in Chapter 15. You can also use iTunes Radio to listen to streaming music. We look at that later in this chapter.

Siri: Playing Music

You can use Siri to play music. Here are some examples:

"Play The Beatles"
"Play Georgia On My Mind"
"Play some blues"
"Play my driving music" (plays the playlist named "driving music")
"Shuffle all songs"
"Skip"
"Pause"

Building a Playlist

Playlists are a way to take the songs you have on your iPad and arrange them in ordered groups. For instance, you can create one to listen to while working, while working out, while trying to go to sleep, or make a party mix for your next get-together.

Creating Playlists

You can create playlists on your Mac or PC in iTunes, but you can also build playlists on your iPad.

1. Tap the Playlists button at the bottom of the main Music app screen.

2. A list of current playlists appears. Tap the New button.

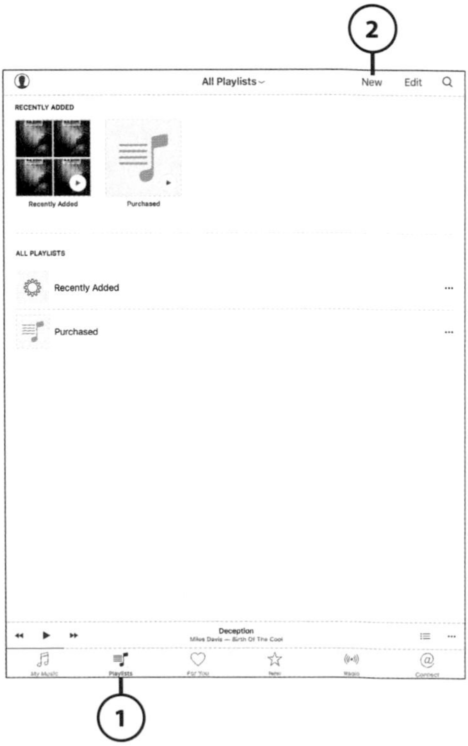

3. Give the new playlist a name, such as *My Playlist*, by tapping here and typing a name.

4. Tap the Add Songs button.

5. A list of sorting options comes up. Tap Songs to see a list of all your songs to choose from. Otherwise, you can choose Artists, Albums, Genres, Composers, or Playlists to view all your music sorted differently.

6. Tap any songs you want to add to the playlist.

7. Use the Search field at the top to find songs faster. If you don't see the Search field, tap and drag your list of songs down so you reveal it at the top of the list.

8. Tap the Done button when you have selected all the songs you want to add to the playlist.

9. On the playlist screen, remove songs from the playlist by tapping on the red buttons. A Remove button appears to the right side of the listing. Tap the Remove button to confirm that you want to remove that song from the playlist.

10. Tap and drag on the three-line buttons to rearrange the songs.

11. Tap the + button to add more songs to the playlist.

12. Tap Done to exit editing the playlist.

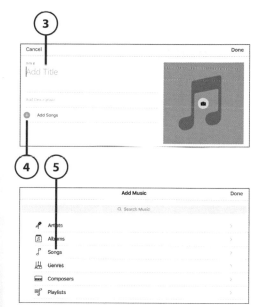

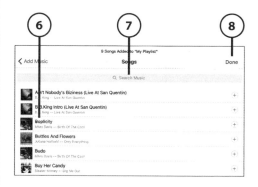

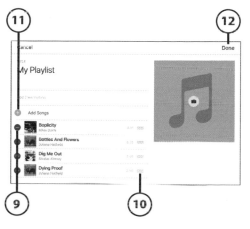

13. You now see your playlist on the
     main Playlists screen. Tap it to start
     playing the songs.

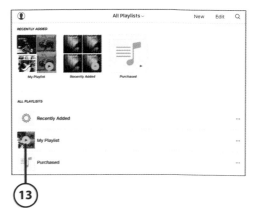

Making iTunes Purchases

You have lots of options when it comes to adding more music to your iPad. You
can simply add more music to your iTunes collection on your computer and then
sync those songs to your iPad. In that case, you can buy them from iTunes, from
another online source, or import them from music CDs.

How Else Can I Get Music?

You can purchase music on your iPad only through the iTunes app. But you can sync
music from your computer that you get from any source that doesn't use special copy protection, like CDs you import into iTunes. You can buy online from places such as Amazon.
com, eMusic.com, cdbaby.com, or even directly from the websites of some artists.

Buying on Your iPad

In addition to syncing music to your iPad
from your computer, you can purchase
music, movies, TV shows, and audio books
directly on your iPad using the iTunes app
and using the same account that you use
in iTunes on your computer.

1. Tap the iTunes Store app icon on
    your Home screen to go to the
    iTunes store. If this is the first time
    you have used the iTunes Store, you
    might be asked about setting up
    Family Sharing. See the next task
    for more information about this.

iTunes Store

2. Initially, you'll be viewing a screen showing featured albums and songs from all genres. But you can select a specific genre of music instead.

3. Swipe left and right to browse more featured albums.

4. Drag the screen up to reveal more lists, such as top albums, top songs, and music videos.

5. Use the Search field at the top to search for an artist, album, or song by name.

6. Select a suggestion from the list, or tap the Search button on the keyboard to complete the search.

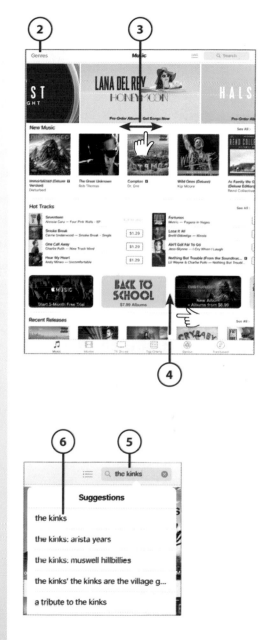

7. Find a song or album you want to buy, and tap its artwork to view more information.

8. If you move down the page by swiping upward, you'll also find ringtones, music videos, movies, and even books that match your search.

9. Tap a song name to listen to a sample of the song.

10. Tap outside the album window to close it and return to the previous view.

11. To buy a song, album, or any item in the iTunes music store, tap the price of that item, and then tap again on the Buy button.

Syncing Devices

After you make an iTunes purchase, the music, TV show, or movie you downloaded should transfer to your computer the next time you sync your iPad. From your computer, you can sync your new purchase to any other device you use that uses your iTunes account.

You can also set iTunes on your computer and your other devices to automatically download new purchases. So when you buy on your iPad, you'll get the new music everywhere. On your iPad, that setting is found in Settings, iTunes & App Store, Automatic Downloads. In iTunes on your computer, it is found in the menu iTunes, Preferences, Store, Automatic Downloads.

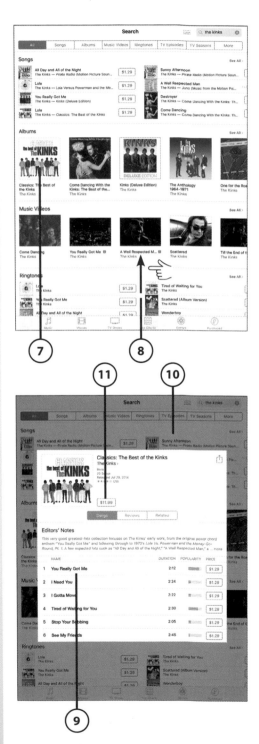

iTunes Match or Apple Music—No Syncing Needed

If you are using iTunes Match, you really don't need to worry about syncing between devices at all. All of the music you purchase will be available when you look in your Music app on iOS devices or iTunes on a Mac or PC.

If you use Apple Music, you have access to all the songs on all your devices. Your playlists and music you have marked as "My Music" would be available everywhere.

Sharing Purchases with Your Family

Family Sharing lets you share items you purchase from iTunes with other members of your household. One family member is set up as the organizer, and his or her iTunes account is the one that will be charged for all purchases.

Each member of the family sharing group can have their own Apple ID and iCloud account, which will be used for email, calendars, and other purposes. Purchases are made through the iTunes account of the organizer's Apple ID.

In addition, those who are part of your Family Sharing group will also have a shared photo stream in the Photos app, a special shared calendar in the Calendar app, a shared Reminder list in the Reminders app, and can see one another's location with the Find My Friends app.

Setting Up Family Sharing

1. The organizer should tap Settings to open her Settings app, and then tap iCloud.

2. Tap Set Up Family Sharing near the top of the iCloud settings side.

3. Next, there is a quick series of screens telling you more about Family Sharing, asking you to read the legal agreement and to confirm your Apple ID and payment information. Tap Get Started to begin working with Family Sharing.

4. After you complete these screens, you are now listed as the organizer for Family Sharing. You can tap your name to alter your settings.

5. You can always turn off purchase sharing. Family Sharing can still be used for other features, such as the shared photos and calendar events.

6. You can now tap Add Family Member to add another family member to the group.

7. Type their Apple ID email address or choose it from your list of contacts.

8. Tap Next.

9. Tap Send an Invitation to send the invitation to the family member's iPad so they can confirm their membership in your Family Sharing group.

10. They will see a notification appear. If they tap it, they will be taken right to the Family Sharing section of the Settings app.

11. They need to tap Accept to join the group.

>>>*Go Further*

PARENTAL GUIDANCE

If a family member younger than 13 years old is added to your group, every time they try to make a purchase, the Family Sharing organizer will get a notification and will have to approve that purchase before it goes through. Also, children ages 13–17 can have this option turned on when they are added to Family Sharing.

The organizer can also tap on any adult family member's name in the Family Sharing settings and then flip the switch labeled Parent/Guardian to enable that adult to approve purchases made by children.

Having It All with Apple Music New!

A popular option for music lovers today is to subscribe to an unlimited music service. Apple now offers such a service, called Apple Music, which is built into the Music app on your iPad.

For a monthly fee, you can play music from a huge collection of millions of songs—nearly everything that is available in iTunes, with only a few notable exceptions, like The Beatles. You can listen to what you want, when you want, on your iPad, iPhone, and Mac. For a modest increase in the monthly fee, you can also share your music access with your family members.

Signing up for Apple Music is fairly easy, and Apple even allows you to try it for a while before you start paying for your subscription. After you are signed up, you can browse Apple Music and pick songs or whole albums to add to your collection in the Music app, and then play those songs any time you want.

Apple Music also includes a For You section that offers specially curated playlists and listening ideas based on your listening preferences and history.

Signing Up for Apple Music

You sign up for Apple Music in the Settings app.

1. In the Settings app, go to Music.

2. Tap Join Apple Music.

3. Tap the button to begin your trial period.

4. Select your plan. The Individual plan is just for you and works on all of the devices and Macs you have set up with your Apple ID. The Family plan also includes others you have set up with Family Sharing. Continue to follow the prompt to complete setup.

Cancelling

Signing up for the trial is low risk as you could always cancel your subscription before the trial period ends. Just tap on the ID button at the top of the Music app (looks like a circle with a head in it), select View Apple ID, then Manage under Subscriptions.

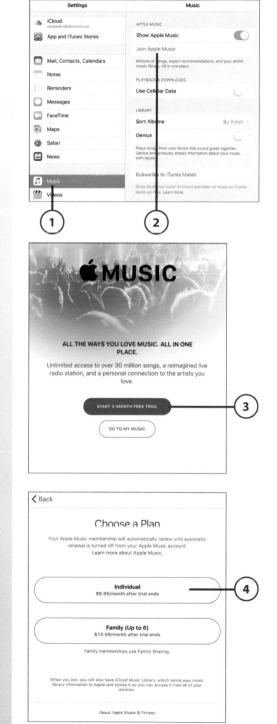

Using Apple Music

After you have signed up for Apple Music, using it is similar to playing songs you have imported from your computer or purchased from iTunes.

1. In the Music app, tap New at the bottom of the screen. This shows you the latest music available in the service.

2. Alternatively, you can go to For You to get recommendations based on your music collection and past listening.

3. Use the Search button to access anything in Apple Music.

4. Type any artist or song name to search.

5. Make sure you select Apple Music instead of My Music. The latter only shows results you have already added to your collection.

6. Tap the result that best matches what you are searching for.

7. The results show artists, songs, albums, and playlists. If you see the item you want, tap it. In this case, tap an album.

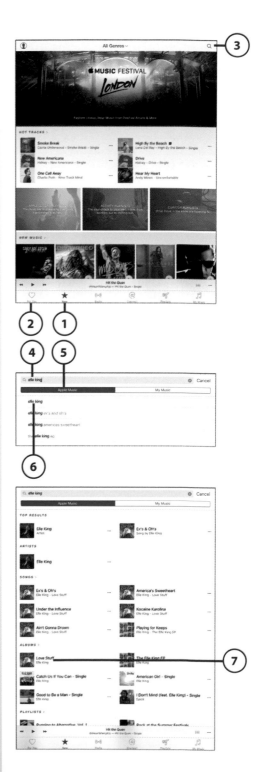

8. A plus button appears next to the album name. Tap it, and it turns into a checkmark. This indicates you have added the album to your collection. It now appears under My Music just as if you had bought it.

9. Alternatively, you can tap the … button to access some options on a per-song basis, including a + button for adding just that one song to your collection.

10. You can also just tap a song to play it immediately.

11. You may be wondering whether you can play Apple Music songs when you are not connected to the Internet. The answer is yes and no. If you tap the … button next to the album and select Make Available Offline, you will have a copy saved to your iPad to play any time. But you need to do that before you go offline, natu-rally. You can select this option for any song or album you have in your collection.

One-Time Setup

These steps are how you play music for the first time, or how to add music from Apple Music to your collection. After you do that, you can replay the songs from My Music just as if you had purchased them, as long as you remain a subscriber. You also now find these added songs on your other iOS devices and Macs.

>>>Go Further
TRY NEW THINGS

One big advantage to a subscription service like Apple Music is you can try new songs as much as you like. If you hear of a new artist, or catch a song on the radio, or hear something in a TV show, you can go to Apple Music and play the album just to see if you like it. That's not easy to do otherwise, as you would end up buying lots of albums that you only listen to once.

Listening to Podcasts

Podcasts are episodic shows, either audio or video, produced by major networks, small companies, and individuals. You'll find news, information, tutorials, music, comedy, drama, talk shows, and more. There is something covering almost any topic you can think of.

Subscribing to Podcasts

To subscribe to and listen to or watch podcasts, you use the Podcasts app from Apple.

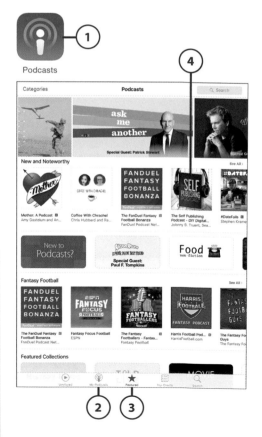

1. Tap the Podcasts app icon on your Home screen.

2. Tap the My Podcasts button to look at the podcasts you've already downloaded. If you start off by looking at your library, you'll see an equivalent button labeled Store at the bottom left that takes you back to this screen.

3. Tap Featured to go to a screen with Apple's currently featured podcasts. Alternatively, if you know what you are looking for, you can tap the Search button at the bottom of the screen to search for a podcast by name or topic.

4. Tap a podcast to get more information about it. You can also swipe right to left to view more in the list.

5. Tap Reviews to see what others have to say.

6. Tap the Play button next to a single episode to play just that episode.

7. Tap Subscribe to subscribe to the podcast. This downloads the latest episode and also automatically gets new episodes as they become available.

8. Using the My Podcasts button from step 2, you can go to the list of podcasts you are subscribed to.

9. Tap the episode to watch or listen to it.

10. Tap the … button and select View Full Description to get more details about an episode. Other options allow you to mark it as played without listening, queue it for future play, or delete it.

11. Tap the settings button to set the sort order and auto-download preferences for the podcast. You would want a current events podcast to put the newest at the top, while a podcast that tells a story or is a learning series would be better suited for oldest on top.

12. Tap Edit to be able to delete podcast episodes from your library.

13. Tap the Edit button at the top left and then use the red buttons next to the podcast names to remove a podcast subscription.

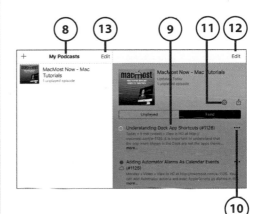

Playing Video

After you have movies, TV shows, and home videos on your iPad, you need to play them using the Videos app.

1. Tap the Videos app icon on your Home screen.

2. The Movies you have on your iPad display by default. Tap Movies, TV Shows, or Home Videos to switch lists. If you don't have videos in one or more of these categories, then that button may not appear at all. Other categories, such as Music Videos, might also appear if you have that kind of video content.

3. Tap a movie to view more information about it. Depending on the type of video, it may just start playing and you have to stop it to see the information. Movies show the information first, but Home Videos will just start playing.

4. Tap the Play button to start the movie.

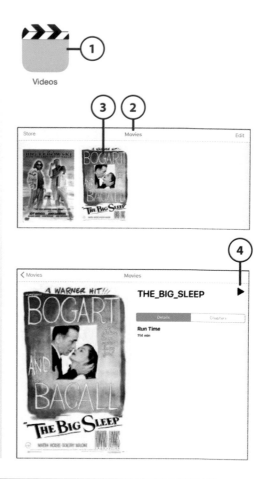

Any Video Alternatives to Apple?

You bet! There is a Netflix app for the iPad that Netflix subscribers can use to stream movies. Amazon also has an Amazon Instant Video app for subscribers to their service. Some companies, such as ABC, have also provided their own apps for viewing their shows on the iPad. You can also view video from any site that has video in standard MP4 formats. The site www.archive.org/details/movies has public domain movies and videos, often in MP4 format. The popular video site http://blip.tv also works well with the iPad.

5. After a movie is playing, tap in the middle of the screen to bring up the controls at the top and bottom of the screen.

How About My Home Videos?

If you shoot a home video with a video camera, or iPod touch or iPhone, you can bring that into iTunes on your Mac or PC and sync it to your iPad. They appear as Home Movies in the menu along the top of the Videos app.

6. Tap the Play/Pause button to pause the movie and then again to resume.

7. Adjust the volume with the volume control.

8. Drag the dot along the line to move to a different section of the movie.

9. Use the Back and Forward buttons to jump between chapters.

10. Tap the Done button to exit the movie and return to the movie information screen.

Changing the Orientation

For most video content, you can rotate your iPad to view in a horizontal orientation and use the Zoom button at the upper right to crop the left and right sides of the video so that it fits vertically on the screen. This is similar to watching a movie on a standard TV.

What About My DVDs?

If you can import CD music content into iTunes, you'd think you'd be able to import video content from your DVDs. Well, technically it is possible (although not necessarily legal) by using programs like Handbrake (http://handbrake.fr/) for your Mac or PC to import DVD content and then drag the resulting file into iTunes. You can then sync it with your iPad. These may also show up as Home Movies, since your iPad doesn't recognize them as official movie content.

>>>Go Further
BUYING AND RENTING VIDEO

Although buying video is similar to buying music, some significant details are different and worth taking a look at.

Copy Protection: Although music in the iTunes store recently became copy-protection free, videos are a different story altogether. Purchased videos can be played back only on the Apple devices you own that use your iTunes account. You can't burn videos to a DVD, for instance, or watch them on a TV unless it is hooked up to an Apple device. Rentals are even more strict because you can watch them only on the device you rent them on.

Collecting Movies: Thinking of starting a collection of videos by purchasing them from Apple? These videos take up a lot of space on your hard drive. An iPad, even a 128GB version, quickly fills up if you start adding dozens of movies. Fortunately, once you purchase a movie with iTunes, you can download it again later. So you can purchase many movies over time, but only put the ones you want to watch on your iPad. Movies you own will appear in your Videos app as well, even if they are not actually on your iPad. You will see a little iCloud download button appear next to them. You can tap that icon to start downloading that movie to your iPad from Apple's servers.

Time-Delayed Rentals: Rentals have some strict playback restrictions. After you download a rental, you have 30 days to watch it. After you start watching it, you have only 24 hours to finish it. This means you can load up your iPad in advance with a few movies to watch on an airplane flight or while on vacation.

TV Show Season Passes: You can purchase seasons of TV shows that aren't complete yet. When you do this, you are basically pre-ordering each episode. You get the existing episodes immediately but have to wait for the future episodes. They usually appear the next day after airing on network television.

Multi-Pass: In addition to season passes, you can also get a Multi-Pass, which is for TV shows that broadcast daily. When you purchase a Multi-Pass, you get the most recent episode plus the next 15 episodes when they become available.

HD Versus SD: You can purchase or rent most movies and TV shows in either HD (high definition) or SD (standard definition). Look for the HD/SD button to the right of the buy buttons on movie purchase pages. The difference is the quality of the image, which affects the file size, of course. If you have a slow connection or limited bandwidth, you might want to stick to SD versions of the shows.

Using AirPlay to Play Music and Video on Other Devices

In iTunes, with the Video app and many other apps that play music or video, you have the option to send the audio or video stream from your iPad to another device that is connected to the same Wi-Fi network, such as an Apple TV.

You need to enable AirPlay on those devices first. For instance, using the Apple TV (2nd generation models or newer), you need to go into settings on the device and turn on AirPlay. You also need to make sure that the device is using the same Wi-Fi network as your iPad.

Accessing AirPlay

1. While using almost any app, bring up the Control Center by swiping upward from the bottom of your screen. (See, "Using Notifications and Control Center" in Chapter 1.)

2. Tap the Airplay button to bring up a list of devices. Note that if you do not have any Airplay devices on your Wi-Fi network, you will not be able to select this.

3. Your iPad will show as the first device. Use this to switch back to playing the media on your iPad if you have switched to something else.

4. Next to each device, you will see either a screen icon or a speaker icon. This tells you whether you can stream video or just audio using that device.

5. Tap on another device, and the music or video currently playing will start to play over that device.

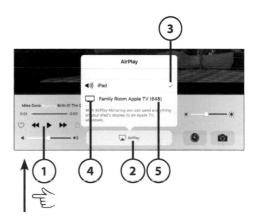

AirPlay Everything

You can also use AirPlay to mirror your iPad's screen with an up-to-date Apple TV. In Control Center, you will see a Mirror switch appear under any video device you select. Use that to turn on mirroring and send your screen to the Apple TV. This is great for apps that do not have a specific video to present, like games or productivity apps. You'll just see your iPad's screen on the TV. Some video streaming apps, however, specifically block this.

Home Sharing

If you are using iTunes on your Mac or PC, you can play this iTunes content on your iPad if it is on the same local network.

1. In iTunes on your Mac or PC, choose Turn On Home Sharing from the File menu. You are prompted to enter your Apple account ID and password.

2. In the Settings App, tap Music.

3. Tap Sign In and enter the same Apple account ID and password used in step 1.

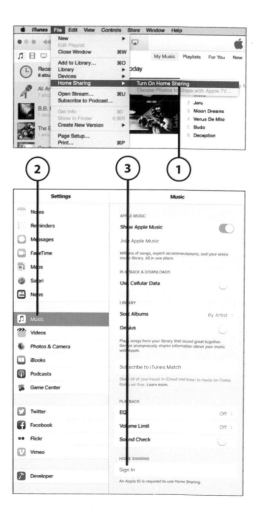

4. In the Music app, tap the list type at the top. It usually reads Artists, Albums, Songs, or Genres.

5. Tap Home Sharing.

6. Then choose the name of the library you want to access. The content in your Music app changes to reflect the content in the iTunes library on your Mac or PC. You can now play songs from your computer without having to transfer them to your iPad first.

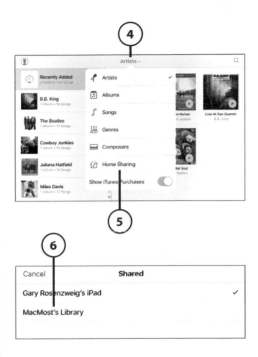

What if My Library Doesn't Appear?

Home Sharing is tricky. It requires that you use the same iTunes account IDs on both your iPad and on your Mac or PC. It also requires that you have the iPad on the same local network as your Mac or PC. In addition, network firewalls and other software may get in the way. It usually works effortlessly, but some users have reported trouble getting Home Sharing to work at all with their particular home network setup.

Listening to iTunes Radio

iTunes Radio is a streaming music service from Apple that is available in iTunes on computers and in the Music app in IOS. You choose a music genre, artist, or song, and then you hear a continuous stream of songs based on that starting point. That stream is saved as a "station," and you can return to it at any time. Meanwhile, you can create other stations with other starting points and switch between them. The music comes from Apple's servers and includes music you already own, as well as music you don't.

In addition, Apple has some specially curated station that you can enjoy as streaming radio. Plus, there is the DJ-hosted Beats 1 Apple radio station that broadcasts live 24 hours a day. You don't need to be a subscriber to Apple Music to listen to these stations.

Selecting a Station

Using iTunes Radio is very easy. You can choose from some sample stations or create your own.

1. Tap the Radio icon at the bottom of the Music app. If this is your first time using iTunes Radio, you might get a welcome message and be prompted with a Start Listening button.

Log In

You must be signed in to your iCloud account to use iTunes Radio. You can sign in using the Settings app in the iTunes & App Stores section.

2. The Beats 1 station is listed at the top. You can tap Listen Now to start streaming it to your iPad. If you don't like what you hear at the moment, keep in mind that Apple runs different programming all day long. So while this particular show may not be for you, one later in the day may be more appealing.

3. You can listen to one of the Featured Stations that Apple provides. There are quite a few of them, so you have to scroll down to see them all.

4. To create your own station, browse your music and select an artist, album, or song. Look for the radio station button to the right of it and tap it. It looks like a dot with curves to the left and right.

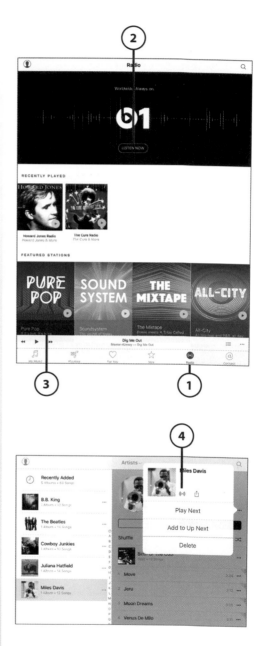

5. It might appear that you are just playing a single song, but you can see in the scrolling description that it is "radio."

6. You can purchase the current song from iTunes.

7. Tap the star button, and you can choose Play More Like This or Play Less Like This. You don't need to do this for every song, but doing it for songs you feel especially fit your idea of this station, or don't fit in at all, helps fine-tune future songs played.

8. You can skip the current song.

9. To stop the station, tap the pause button. It changes to a play button so you can resume later.

After you have created a station, it appears as a recently played station on the main Radio screen, just above the present Apple stations in step 3.

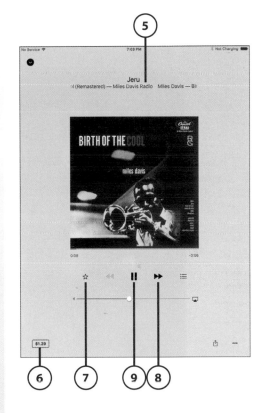

What About Bandwidth?

iTunes Radio streams music from the Internet. This means it uses bandwidth. If you are using your iPad with a mobile network or have limited bandwidth at home, that is something to be aware of. However, audio streams do not use as much as video streams, so you may be surprised at how little bandwidth an hour or so of music uses compared to watching a few YouTube videos.

And Now a Message from Our Sponsor

iTunes Radio is free, but sometimes includes commercials. Every so often you'll hear a sponsored message between songs on stations you create. Beats 1 occasionally has "sponsored by" messages. But if you have an iTunes Match account and are signed into it, as a bonus you get to listen to the station you created in iTunes Radio commercial-free!

Purchase and read
books with the iPad's
ebook reader.

In this chapter, find out how to purchase books from the iBooks store and how to read them on your iPad.

Reading Books

As an ebook reader, your iPad gives you access to novels, textbooks, and more, storing hundreds inside. Plus, you can purchase more books right from the iPad.

A single app, the iBooks app, allows you to both read and purchase new books. You can also download and add books from other sources, including the Kindle app.

Buying a Book from Apple

The first thing to do with the iBooks app is to get some books! You can buy books using the store in the app. You can also find some free books there.

1. Tap the iBooks app icon to launch iBooks.

2. If you have previously purchased and downloaded books, you see those when iBooks opens.

3. Tap one of the buttons such as Featured, NYTimes, Top Charts, or Top Authors to switch to the iBooks store.

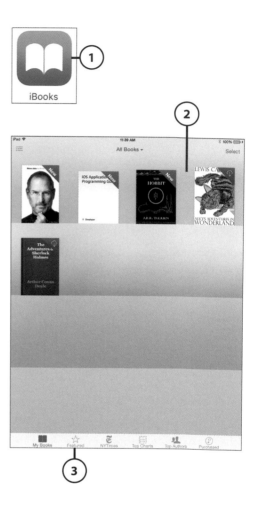

Don't Want to Purchase from Apple?

You don't necessarily need to buy books from Apple. You can buy from any seller that sends you an ePub or PDF formatted file with no copy protection. If you receive the file on a computer, just drag and drop it into iTunes. It will add it to your books collection there, ready to be synced to your iPad.

You can also add PDFs you find on the web or receive in email to your iBooks library. While viewing a PDF on your iPad in Safari, tap once in the middle of the screen, and an Open in iBooks option appears at the top. While viewing a PDF attached to an email message, you can use the Share button to open it in iBooks. Many other third-party apps also allow sharing PDFs to iBooks this way. Text and ePub-formatted documents often work as well. When you open a document in iBooks, a copy is placed in your iBooks library.

4. Swipe left and right to browse more featured books.

5. Tap the Categories button to go to a list of book categories.

6. Tap Top Charts button to see a list of bestsellers.

7. Swipe up to see more featured categories.

8. Use the search field to search for book titles and authors.

9. Tap any book cover to view more information about the book.

10. Tap the price next to a book to purchase it. The price button changes to Buy Book. Tap it again to continue with the purchase.

11. Tap the Sample button to download a sample of the book.

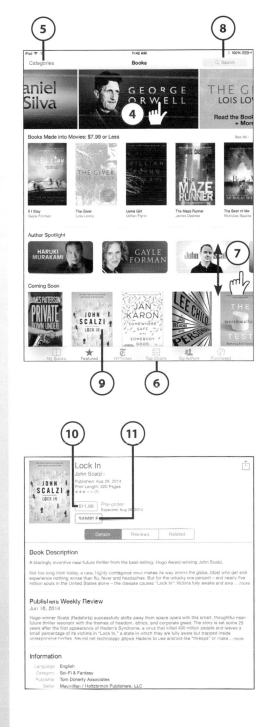

Reading a Book

Reading books is a simple process. Following are the basics of reading your downloaded books.

1. Tap the iBooks app icon to launch iBooks.

2. If you are still in the store section of the app, tap My Books at the bottom to go to your iBooks library. Then, tap a book to open it.

Can't Find Your Book?

Did you download a book only to discover that you can't see it in your Library? Try tapping the Collections button at the top of the screen and switching to a different collection. For instance, by default, PDF documents are put in the PDF collection, not in the Books collection.

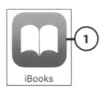

3. To turn a page, tap and hold anywhere along the right side of the page, and drag to the left. A virtual page turns.

4. Tap and drag from the left to the right or simply tap the left side of the page to turn the page back.

5. To move quickly through pages, tap and drag the small marker at the bottom of the page along the dotted line. Release to jump to a page.

6. Tap the Table of Contents button at the top to view a table of contents.

INTRODUCTION

How This Book Came to Be

In the early summer of 2004, I got a phone call from Steve Jobs. He had been scattershot friendly to me over the years, with occasional bursts of intensity, especially when he was launching a new product that he wanted on the cover of *Time* or featured on CNN, places where I'd worked. But now that I was no longer at either of those places, I hadn't heard from him much. We talked a bit about the Aspen Institute, which I had recently joined, and I invited him to speak at our summer campus in Colorado. He'd be happy to come, he said, but not to be onstage. He wanted instead to take a walk so that we could talk.

That seemed a bit odd. I didn't yet know that taking a long walk was his preferred way to have a serious conversation. It turned out that he wanted me to write a biography of him. I had recently published one on Benjamin Franklin and was writing one about Albert Einstein, and my initial reaction was to wonder, half jokingly, whether he saw himself as the natural successor in that sequence. Because I assumed that he was still in the middle of an oscillating career that had many more

7. Tap anywhere in the table of contents to jump to that part of the book.

8. Tap the Resume button to return to the page you were previously viewing.

9. Tap the Library button to return to your books. If you return to the book later, you return to the last page you viewed. No need to stick a bookmark or piece of scrap paper into your iPad.

Using Reading Aids

iBooks has a variety of ways you can customize your reading experience. You can change the font size, the font itself, and even turn your iPad on its side to see two pages at one time.

1. While viewing a page in iBooks, tap the display adjustment controls at the top of the screen. If you don't see the controls, tap once in the middle of the screen to bring them up.

2. Drag the brightness control left or right. Dragging to the left makes the screen dim, which you might use if you're reading in a dark room. Dragging to the right makes it bright, which could make reading easier while outdoors.

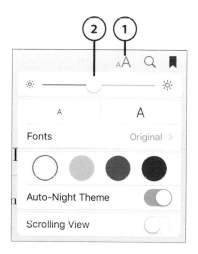

3. Tap the smaller "A" button to reduce the size of the text.

4. Tap the larger "A" button to increase the size of the text.

5. Tap the Fonts button to choose from a few font options.

6. Tap to select one of four color themes.

7. The Auto-Night Theme switch monitors the light around your iPad and switches to Night mode when it is dark.

8. Turn on Scrolling View to read your book as one long scrolling page.

9. Turn your iPad on its side to change to a two-page view. (Make sure your orientation lock is not on.)

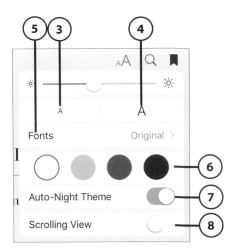

Where Did the Buttons Go?

If you tap in the middle of the screen, the buttons at the top and the dotted line at the bottom disappear. You can still turn the pages; you just don't have access to these buttons. To see the buttons again, tap in the middle of the screen.

Adding Notes and Highlights

Each time you launch iBooks, your iPad returns you to the page you were last reading. However, you might want to mark a favorite passage or a bit of key information.

1. Go to a page in a book in iBooks. (See the previous tasks in this chapter to find out how to access a book.)

2. Tap a word and hold your finger there for about a second.

3. Release your finger and you see six choices: Copy, Define, Highlight, Note, Search, and Share.

Define, Search, and Share

Tapping Define brings up a definition of the word. Tapping Search brings up a list of the locations of the word throughout the text. When you choose Share, you can send the excerpt you have selected to someone else using email, a text message, Twitter, or Facebook.

4. Drag the blue dots to enlarge the section of text that is highlighted.

5. Tap Highlight. Alternatively, you can tap a word and hold for a second and then immediately start dragging to highlight text.

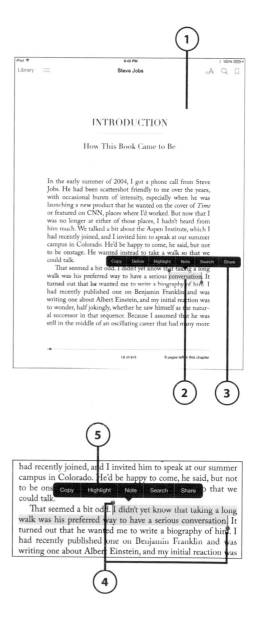

6. The text is now highlighted.

7. Tap the first button to change the type of highlighting. You can choose from various colors or a simple red underline.

8. Tap the second button to remove the highlight completely.

9. Tap Note instead of Highlight to bring up a yellow pad of paper and add a note.

10. Tap in the note to bring up the keyboard and start typing.

11. Tap outside the yellow paper to finish the note. It will then appear as a small yellow sticky note to the right side of the page. Tap it any time you want to view or edit the note. You can delete a note by removing all text in the note.

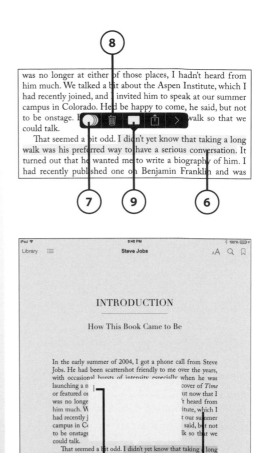

Adding Bookmarks

You can also bookmark a page to easily find it later.

1. Tap the bookmark button at the top of a page to bookmark the page. You can bookmark as many pages as you want in a book. If you don't see the bookmarks button, tap once in the center of the screen to bring up the controls.

2. Tap it again to remove the bookmark from the page.

3. Tap the Table of Contents button to go to the table of contents.

4. Tap the Bookmarks button at the top of the table of contents to see a list of all the bookmarks, highlights, and notes you have added to the book.

5. Tap any bookmark, note, or highlight to jump to it.

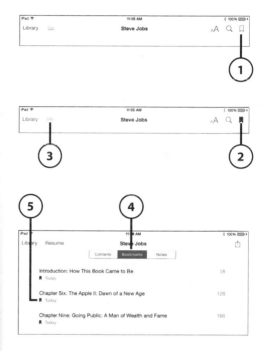

Organizing Your Books

Like to read a lot? You aren't alone. Many people gather massive collections of ebooks on their iPads. Fortunately, iBooks includes a few great ways to organize your ebooks.

1. If you are on the iBook store screen, tap My Books to view your library. If you are viewing a book, tap Library in the upper-left corner to return to the book library.

2. The heading at the top of the screen shows which collection you are viewing. Tap it to see a list of collections.

3. Tap a Collection name to jump to that collection. You can think of collections as different bookcases filled with books.

4. Tap New Collection to create a new collection.

5. The New Collection option changes to an editable text field, and the keyboard appears. Type the name of the new collection.

6. The Collections list now features your new collection. Tap Done. If you ever want to delete or rearrange collections, the Edit button at the top of this list allows you to do that.

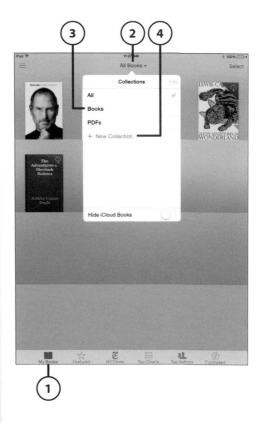

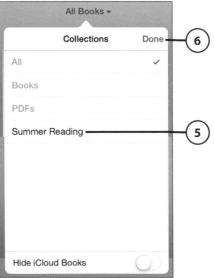

Books in the Cloud

When you view your Purchased Books collection, you will see all the books you have bought in the past, even if that book is no longer on your iPad because you removed it. These books will have a little iCloud icon in the upper-right corner; when you select one, it will download. If you then delete the book, you can always re-download it by tapping on the Purchased button at the bottom of the Collections screens, selecting Not on This iPad from the top, and tapping the download button next to that book.

7. The new collection doesn't have any books in it yet, so selecting it now only brings up a blank list. Instead, tap on All or Books to return to your list of books.

8. After you have returned to your list of books, tap Select to start selecting books to move to the new collection.

9. Tap on several books to select them. You'll see a checkmark appear in the bottom-right corner of each book.

10. Tap Move. (While in this mode, you can also tap Delete, which removes the books from your iPad.)

11. Tap the name of your new collection to move your books there.

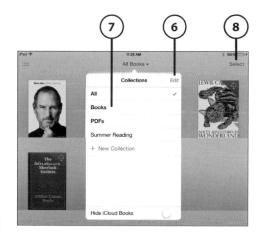

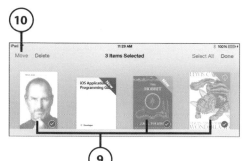

12. Bring up the Collections list again and switch to your new collection.

13. The books you selected to move will now appear here.

14. To re-arrange your books inside a collection, tap and hold any book. The book's picture will get a little larger and start to follow your finger. Drag it around on the screen and release to place it before or after another book.

15. Tap the button at the top left to switch to list view.

16. The list view allows you to sort your books by author or category.

17. Tap the button at the top left to return to the bookshelf view.

Another Way to Delete

You can also delete books in list view by swiping from left to right across the title of a book. A Delete button appears to the right. Tap it to delete the book.

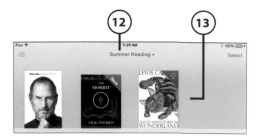

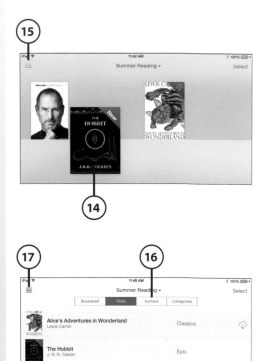

Using iBooks Alternatives

You can purchase and read books from other sources in addition to Apple. The Kindle app allows you to buy books from Amazon.com, or read ones you have already purchased on a previous device. You can also find many small independent publishers and authors in Amazon's catalog that aren't available in iBooks.

You can use the App Store app to search for and install the free Kindle app. See "Purchasing an App" in Chapter 15 to learn how to get third-party apps.

1. Tap the Kindle icon to launch the Kindle app. You see a screen that displays your library. There are two modes: Cloud and Device. Cloud shows all ebooks you have purchased from Amazon. Device shows the books you have already downloaded onto your device.

2. Tap a book to open it.

3. Tap the middle of the page to bring up controls at the top and bottom.

4. Tap the Font button to change the font size, brightness, and background.

5. Tap the right side to flip to the next page.

6. Use the slider at the bottom to quickly move to other pages in the book.

7. The button at the top left allows you to jump to chapters or sections.

8. You can add your own bookmarks just like in iBooks.

9. Tap the Search button to search text in the book.

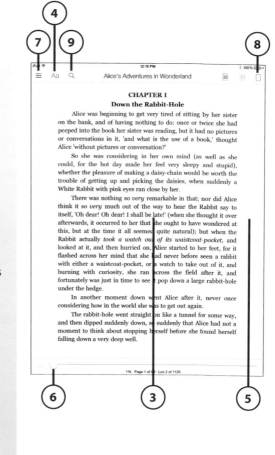

Cloud Versus Device

The Kindle app has a Cloud/Device control at the bottom of the screen. You can tap on a book on the Cloud screen to download it to your device. You can tap on it again, after it has been downloaded, to read it.

More eBook Alternatives

If you like to buy your books from Barnes & Noble, you can also get the Nook app. This lets you read books that can be purchased in the Nook store. If you own a Nook and have already bought books, you can access those books and load them onto your iPad.

Another App you can get is the Google Play Books app. This works with books purchased in the Google Play store, which is similar to the Amazon Kindle store or the iBookstore. You can choose whether you want to buy from Apple, Amazon, Barnes & Noble, or Google.

Track your
appointments
and events.

Store and
search
all your
contacts.

Take notes
and create
lists.

Set reminders.

In this chapter, we learn how to add and look up contacts and calendar events. We also look at the Notes and Reminders apps.

→ Adding a Contact

→ Searching for a Contact

→ Working with Contacts

→ Creating a Calendar Event

→ Using Calendar Views

→ Creating Calendars

→ Creating Notes

→ Creating Checklists in Notes

→ Adding Photos and Sketches to Notes

→ Setting Reminders

→ Setting Clock Alarms

Organizing Your Life

Whether you are a well-connected businessperson or just someone who has lots of friends, you can use the iPad to organize your life with the default Contacts, Calendar, Notes, and Reminders apps. Let's take a close look at some of the things you can do with these apps.

Using the Contacts App

The primary way iPad users store their contacts is to use Apple's iCloud service. This places your contacts database on Apple's servers, making them available to you on any iOS device or Mac you use. You can even access them from a PC with Apple's iCloud.com website. It also keeps all these devices in sync; so any time you add or edit a contact, the change will show up everywhere. The Contacts app on your iPad is how you access and modify your contacts.

Adding a Contact

Let's start by adding a new contact from scratch.

Contacts

1. Tap the Contacts app icon to launch the app.

2. Press the + button near the top of the screen. A New Contact form and keyboard appear.

3. Type the first name of the contact. No need to use Shift to capitalize the name because that happens automatically.

4. Tap the return key on the keyboard to advance to the next field and type the last name for the contact. If you are adding a company instead of a person, skip the first and last name fields and use only the Company field. The contact will be listed under the company name.

5. To add more information, like a phone number, tap the green + button next to the field name.

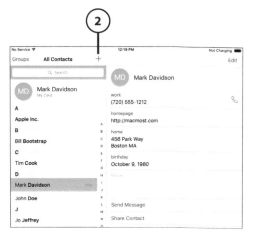

6. Type the phone number.

7. If you ever want to remove some information from the contact, you can use the red – buttons.

8. You can add more than one phone number per contact. Some contacts may have many: home, work, mobile, and so on.

9. Tap Add Photo to add a photo from one of your photo albums or take one right now using your iPad's camera.

Don't Worry About Formatting

You don't need to type phone numbers with parentheses or dashes. Your iPad formats the number for you.

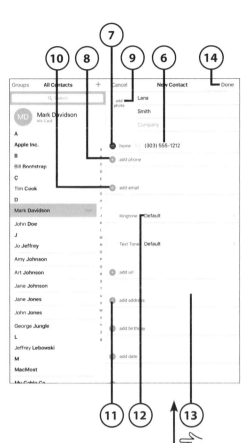

10. You can add one or more email addresses to the contact as well. These will be used in your Mail app when you compose a new message. You will only need to type the person's name, or choose them from a list, instead of typing their email address.

11. You can add one or more physical addresses for the contact.

12. You can select a specific ringtone for the contact that is used when they call you via FaceTime. You can also set a specific Text tone for Messages.

13. You can swipe up to see more fields. You can even add custom fields and notes to a contact.

14. Tap the Done button to finish.

Siri: Call Me Ray

You can set a nickname field in a contact. When you do this, and the contact happens to be yours, Siri will call you by that name. You can also tell Siri: "Call me *name*" and it will change your nickname field even if you are not in the Contacts app at the moment.

You can also set relationships in your contacts by saying things like "Debby is my wife."

Searching for a Contact

If you didn't have a lot of friends before, I'm sure you gained quite a few since you got a new iPad. So how do you search through all those contacts to find the one you want?

1. Tap the Contacts app icon to launch the app.

2. Tap in the Search field. A keyboard appears at the bottom of the screen.

Other Ways to Find Contacts

You can also drag (or flick to move quickly) through the contact list to find a name. In addition, the list of letters on the left side of the Contacts app enables you to jump right to that letter in your contacts list.

Contacts

Siri: Show Me

You can also use Siri to find a contact.
Try these phrases:

"Show me John Smith."
"Show me my contact."
"Show me my wife."

3. Start typing the name of the person you are looking for. As soon
    as you start typing, the app starts
    making a list of contacts that contain the letters you've typed. Keep
    typing until you narrow down the
    list of names and spot the one
    you are looking for.

4. Tap the name to bring up the
    contact.

5. Tap the Cancel button to dismiss
    the search.

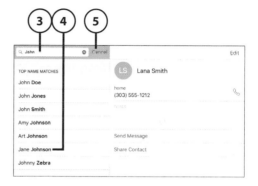

Working with Contacts

After you have contacts in your iPad, you can do a few things from a contact in the Contacts app.

1. Tap and hold the name to copy it to the clipboard buffer.

2. Tap and hold the phone number to copy it to the clipboard buffer.

3. Tap the phone icon to call the number. Tap the message button to send a text message to the contact using that phone number. You can also tap Send Message near the bottom of the contact. See "Conversing with Messages" in Chapter 8.

4. Tap the FaceTime button to start a video chat with the user, providing they are also on an iOS device (or a Mac) and have set up FaceTime. You can start a FaceTime video call, or tap the phone-like button for an audio-only call.

5. Tap the email address to start composing a new email in the Mail app.

6. Tap to the right of Notes to add more information without entering Edit mode.

7. Tap Share Contact to send the contact information via a text message, email, or using AirDrop.

8. Tap Edit to enter Edit mode, which gives you the same basic functionality as entering a new contact.

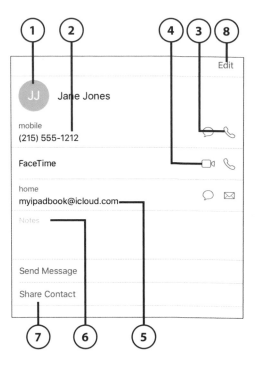

Using the Calendar App

Now that you have people in your Contacts app, you need to schedule some things to do with them.

Calendars, like contacts, are stored using Apple's iCloud service. So, your calendars will sync over the Internet to your other iOS devices and even your Mac, as long as you use the same iCloud account for each device.

Let's look at some things you can do with the Calendar app.

Creating a Calendar Event

1. Tap the Calendar app icon on the Home screen.

2. Tap the + button at the upper right.

3. Enter a title for the event.

4. Enter a Location for the event, or skip this field.

5. Tap the Starts field to bring up a control for setting the starting time.

6. Tap the Ends field to bring up a control for setting the ending time for the event.

7. If the event covers the entire day, or a series of days, then slide the All-day switch on. The Starts and Ends fields will now be dates only, and won't include a specific time.

8. Tap Repeat to set an event to repeat every day, week, 2 weeks, month, or year.

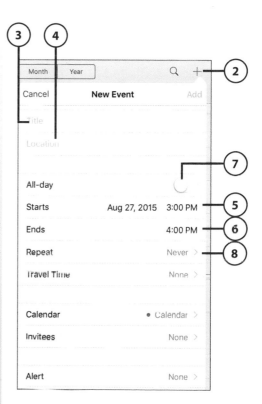

9. Tap Invitees to send an email invitation to another person for this event, if your calendar system allows this. If you and the other person are both using iCloud, they will get a notification of the event and have the option to accept or decline. If they accept, the event will be added to their calendar. You will then be able to look at your event's invitation list in this same location and see if they have accepted or declined.

10. Tap Alert to set the time for a notification alert to appear. This can be at the time of the event, or before the event, such as 5 minutes, 15 minutes, or even as much as a week before.

11. In addition, if you set Travel Time, your alert will be adjusted so you have enough time to get to the event's location.

12. Tap Add to complete the event.

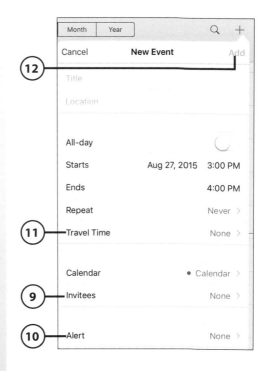

Siri: Creating Events

You can use Siri to create new events even when the Calendar app is not on your screen.

"Schedule a doctor appointment for 3 PM next Wednesday."
"Set up a meeting with John tomorrow at noon."
"Cancel my dentist appointment."

Deleting Events

To delete an event, scroll to the bottom of the event information while editing it to reveal a Delete Event button. This button also appears when you tap the event in any of the Calendar views. There is no real need to delete past events from your calendar—they take up almost no space and could be useful as a record of your past appointments.

Using Calendar Views

There are three main ways to view your calendar: Day, Week, and Month. Let's take a look at each.

Exploring Day View

The Day view is broken into two halves: the left side shows a timeline from morning until evening. Events are shown as blocks of color in this vertical timeline. The right side shows information for the event selected, if any.

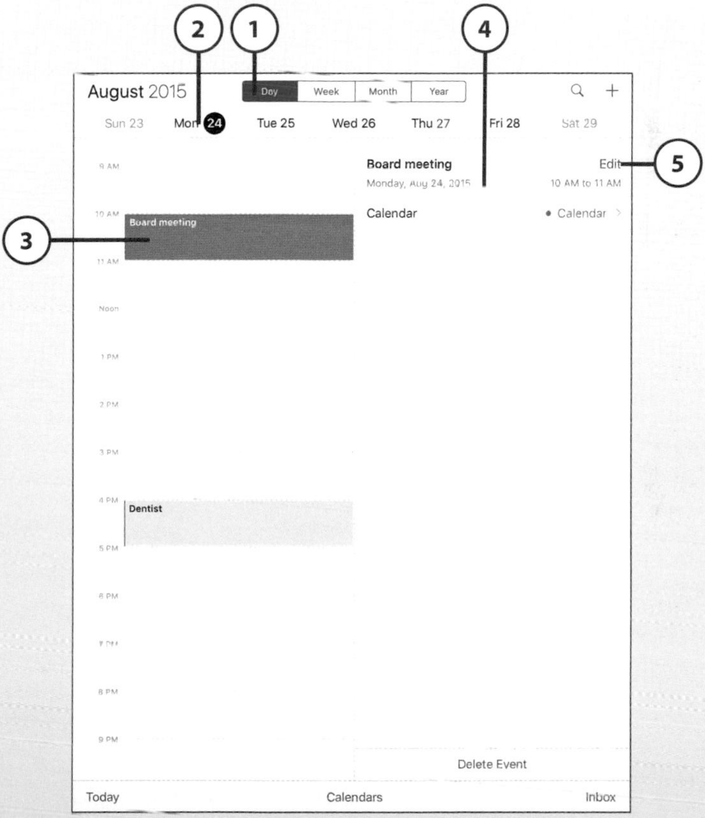

1. Tap Day to enter Day view mode.
2. You can tap any day shown at the top to jump to the list of events for that day. You can also drag left and right here to see previous days and upcoming ones.
3. Tap any event shown to view information about that event.
4. The information appears on the right.
5. You can tap Edit to edit that event and change any aspect of it, or delete it.

6. You can drag up and down to view the entire day.

7. Tap Today to jump to the current day, in case you have moved to another day and want to return quickly.

8. Tap Calendars to select which calendars are shown. This is useful if you have set up multiple calendars in iCloud, or have subscribed to public calendars.

9. Tap Inbox to view any invitations you may have received via email or messages. You can accept or reject them. Accepted invitations will be added to your calendar.

10. Tap + to add a new event.

Year View

There is also a Year view, as you may have already noticed since there is a Year button at the top of the screen. This shows you 12 very small monthly calendars, with colored-in spaces on days where you have events. You can use this view to quickly navigate to an event in a different week or month. Or, you can use it to see when the days fall in the week.

Exploring Week View

To get a view of all the events for the week, switch to Week view. This gives you seven days across, but less space to preview each event. You can still select and edit events.

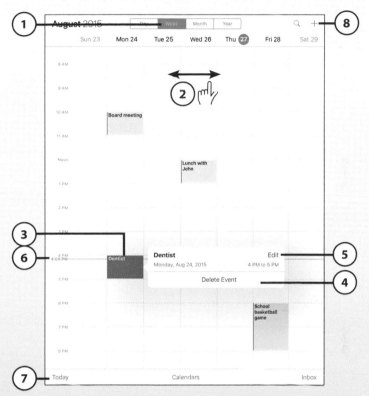

1. Tap Week to go to the Week view.

2. You can move to the previous week or the next by tapping and dragging in any blank part of the calendar. You can also drag vertically to see earlier in the morning or later in the evening.

3. Tap an event to view more information about it.

4. The information appears in a box to the left or right of the event.

5. You can tap Edit to edit the event right here. The familiar editing interface will appear in an expanded box while you remain in the Week view.

6. You can see the current time represented by a red line.

7. Tap Today if you have navigated away from the current week and want to get back.

8. Tap + to add a new event while remaining in Week view.

Exploring Month View

To see the "big picture," you may want to use Month view. This gives you a grid of seven days across and six or more weeks vertically. While this view is similar to a monthly calendar, it doesn't necessarily have to show a single month. It can be used to show any group of six consecutive weeks.

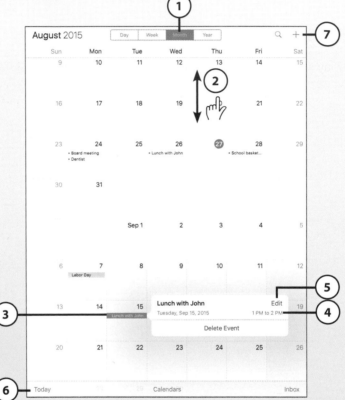

1. Tap Month to enter Month view.

2. While in Month view, you can tap and drag in blank areas to scroll up and down.

3. Tap an event to view more information.

4. The information appears in a box, like in Week view.

5. Tap Edit to edit the information right here in Month view. The editing interface will appear inside an enlarged box.

6. Tap Today to return to the current day if you have scrolled away from it.

7. Tap + to add a new event right here in Month view.

Siri: Checking Your Schedule

You can use Siri to see what events you have coming up.

"What do I have going on tomorrow?"

"What is on my calendar for this week?"

"When is my dentist appointment?"

Creating a Calendar

You may have noticed in the previous tasks that you can select a calendar when you create an event. You can create multiple calendars to organize your events. For instance, you may want to have one for work and one for home.

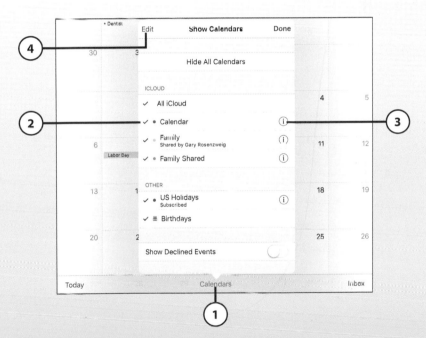

1. From any calendar view, tap the Calendars button at the bottom center.

2. You can scroll up and down this list and disable or enable calendars by tapping on the checkmarks. A calendar without a checkmark is hidden and won't appear in your views.

3. You can also view and change information about a calendar, such as changing the color used as a background for events. You can also share calendars with other iCloud users.

4. Tap Edit to go into editing mode.

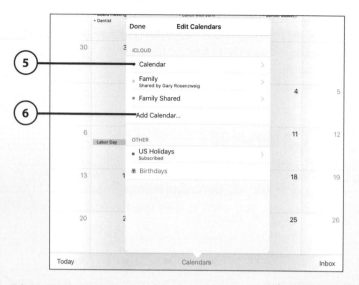

5. In Editing mode, you can also select calendars to change their color and which other people they are shared with.

6. Tap Add Calendar to create a new calendar.

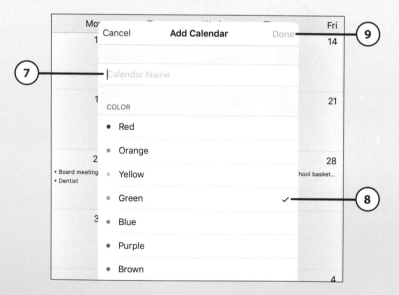

7. Give the new Calendar a name.

8. Set the color for the calendar.

9. Tap Done.

Deleting a Calendar

You can delete a calendar by following the previous steps 1–4 and then selecting a calendar to edit. Scroll to the bottom below the list of colors and choose Delete Calendar.

Default Calendar

Which calendar will be used when you create a new event? The default calendar is a setting you can find in the Settings app, under Mail, Contacts, Calendars, way near the bottom of the list of preferences on the right.

>>>Go Further

SHARING CALENDARS

When you edit a calendar's information, you can also use the Add Person button that appears above the list of colors to share a calendar with a specific iCloud user. Below the colors list, you can choose to set the calendar to "public" and then share an Internet link that others can use to subscribe. For instance, you can create a schedule for your softball team and make it public, and then put a link to the calendar on the team's website. Anyone can subscribe to this calendar, but only to view it. By default, others can edit it, but you can turn off Allow Editing by tapping the i button for the calendar, and then View & Edit next to the person's name with whom you are sharing it.

Using the Notes App

Another organization app that comes with your iPad is the Notes app. Although this one is much more free-form than a Contacts or Calendar app, it can be useful for keeping quick notes or to do lists.

Creating a Note

1. Tap the Notes icon on your Home screen.

2. Notes opens up the note you were previously working on. To type, tap on the screen where you want the insertion point, and a keyboard appears.

What's in a Name

The filename for a note is just the first line of the note, so get in the habit of putting the title of a note as the first line of text to make finding the note easier.

3. To start a new note, tap the Compose button at the upper right.

4. To view a list of all your notes, and to jump to another note, tap the Notes button.

5. Tap the name of the note you want to switch to.

6. Tap and type in the Search field to find text inside of notes. If you don't see the Search field, tap and drag down on the list of notes to reveal it just above the first note in the list.

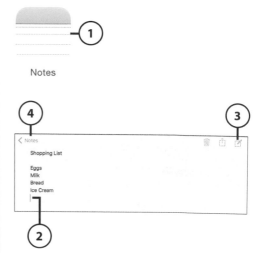

7. Turn your iPad to horizontal orientation, and you'll have a permanent list of notes on the left. In this view, you don't need to tap Notes, as you did in step 4, to see the list.

8. Tap the Trash button at the top-right of the screen to delete the note you are viewing.

9. Tap the Share button at the top-right of the screen to share the note in a number of ways. For instance, you can start a new email message in the Mail app using the contents of the note, or print the note using AirPrint.

Notes Isn't a Word Processor

You can't actually use Notes for serious writing. There are only basic styles and no formatting choices. You can't even change the display font to make it larger. If you need to use your iPad for writing, consider Pages or a third-party word processing app. If you want to make some text bold, italic, or underlined, you can tap and hold a word, adjust the selection, and use the **B/U** button next to Cut, Copy, and Paste to apply a simple style to the selection.

Notes in the Cloud

Notes are stored on Apple's iCloud server, just like calendar events and contacts. If you are using the same iCloud account on your Mac, for instance, you should see the notes appear almost instantly on your Mac, synced through iCloud. They will also appear on your other iOS devices.

Creating Checklists in Notes New!

You can already see that Notes is useful for creating lists. Apple has built in a list function to make it even easier to use in this way.

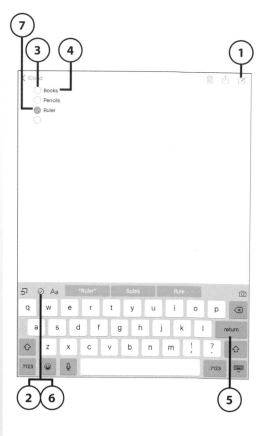

1. Start a new note, or continue typing in an existing one.

2. Tap the checklist button when you want to start a list. You can have text before and after the list, it doesn't have to be at the top of the note or the only thing in the note.

3. You'll see an empty circle appear on the line you are typing.

4. Type the first item in the list.

5. Hit Return on the on-screen keyboard and you can continue entering more items, each with an empty circle to its left.

6. Tap the checklist button again when you want to resume typing normal non-list text.

7. You can tap any empty circle in the list to fill it with a checkmark.

Notes vs. Reminders

Checklists in Notes are good for things like shopping lists, packing lists, party invitation lists, and so on. For to-do lists, use the Reminders app, which we will look at later in this chapter.

Adding Photos and Sketches to Notes New!

You can also insert photos from your photo library into notes, take photos with the camera, or draw sketches with your finger to include in your notes.

1. Create a new note or use an existing one. Photos and sketches can co-exist with other text in any note.

2. Position the cursor where you want to insert the photo or sketch.

3. Tap the Photo button to choose a photo from your library, or take one with the camera. It is the same way you insert a photo into an email message or text message. You are asked to choose a photo from your library or shown the camera interface to take a picture.

4. Tap the sketch button to enter the sketching screen.

5. On this screen, you can draw anything you like using a few simple tools. Select the pen, marker, or pencil tool at the bottom.

6. Select a color. You can swipe from left to right across the colors to see two more sets of colors.

7. Tap and drag your finger to draw.

8. The eraser tool enables you to clear marks you have made.

9. You can use the undo and redo buttons to help draw.

10. When you are done, tap Done to return to the note.

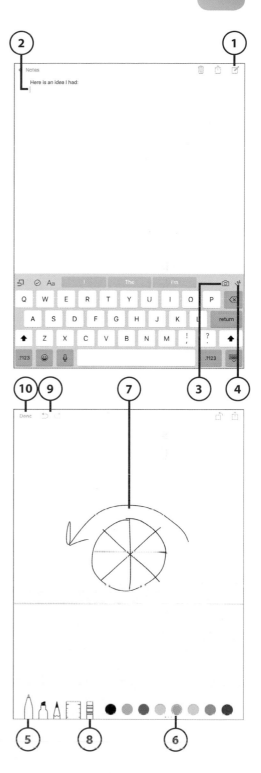

11. The sketch appears in your note. Tap it to return to the sketch screen to edit it. If you tap and hold the sketch instead, you get Cut, Copy, Delete, and Share options.

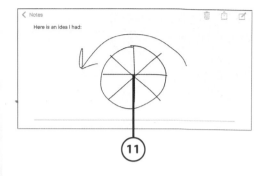

Multiple Sketches

You can add more than one sketch to a note. If you need to move a sketch to a different location in your note, or to a different note, tap and hold the sketch until you get the options menu. Then use Cut to remove it and later use Paste to place it elsewhere.

It's Not All Good

Don't See the Photo or Sketch Buttons?

These buttons only appear on more recent iPad models and only if your notes are being stored in the latest version of iCloud notes. For instance, if you share your notes with a Mac using an older version of OS X, or an iPhone using an older version of iOS, then you can't create sketches in your notes because they are not compatible with the Notes app on those other devices.

Using the Reminders App

Reminders is a to-do list application available on iPad, iPod touch, iPhone, and Macs. This app is for creating an ongoing list of tasks you need to accomplish or things you need to remember. These reminders can be similar to calendar events with times and alarms. Or, they can be simple items in a list with no time attached to them.

Setting a Reminder

1. Tap the Reminders icon on your Home screen.

2. Select the list you want to add a new Reminder to.

3. Tap in a new line to create a new reminder.

4. Type the reminder and close the keyboard when done.

5. Tap the i button next to the reminder to bring up the Details dialog. If you don't see an i button, then tap any reminder item first.

6. Tap here to edit the reminder.

7. Slide the Remind me on a day switch to on to set a reminder alert.

8. Set a time for the alert to occur.

9. Add a note to the reminder if you want to include more details.

10. Tap outside of the Details box when you are finished editing the reminder.

Reminders

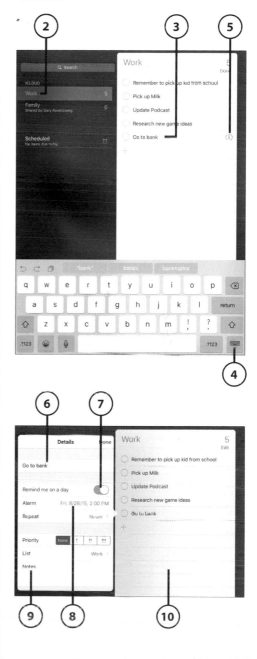

Siri: Remind Me

You can create new reminders using Siri like this:

"Remind me to watch Doctor Who tonight at 8 PM."
"Remind me to pick up milk when I leave work."
"Remind me to check my stocks every day at 9 AM."

11. Tap the button next to the reminder when you have completed the task. It will remain in the list temporarily.

12. Tap Add List to add a new reminders list.

13. Tap Show Completed to see completed reminders.

14. You can also search for reminders by typing the title or something from the content.

15. Tap Edit to remove reminders.

16. Tap the red button next to a reminder to delete it.

17. Tap and drag the right side of the reminders to re-order them.

18. Tap Done when you are finished deleting and re-ordering the reminders.

19. You can also delete the entire list before leaving editing mode.

20. You can also share a Reminders list with another iCloud user before leaving editing mode. Tap Sharing, and you can add one or more people from your contacts or manually add people with their Apple ID. Shared Reminders lists will sync items to all people sharing it.

iCloud

Reminders sync by using the iCloud service from Apple. So, they are automatically backed up and should also appear on your Mac in the Reminders app, if you have OS X 10.8 Mountain Lion or newer. And if you use an iPhone, they should appear there as well.

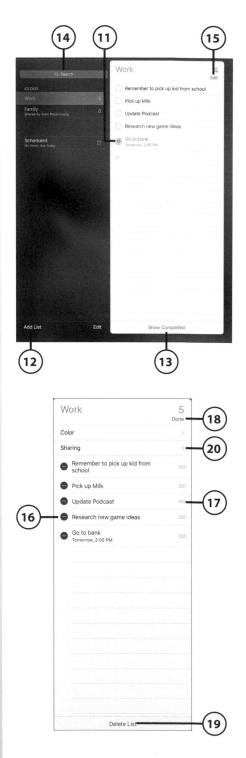

Using the Clocks App

The advantage of using an alarm rather than a reminder is that an often-recurring alarm, like your morning wake-up call, or a reminder on when to pick up your child at school, won't clutter up your Reminders list or calendar.

Setting Clock Alarms

1. Tap the Clock app.

2. The main screen shows up to six clocks in any time zone you want. Tap a clock to have it fill the screen.

3. Tap an empty clock to add a new city.

4. Tap Edit to remove or rearrange the clocks.

5. Tap Alarm to view and edit alarms.

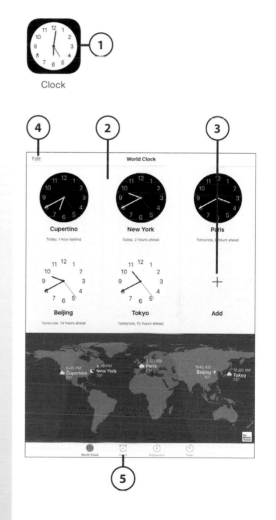

6. To add a new alarm, tap the + button.

7. Select a time for the alarm.

8. Select the days of the week for the alarm. Leaving it set to Never means you just want the alarm to be used once, as you might do if setting an alarm to wake you up early so you can catch a plane the next day. Otherwise, you can select from seven days of the week. So, you can set an alarm for Monday through Friday and leave out the weekend.

9. Tap Label to give the alarm a custom name.

10. Select a sound for the alarm. You can choose from preset sounds or your ringtone collection.

11. Leave the Snooze switch on if you want the ability to use snooze when the alarm goes off.

12. Tap Save to save all your settings and add the alarm.

13. The alarm now appears in the special Clock calendar. This alarm was set for Monday, Tuesday, Thursday, and Friday, so only those four days are indicated.

14. You can switch off the alarm, while leaving it in the calendar for future use.

15. Tap Edit on an alarm to edit or delete it.

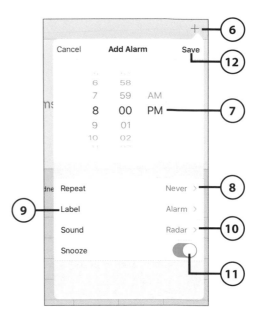

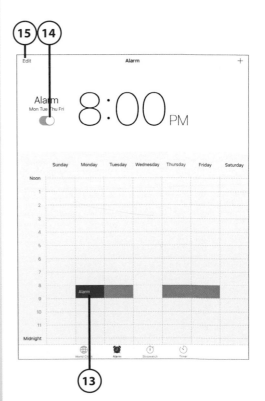

16. The alarm will sound and a message will appear when it is time. This will appear as a message in the middle of your screen. But even if your iPad is sleeping, it will wake up and display a message on the lock screen.

17. If you've enabled snooze, tapping here will silence the alarm and try again in 9 minutes.

18. To silence the alarm normally, assuming it has sounded while the iPad is asleep and locked, you need to swipe the lock switch. If the iPad was awake when the alarm went off, you simply get a button to tap.

Wake Up!

When you set an alarm, it will sound even if you lower your volume to nothing, mute the sound with the side switch or Control Center, and switch into Do Not Disturb mode. This way, you can't accidentally turn off an alarm just because you wanted to avoid other distractions.

Siri: Create Alarms

You can use Siri to create and delete alarms. Try these phrases:

"Set an alarm for weekdays at 9 AM."
"Create an alarm for tomorrow at 10 AM."
"Cancel my 9 AM alarm."
"Turn on my 9 AM alarm."
"Turn off my 9 AM alarm."

The Web is at your
fingertips with iPad's
Safari web browser.

In this chapter, you learn about Safari, the browser built in to the iPad. You can use it to browse the Web, bookmark web pages, fill in forms, and search the Internet.

→ Browsing to a URL and Searching
→ Viewing Web Pages
→ Opening Multiple Web Pages with Tabs
→ Bookmarks, History, and Reading List
→ Deleting Your Bookmarks
→ Creating Home Screen Bookmarks
→ Viewing Articles with Safari Reader
→ Filling in Web Forms
→ Saving Time with AutoFill

Surfing the Web

The iPad is a beautiful web surfing device. Its size is perfect for web pages, and your ability to touch the screen lets you interact with content in a way that even a computer typically cannot.

Getting Started with Safari

Undoubtedly, you know how to get to web pages on a computer using a web browser. You use Safari on your iPad in the same way, but the interface is a little different.

At the top of the Safari browser is a toolbar with just a few buttons. In the middle, the largest interface element is the address field. This is where you can type the address (URL) of any web page on the Internet, or enter a search query.

Tips for Typing a URL

- A URL is a Universal Resource Locator. It can be a website name or a specific page in a website.

- For most websites, you don't need to type the "www." at the beginning. For instance, you can type **www.apple.com** or **apple.com**, and both take you to Apple's home page. You never need to type "http://" either, though occasionally you need to type "https://" to specify that you want to go to a secure web page.

- Instead of typing ".com." you can tap and hold the period button on the iPad keyboard. You can select .com, .edu, .org, .us, or .net.

Browsing to a URL and Searching

1. Tap the Safari icon on your iPad to launch the browser. Unless you have rearranged your icons, it is located at the bottom of the screen, along with your other most commonly used applications.

2. Tap in the field at the top of the screen. This opens up the keyboard at the bottom of the screen. If you were already viewing a web page, the address of that page remains in the address field. Otherwise, it will be blank.

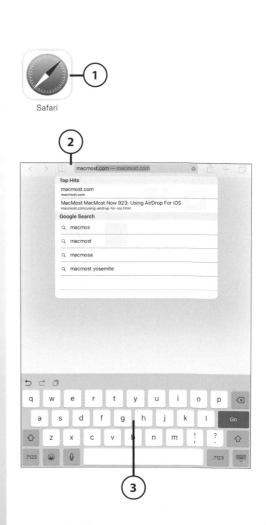

Clear the Slate

To clear the field at any time, tap the X button located inside the field all the way to the right.

3. Start typing a search term or a URL such as apple.com or macmost.com.

4. The area to the right of where you are typing will fill with a complete address and description, trying to predict the URL you want. You can ignore this and keep typing until you have completed the URL. You can then skip to step 6.

5. As you type, suggestions based on previous pages you have visited and past web searches from other users appear. To go directly to one of these pages, tap the page in the list.

Search This Page

Below the Google suggestions in the search suggestions drop-down menu is a list of recent searches and the occurrences of the phrase on the web page you are viewing. Use the latter to find the phrase on the page.

6. Otherwise, tap the Go button on the keyboard when you finish typing. If you typed or selected a URL, you will be taken to that web page.

7. Notice that the address field at the top of the screen shows you the domain name for the website you are visiting, but doesn't display the complete URL of the specific page of that site you are on.

   If you typed a search term, or selected a search from the list, the term will remain at the top and you will get a page of search results.

8. Tap on any result to jump to that page.

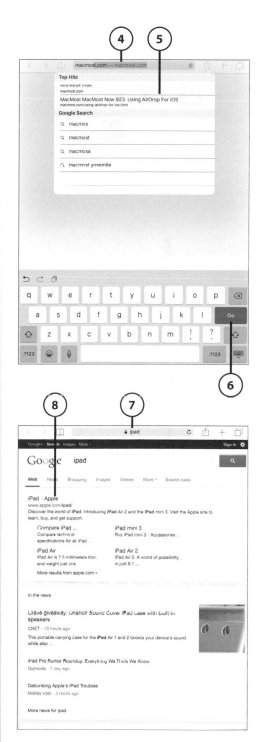

Siri: Search the Web

You can use Siri to search the web, even if you are not currently looking at the Safari screen. Sometimes Siri will also answer general questions by suggesting a web search:

"Search the web for iPad tutorials."
"Search for local plumbers."
"Search for MacMost.com."
"Search Wikipedia for Paris."
"Show me some websites about geology."
"Google Denver news."
"Search for iPad tutorials on MacMost.com."

Nothing Special, Please

Some websites present you with a special iPad version of the site. This is not as common as the special iPhone or iPod touch versions that many sites offer. If a website does not look the same on your iPad as it does on your computer, you might want to check to see if a switch is on the web page provided by the site to view the standard web version, instead of a special iPad version. You can also tap in the address field in Safari, and then drag down on the list of Favorites that appears to reveal a Request Desktop Site option. This is especially useful if a site has lumped the iPad together with the iPhone and provided a needlessly simplified version.

>>>*Go Further*

TIPS FOR SEARCHING THE WEB

- You can go deeper than just typing some words. For instance, you can put a + in front of a word to require it and a – in front to avoid that word in the results.

- You can use special search terms to look for things such as movie times, weather, flight tracking, and more. See https://support.google.com/websearch/answer/134479 for all sorts of things you can do with a Google search.

- Using iPad's Settings app, you can choose the search engine that Safari uses as its default. Tap the Settings icon and choose Safari on the left, and then look for the Search Engine setting. You can choose Bing, Yahoo!, or Duck Duck Go instead of Google, for instance.

- Using Google, you can search for much more than text on web pages. Look at the top of the search results, and you see links such as Images, Videos, Maps, News, and Shopping. Tap More and you can also search for things such as Blogs and Books.

- To explore the search results without moving away from the page listing the results, tap and hold over a link to see a button that enables you to open a link in a new tab, leaving the results open in the current tab.

- You can use many search settings with Bing or Google. These are not specific to the iPad but work on your computer as well when performing searches. Tap the settings button (looks like a small gear) in the upper-right corner of the search results page to choose a language, filters, and other settings. Set up a Bing or Google account and log in to save these search preferences and use them between different devices.

Viewing Web Pages

Whether you typed in a URL or searched for a web page, after you have one open on your iPad screen, you can control what you view in several ways. You need to know these techniques to view the complete contents of a web page and navigate among web pages.

1. Navigate to any web page using either of the two techniques in the previous step-by-step instructions. When you arrive at the page, only the domain name shows at the top.

2. When you are viewing a page, you can touch and drag the page up and down with your finger. As you do so, notice the bar on the right side that gives you an indication of how much of the complete web page you are viewing at one time.

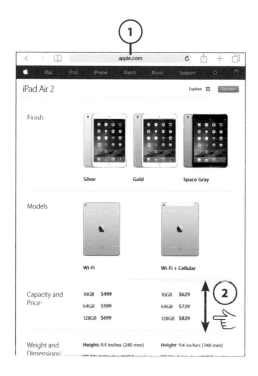

3. To zoom in on an area in the page, touch the screen with two fingers and move your fingers apart. This is called an unpinch. You can also move them closer together (pinch) to zoom back out. A double-tap restores the page to normal scaling. This works well on websites made for desktop computers, but mobile sites usually are set to already fit the screen at optimal resolution.

4. You can also double-tap images and paragraphs of text to zoom in to those elements in the web page. A second double-tap zooms back out.

5. While zoomed in, you can also touch and drag left and right to view different parts of the web page. You see a bar at the bottom of the screen when you do this, just like the bar on the right side in step 2.

6. To move to another web page from a link in the current web page, just tap the link. Links are usually an underlined or colored piece of text; however, they can also be pictures or button-like images.

It's Not All Good

Where's the Link?

Unfortunately, it isn't always easy to figure out which words on a page are links. Years ago, these were all blue and underlined. But today, links can be any color and may not be underlined.

On the iPad, it is even more difficult to figure out which words are links. This is because many web pages highlight links when the cursor moves over the word. But with the touch interface of the iPad, there is no cursor.

Opening Multiple Web Pages with Tabs

Safari on the iPad enables you to open multiple web pages at the same time. You can view only one at a time, but you can hold your place on a page by opening a new tab to look at something on another page.

1. View a web page in Safari that has links to other pages, such as MacMost.com. Instead of tapping on a link, tap down and hold your finger there until a contextual menu pops up above your finger.

2. Tap Open in New Tab.

3. Alternatively, you can tap the + button at the top of the screen to open a new tab that shows icons linking to the websites you have put in your Favorites.

4. You see two tabs at the top of the screen now. The one on the right is in front of the one on the left and represents the page you are looking at below. You can tell which tab is the active one—it is in a lighter shade of gray than the others, and the Close Tab button (shown as an X) is visible.

5. You can switch tabs by tapping on the other tab; that tab now appears front of the one on the right, and the screen area below shows that page.

6. When you enter a new web address, search, or use a bookmark, it changes the page of the current tab, but doesn't affect the other tab.

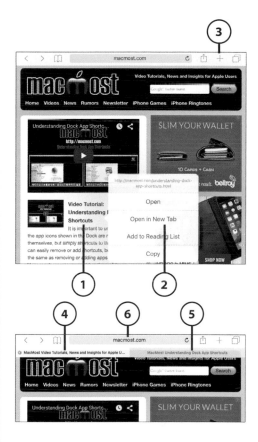

7. You can close the current tab by tapping the X button to the left of the tab's name.

8. Tap the Tabs button at the upper right to see all your tabs presented on one screen.

9. Each tab will appear. You can now tap any tab to jump to it.

10. In addition, you'll also see the titles of tabs open on other devices that are using the same iCloud account. The size of these previews will shrink depending on how many tabs are open. You can tap these to open their pages on your iPad.

11. Tap Done to return to the tab you were viewing previously.

Private Browsing

When you use the tabs screen to select which tab to view, you also see a Private button at the top. Tap that and a new tab opens in private browsing mode. Web pages you view in this tab are not stored in your history. In addition, browser cookies are deleted after you close the tab. This does not hide your browsing behavior from your ISP or employer, but it could help you keep the surprise when buying a birthday present for someone who uses the same iPad.

Viewing Articles with Safari Reader

Web pages on the iPad can be vibrant and pretty. But sometimes the website tries to cram so much text and other junk onto a page that it can be painful to read. You can clear away all the clutter to reveal the text of a news article or blog post using the Reader feature.

1. Look for the Reader button in the address field. If it is there, that means you can tap it to switch to Reader mode for this article.

2. In Reader mode, only the text and inline images of the article appear.

3. Tap the text appearance button to the right of the web address to view options.

4. Tap the large or small "A" buttons to make the text size larger or smaller.

5. Tap the background color buttons to adjust to your liking.

6. You can also select from a short list of fonts.

7. Tap Reader again to return to the regular view of the page.

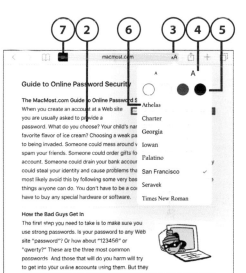

Bookmarks, History, and Reading List

You can always visit a web page by typing its address in the field at the top of Safari. But the app also has a way for you to get to your most frequently visited sites easily, find a page you recently visited, or save a page to read later.

Using Bookmarks and Favorites

Bookmarks allow you to save the web pages you visit most often and then access them with just a few taps. Favorites are bookmarks that appear at the top of the Safari browser for easier access.

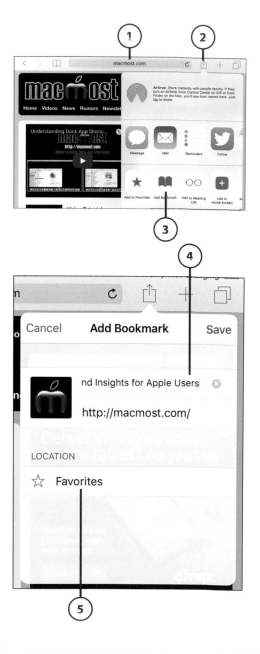

1. Use Safari to navigate to any web page.

2. Tap the Share button at the top of the screen.

3. Tap Add Bookmark.

4. Edit the title of the bookmark. The official title of the web page is prefilled, but you can use the keyboard to change it. You can tap the X to clear the text and start fresh.

5. Tap Location to place the bookmark in a bookmarks folder.

6. You can choose to place the bookmark in Favorites, so it will appear at the top of the Safari window where you can easily find it.

7. Or you can put it in Bookmarks, where you can select it from the Bookmarks menu.

8. Tap Save to finish creating the bookmark.

9. To use a bookmark, first tap the Bookmarks button. This opens up a sidebar on the left. In vertical orientation, this sidebar closes when you choose a web page to view. In horizontal orientation, the sidebar stays until you tap the Bookmarks button again.

10. Find the bookmark in the list and tap it to go to that web page. These would be any bookmarks you saved by using step 7.

11. If you put the bookmark in Favorites or another folder, such as in step 6, you have to tap that folder name first to dig down to find the bookmark.

12. When you create a new tab, the bookmarks you put in your Favorites folder will appear as icons for quick access to those pages. For more about tabs, see "Opening Multiple Web Pages with Tabs" earlier in this chapter.

>>>*Go Further*

TIPS FOR BOOKMARKING WEBSITES

- The titles of web pages are often long and descriptive. It is a good idea to shorten the title to something you can easily recognize, especially if it is a web page that you plan to visit often.

- To create folders inside the Bookmarks folder, tap the Bookmarks button at the top of the Safari screen. Then choose the Bookmarks button at the top. At the bottom of that menu, tap Edit and then tap New Folder.

- You can create folders of bookmarks under Favorites. These appear as their own pop-up menu when you tap them, giving access to a subset of your bookmarks.

Using History

Safari keeps track of which web pages you have visited. You can use this history to find a page you went to earlier today, yesterday, or even several days back.

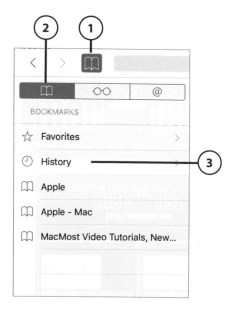

1. After using Safari to view several pages, tap the Bookmarks button at the top of the screen.

2. Tap the first tab at the top of this menu to view your bookmarks and history folders.

3. You may already be viewing your history at this point. If the top of this menu reads History instead of Bookmarks, then you are. Otherwise, tap the History item to go into your history. It is also possible that you have dug down into a bookmarks subfolder. If you see a label with a left-facing blue arrow at the top of the list, tap it to move up a level until you get to the main bookmarks list that includes Favorites and History.

4. Tap any item in the list to jump to that web page.

5. Previous pages you have visited are broken into groups by date.

6. Tap the Clear button if you want to clear out your browsing history. For instance, are you about to hand your iPad to your spouse right after shopping for their birthday present?

History/Bookmarks

Safari treats both history and bookmarks the same. They are both just lists of web pages. Think of your history as a bookmark list of every site you have visited recently. If you think you may need to go to a web page later the same day or this week, you can always use your History instead of creating a new bookmark. Use bookmarks only for truly important pages that you know you'll need often or later on.

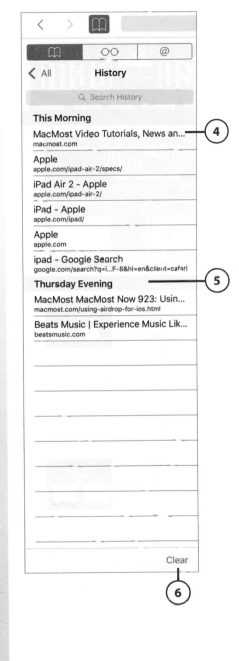

Deleting Your Bookmarks

Adding and using bookmarks is just the start. You eventually need to delete ones you don't use. Some might link to missing or obsolete pages, or some you simply no longer use.

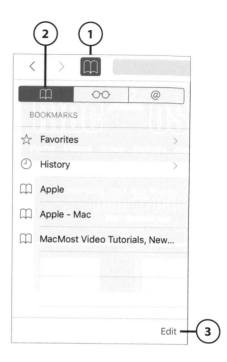

1. Tap the Bookmarks button at the top of the Safari screen.

2. Navigate to the Bookmarks section of that menu. If the bookmark you want to delete is in a folder, tap that folder to navigate into it so you can see the bookmark.

3. Tap Edit.

4. Tap the red button next to a bookmark.

5. Tap the Delete button to remove the bookmark. The bookmark is instantly deleted.

6. Tap Done when you finish deleting bookmarks.

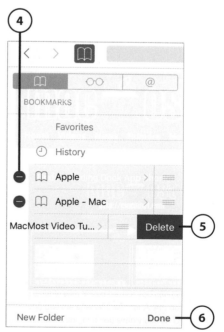

Sync Your Bookmarks

If you are using iCloud, your bookmarks should sync between all your iOS and Mac devices. Safari on your computer gives you greater control over moving and deleting bookmarks. So just do your wholesale editing on your computer and those changes should be reflected in your iPad's bookmarks as well.

Creating Home Screen Bookmarks

If a web page is so important to you that you want even faster access to it than via a browser bookmark, you can save it as an icon on your iPad's Home screen.

1. Use Safari to navigate to any web page.

2. Tap the Share button at the top of the screen.

3. Tap Add to Home Screen. Note that the icon shown here will change to use the icon for that website or to a small screen capture of the site.

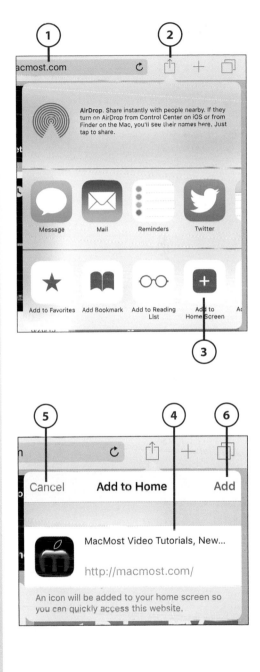

Managing Home Screen Bookmarks

You can arrange and delete Home screen bookmarks just like icons that represent apps. See "Arranging Apps on Your iPad" in Chapter 15 for details.

4. You can now edit the name of the page. Most web page titles are too long to display under an icon on the Home screen of the iPad, so edit the name down to as short a title as possible.

5. You can tap Cancel to leave this interface without sending the bookmark to the Home screen.

6. Tap Add to complete adding the icon to the Home screen.

7. Press the Home button to return to your Home screen (not shown).

8. Look for the new icon on your Home screen that represents this bookmark. You may need to swipe through the pages of your Home screens to find it. Then, you can move it to any page or into a folder. The icon acts just like the app icons on your Home screen. See "Arranging Apps on Your iPad" in Chapter 14.

Website Icons

The icon for this type of bookmark can come from one of two sources. Web page owners can provide a special iPhone/iPad icon that would be used whenever someone tries to bookmark her page.

However, if no such icon is provided, your iPad takes a screen shot of the web page and shrinks it down to make an icon.

Building a Reading List

Your reading list is similar to bookmarks. You can add a page to your reading list to remember to return to that page later. When you do, it is removed from the Unread section of your reading list, but still appears in the All section.

1. Find an article you want to read later.

2. Tap the Share button.

3. Tap Add to Reading List.

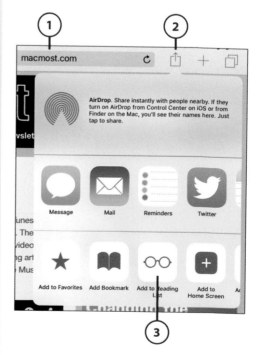

4. To see your reading list, tap the Bookmarks button.

Take it Offline

Pages you add to your reading list are downloaded to your iPad so that you can read them later, when not connected to the Internet.

5. Tap the Reading List button.

6. Tap any item to view the page. Even if you are not connected to the Internet, the page will show because Safari stored the content when you added the page to the Reading List.

7. At the bottom you see either Show All or Show Unread. This lets you switch between the two lists. Show All shows everything in your Reading List. Show Unread does not show items you have already opened from the Reading List.

Reading List Syncing

The Reading List also syncs across your iOS devices and Macs using iCloud. So you can add it on your Mac and then see it appear in your Reading List on your iPad.

Shared Links

In addition to Bookmarks and Reading List, there is a third button that looks like an @ symbol that appears only if you are signed into social media networks like Twitter or Facebook in the Settings app. Here you find shared links. Recently shared links from those networks appear in this list.

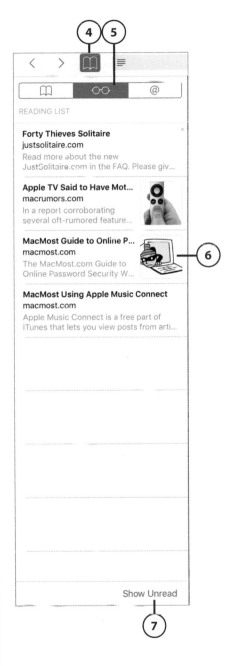

Working with Web Forms

The Web isn't a one-way street. Often you need to interact with web pages, filling in forms or text fields. Doing this on the iPad is similar to doing it on a computer, but with a few key differences.

The keyboard shares screen space with the web page, so when you tap on a field, you bring up the keyboard at the bottom of the screen.

Also pull-down menus behave differently. On the iPad, you get a special menu showing you all the options.

>>>Go Further

SCANNING YOUR CREDIT CARD

When encounter a web form that asks you to enter a credit card number, it can be a pain to have to enter all those digits. Instead, you can have your iPad read the number right from the card using your iPad's camera. Just tap in the credit card number field, and you see a Scan Credit Card button appear above the keyboard. Tap that and you are instructed to hold your card up to the camera. If the lighting is good and your number is clearly visible, it will be read by the camera and inserted into the field. If you don't see the Scan Credit card button, it could be because the web page isn't labeling its fields in a way that Safari can recognize. In that case, you need to enter the number manually.

Filling in Web Forms

1. Use Safari to navigate to a web page with a form. For demonstration purposes, try one of the pages at http://apple.com/feedback/.

2. To type in a text field, tap that field.

3. The keyboard appears at the bottom of the screen. Use it to type text into the field. The features of the keyboard will depend on cues from the website. For instance, a site can set a text field to only accept numbers, so you'll see a numeric keyboard instead of a full keyboard.

4. Tap the Go button when you finish filling in all the required fields.

5. To select a check box or radio button, tap it just as you would click on it on your computer using the mouse.

6. To select an item in a pull-down menu, tap the menu.

7. The special iPad pull-down menu reacts like any other iPad Interface. You can tap an item to select it. You can touch and drag up and down to view more selections if the list is long.

8. A check mark appears next to the currently selected item. Tap that item or any other one to select it and dismiss the menu.

Special Menus

Some websites may use special menus that they build from scratch, rather than these default HTML menus. When this is the case, you get a menu that looks exactly like the one you get when viewing the web page on a computer. If the web page is well coded, it should work fine on the iPad, though it might be slightly more difficult to make a selection.

>>>*Go Further*

TIPS FOR FILLING IN FORMS

- You can use the AutoFill button just above the keyboard to fill in your name, address, and other contact info instead of typing on the keyboard. To enable AutoFill, go into your iPad Settings and look for the Passwords & AutoFill preferences under Safari. Also make sure your own information is correct and complete in your card in the Contacts application. See "Saving Time with AutoFill," later in this chapter.

- To move between fields in a form, use the flat left and right arrow buttons just above the keyboard that move to the Previous or Next field. You can quickly fill in an entire form this way without having to tap on the web page to select the next item.

Saving Time with AutoFill

When you go to websites and fill out forms, it can be annoying to type out basic information like your name and address, or your user ID and password. Furthermore, if you have to type your password every time you visit a site, or even on a daily or weekly basis, this encourages you to use simple, easy-to-guess passwords so you don't have to type long complex strings of characters.

The Keychain function built into Safari allows you to automatically fill in forms and login prompts. After you enter your information the first time, you never have to do it again for that website.

Setting Up AutoFill

To set up AutoFill in Safari, start by going to the Settings app.

1. Tap Safari in the Settings app.

2. Tap AutoFill.

3. Slide the Use Contact Info switch on, if it's not. Now any time you go to a web page with a form that asks for basics like name, address, or telephone number, AutoFill uses your contact information in the Contacts app to fill those fields automatically.

4. Tap My Info to tell Safari which contact in the Contacts app is you.

5. Slide the Names and Passwords switch on to have Safari remember user IDs and passwords when you log on to websites. As you will see in the next section, Safari prompts you each time you enter a new User ID and Password so you can decide the passwords that are saved.

6. After you have visited some sites and saved some passwords, you can access the list of saved passwords by going back to the main Safari settings screen and tapping Passwords.

7. Tap on any entry to view the ID, password, and the website it belongs to. This can come in handy if you need to view or copy and paste a password. For instance, you can grab your Amazon password to paste it into the Kindle app.

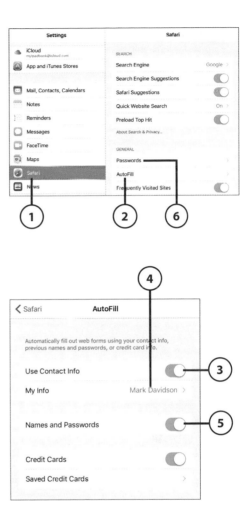

8. You can enter Edit mode to delete entries.

9. You can manually enter new passwords right here as well.

10. Safari can also remember credit card information. Those settings are found back on the AutoFill settings screen. Slide the Credit Cards switch to on for this information to be saved.

11. Tap Saved Credit Cards to see a list of your saved credit cards and to add new ones. When you add a credit card, include your name, the card number, the expiration date, and a short description. However, the security code for the card is not saved. Most websites will ask you for this even after Safari has autofilled in the information it has saved.

>>>*Go Further*
SAFETY AND SECURITY

If you add your passwords and credit card information for Safari to automatically fill in, isn't that incredibly insecure? Well, it is if you have not set a passcode for your iPad. The Settings app recommends this when you turn these options on.

You should set a passcode under Settings, General, Passcode Lock. Then, you should set the Require Passcode option to Immediately so as soon as you lock your iPad by closing the Smart Cover or pressing the sleep button, the passcode is required to use it.

Even with the security enabled, using a simple passcode like 1234 or letting it sit around unlocked still presents a problem. You don't need to use AutoFill on every website. You could use it for unimportant sites like games and forums, and avoid using it for bank accounts and social media sites.

The advantage to using AutoFill for passwords is that you can use a long, random password for an account rather than a short, memorable one. It is more likely that your account will be broken into remotely when you use a short, common password than someone stealing your iPad and using it to gain access to that website. And even if they do, you can simply change your important passwords if your iPad is stolen.

Using AutoFill

After you have AutoFill set up, using it is relatively simple. You can use it with a form that asks for basic contact information, or for a login form. The process is the same. Let's look at using it with a simple login form.

1. Enter an ID or password at a website.

2. If AutoFill is enabled, you may be prompted by Safari to save the password.

3. Tap Save Password to save the user ID and password.

4. Alternatively, you can tell Safari that you don't want to save the password for this site, and not to ask again.

5. You can also skip this for now. This is useful if you have multiple logons for a site and don't want to save the one you are using at this moment.

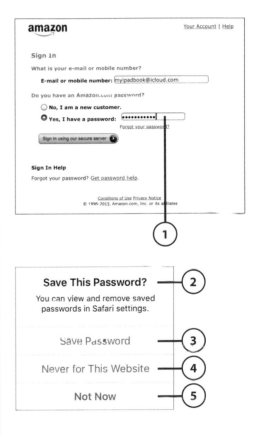

6. Log out and then return to the same website.

7. You'll notice that the ID and password are already filled in. The fields turn yellow to show that AutoFill has been used to fill them in.

8. Tap the button used by the site to complete the login.

9. If your ID and password don't appear at first, look for the Passwords button on top of the keyboard. This button will also allow you to select from multiple sets of IDs and passwords if you have more than one account at the site.

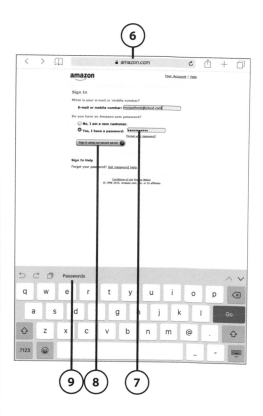

Changing Passwords

So what happens if you change passwords for a site? Simply use the keyboard to erase and retype the password when logging into that site the next time. AutoFill will prompt you, asking if you want to save the new password, replacing the old one in its database.

It's Not All Good

AutoFill Not Working?

AutoFill works because forms use typical names for fields: id, password, name, firstname, lastname, zip, and so on. If a website wants to get creative, or intentionally block AutoFill functions of browsers, then the site may obfuscate the names of fields to make it impossible for AutoFill to tell which field is which. Therefore, some websites might not work with AutoFill, while others do.

>>>Go Further

SAFARI EXTENSIONS

You can add new functionality to Safari with third-party extensions. For instance, you can use the popular 1Password app to insert passwords into login pages. You can use the Pinterest extension to pin web pages without leaving Safari.

To install an extension, first install the app from the App Store as you would any other app. (See Chapter 15 to learn how to find and install apps.) After you have installed an app that offers a Safari extension, tap the Share button at the top of Safari to start the process of activating it. This is the same button used to add a bookmark.

In the menu that appears, you see a list of ways to Share the page you are viewing, such as Message and Mail. You also have a list of more actions you can take with the page, such as Add Bookmark and Copy. Swipe either of these lists from right to left, and you see a More button as the rightmost item in the list. If the extension adds a way to share a web page, you find it by using the More button in the first list. Other extensions are behind the More button in the second list. Either way, switch the extension on to activate it.

After that, you'll find the extension along with the other items in either of these two lists as a button. For instance, with the Pinterest extension, you can tap the Share button, and then tap the Pinterest button to quickly add an image on the current page to one of your boards.

Send and receive messages from other iOS and Mac users.

Send and receive email from your ISP or a variety of popular email services.

In this chapter, you learn how to configure and use the Mail app to correspond using email and how to use the Messaging app to send and receive messages.

→ Configuring Your iPad for Email
→ Reading Your Email
→ Composing a New Message
→ Deleting and Moving Messages
→ Searching Email
→ Configuring How Email Is Received
→ Creating a Signature
→ More Email Settings
→ Setting Up Messaging
→ Conversing with Messages

Communicating with Email and Messaging

Now that you have an iPad with a battery that seems to last forever, you have no excuse for not replying to emails. You need to be comfortable using the built-in Mail app that enables you to connect with your home or work email using standard protocols such as POP and IMAP. You can even connect with more proprietary systems such as AOL, Exchange, Gmail, and Yahoo!. You can also send messages to your friends using Apple's iMessage system.

Configuring Your iPad for Email

It's easy to set up your email if you use one of the popular email services like Gmail, Yahoo!, AOL, or Microsoft. But if you use another kind of service, such as the email given to you by your local ISP or the company you work for, you need to enter more detailed information such as server addresses.

It is possible that your email account has already been set up for you. If you use Apple's iCloud as your email service, when you answered some questions while setting up your new iPad, you probably already gave your iPad your Apple ID and password and it set up your email automatically. You can use these steps to check to make sure that account is there, or add an additional account from another provider.

If you are using iCloud, Gmail, or any of the other services listed on the Add Account screen, all you really need to do is enter your email address and password. Your iPad will set up the account from those two pieces of information. But if you are using another type of email account, you need to enter several details about your account.

Set Up Your Email Account

1. Tap the Settings icon on your Home screen.

Settings

2. Tap Mail, Contacts, Calendars.

3. If you are using iCloud and set up your Apple ID when you first started your iPad, you should see your iCloud account listed. If this is your only email account, you don't need to do anything else.

4. If you have another email account you want to add, tap Add Account.

5. If you have an iCloud, Microsoft Exchange, Google, Yahoo! Mail, AOL, or Outlook.com account, tap the corresponding button. In the figure, we selected Google to access a Gmail account.

Other

If your email account is from a cable or DSL internet provider, or employers (depending on their system), you need to tap Other when setting up your account. Gather information like your ID, password, email server address, and account type (such as POP or IMAP) before starting. Check with your provider's support departments if you get stuck.

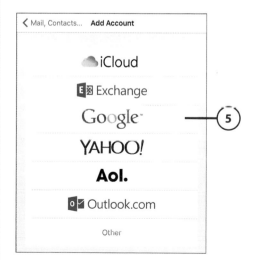

6. The next screen varies depending on the service you are using. Here you can see Google's authentication screen. If you chose Yahoo!, you would see Yahoo's authentication screen, which looks different. Some account types, like AOL, simply offer a few text entry fields and no logo or other buttons.

7. For Google's screen, start by entering your email address. Make sure you enter it perfectly, as this is your ID for logging into this email service.

8. Enter your password for this email account.

9. Tap Sign-In.

10. The next screen shows you what services the provider offers. For instance, Google's accounts not only provide email, but also contacts, calendars, and notes. You can leave all these turned on, or turn some off if you prefer not to use a service from that provider on your iPad.

11. Tap Save to continue.

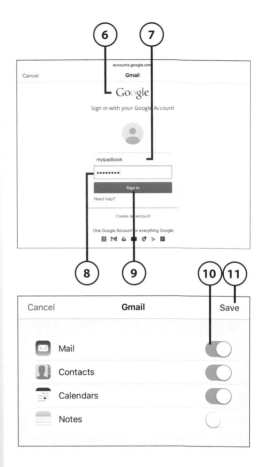

>>>Go Further
CHOOSING AN EMAIL PROVIDER WISELY

If you are using a cable or DSL provider, you might have an email address assigned to you by them. There are many good reasons to avoid using these email addresses and instead sign up for one such as Apple's iCloud or Google's Gmail service. The main reason is transportability. If you have a cable network email address now, you will lose it if you switch to another provider or you move out of your provider's territory. Another reason is that these ISP-provided email services tend to lack features like good junk mail filtering and the ability to send and receive email from multiple devices seamlessly.

Reading Your Email

You use the Mail app to read your email, which is much easier to navigate and type with your iPad turned horizontally. In horizontal mode, you can see the list of messages to the left while you view the message content to the right. In vertical mode, you view only one of these at a time. Let's start by reading some email.

1. Tap the Mail app icon on the Home screen.

Mail

2. On the left, you see a list of incoming mail. Tap a message in the list to view it.

3. On the right, you see the selected message.

4. If you want to check for new mail, drag the list of messages down and release. It will spring back up and ask the server to see if there are new messages.

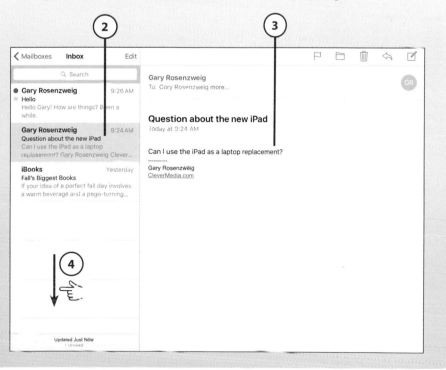

5. Tap the name or email address of the sender.

6. Tap Create New Contact to add the sender to your contacts.

7. Tap Add to Existing Contact to add the email address to a contact you already have in your Contacts app.

8. Tap the Folder button at the top of the message.

9. Tap a folder to move the current message to that folder.

10. Tap the Trash button at the top of the message to send the message directly to the Trash folder.

11. Tap the arrow button at the top of the message to reply or forward the message.

12. If you tap and swipe right to left or left to right across the message in the left sidebar, you get more options. Be careful not to swipe too fast; instead of options, you will quickly put the message in the trash.

13. Options include things like flagging or deleting the message.

Customization

You can customize this by going to the Settings app, selecting Mail, Contacts, Calendars on the left, and then Swipe Options. For instance, you can change the Swipe Right action from the default Mark as Read, to Archive.

14. If you tap More, you see a list of more options appear.

15. In addition to actions like Reply and Forward, you can also select Notify Me, which gives you an alert when someone else replies to this message thread (any message with the same title).

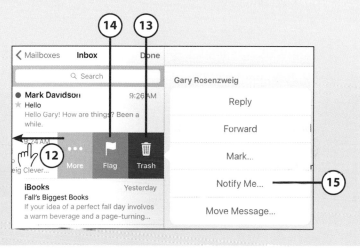

Multiple Inboxes

If you have more than one email account, you can choose to look at each inbox individually or a single unified Inbox that includes messages from all accounts. Just tap the Mailboxes button at the upper-left corner of the screen and choose All Inboxes. You can also choose to look at the inbox of a single account, or dig down into any folder of an account.

How Do You Create Folders?

For most email accounts—particularly IMAP, Gmail, and iCloud accounts—you can create folders using the Mail app. Use the back arrow at the upper-left corner of Mail and back out to the list of inboxes and accounts. Choose an account. Then tap the Edit button, and you'll see a New Mailbox button at the bottom of the screen.

VIPs

You can make a contact a VIP when you select the sender's name in an incoming email. Then, their messages will continue to appear in your inbox as normal, but they will also appear in the VIP inbox. So if you get a lot of email and want to occasionally focus only on a few very important people instead of everyone, choose your VIP inbox rather than your inbox.

If you are using VIPs with your iCloud email accounts, you'll see the same VIPs for your Mac and other iOS devices using that iCloud account.

Composing a New Message

Whether you compose a new message or reply to one you received, the process is similar. Let's take a look at composing one from scratch.

1. In the Mail app, tap the Compose button.

2. Enter a To: address.

3. Alternatively, tap the + button to bring up a list of contacts, and choose from there.

4. Tap in the Subject field and type a subject for the email.

5. Tap below the subject field in the body of the email, and type your message.

6. Tap the Send button.

Siri: Sending Email

You can use Siri to send email by asking it to "send an email to" and the name of the recipient. It will ask you for a subject and a body to the message, and then display it. You can choose to send it or cancel. You can even do the whole thing through Siri by saying something like "Send an email to John Johnson with the subject hello and the body how are you doing."

Including Images

You can copy and paste inside a Mail message just like you can inside of any text entry area on your iPad. But you can also paste in images! Just copy an image from any source—Photos app, Safari, and so on. Then tap in the message body and select Paste. You can paste in more than one image as well.

>>>Go Further

HANDOFF TO YOUR OTHER DEVICES

Starting with version 8, iOS has a feature called Handoff, which helps those who use multiple iOS devices and Macs. If you are in the middle of composing an email on your Mac or other iOS device, and then you look at the lock screen on your iPad, you should see a small Mail app icon at the lower left. Tap that icon and swipe up, and your iPad will automatically launch Mail and bring up the message composition window with the contents of the message you were writing on the other device. Meanwhile, the other device will close the composition window.

So, one device "hands off" the message to the other. You could be writing an email on your iMac and then grab your iPad and finish it there. Or vice versa. This also works with viewing Web pages in Safari and with Apple-created apps like Pages, Numbers, Keynote, and Maps.

There is a Handoff setting in the Settings app under General. It should be on by default. On Macs, there is a setting in System Preferences under General. But keep in mind that you'll need a pretty recent Mac running at least Mac OS X Yosemite for this to work. And both machines should be nearby with Wi-Fi and Bluetooth turned on. See the information at support.apple.com/HT204678 for setup help and troubleshooting.

Deleting and Moving Messages

While viewing a message, you can simply tap the Trash Can icon and move it to the trash. You can also move a group of messages to a folder or the trash.

1. In the Mail app, go to any mailbox and any subfolder, such as your Inbox.

2. If you are viewing a message, you can delete it by tapping the trash can icon.

3. You can also start the process of deleting a message or several messages by tapping the Edit button.

4. Tap the circles next to each message to select them.

5. They will be added to the middle of the screen in a neat stack.

6. Tap the Trash button to delete the selected messages.

7. Tap the Move button, and the left side of the screen changes to a list of folders. You can select one to move all the messages to that folder.

8. Tap the Cancel button to exit without deleting or moving any messages.

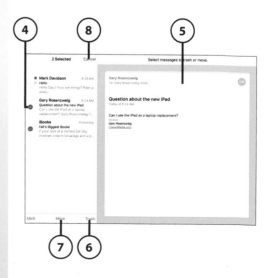

9. Alternatively, you can delete a single message by dragging just slightly right to left across the message in the list. This reveals Trash, Flag, and More buttons. If you drag all the way from the right to the left side of the screen, the Trash button enlarges and fills the space, and then the message is deleted with just this one gesture.

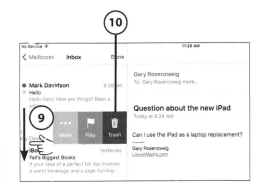

10. Tap the Trash button to delete the message. The More button allows you to reply, forward, flag, move, and perform various other actions on the message.

Oops—How Do I Undelete?

So you just tried to use step 9 to see what those buttons looked like, and you deleted the message by accident? You can always look in your Trash folder to select the message and move it back to the Inbox. But you can also give your iPad a quick shake, and you'll be prompted to undo the deletion.

Where's the Trash?

If you are just deleting the single message that you happen to be viewing, you can tap the trashcan icon at the top. But sometimes that icon isn't there. Instead, you may see an icon that looks like a file box. This is an Archive button. Some email services, like Gmail, insist that you archive your email instead of deleting it. To facilitate this, they provide a nearly infinite amount of storage space, so you might as well use that Archive button.

What About Spam?

Your iPad has no built-in spam filter. Fortunately, most email servers filter out spam at the server level. Using a service such as Gmail means that you get spam filtering on the server and junk mail automatically goes to the Junk folder, not your Inbox.

Searching Email

You can also search your messages using the Mail app.

1. The Search field is at the top of the messages list in the left sidebar in the Mail app. It won't be visible at first. To see it, tap and drag down the messages in the left sidebar.

2. Tap in the Search field.

3. Type a search term.

4. You see people and messages in the results. Select a message to view it from the search results.

5. Tap Cancel to exit the search and return to the mailbox you were previously viewing.

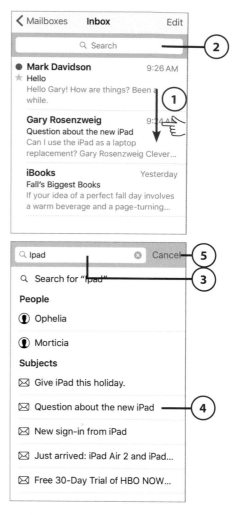

Search What?

Searches work on From, To, Subject fields and the body of the message. Any messages you have in your inbox will pop up right away, but any archived messages or ones stored in folders may or may not appear after a few seconds. The Mail app relies on your email server to return these results. Depending on what type of email server you have, it could take a while. Older results may not appear at all.

Customizing Your Email

You have more settings for email beyond the basic account setup. For instance, you can decide how you want to receive email, using either push delivery or fetch delivery (or manual). There are even more Email settings in the Settings app.

No Thanks—I'll Do It Myself

The Manual setting is useful if you don't want to be disturbed throughout the day as you receive email. These accounts will only be checked when you open the Mail app and look at the inbox for that account. Another reason to use Manual is to preserve battery as your iPad won't use Wi-Fi or your mobile connection as often. You also might want to use Manual if you are concerned about bandwidth, like when traveling internationally and only want to check email when using Wi-Fi.

Configuring How You Receive Email

When you receive email, it is either fetched, pushed, or delivered manually when you choose. Fetch checks for email at regular intervals, whereas push receives messages soon after they have arrived at your email service. Depending on what your provider supports, you can choose between these settings.

1. Go to the Settings app and tap on Mail, Contacts, Calendars.

2. Tap Fetch New Data.

3. Turn on Push to use push email reception, if you use email accounts that can send email via push.

4. Otherwise, select how often you want your iPad to go out to the server and fetch email.

5. Tap one of your email accounts to customize the settings for that particular account. Note that even some subscribed calendars have the ability to be set to push or fetch.

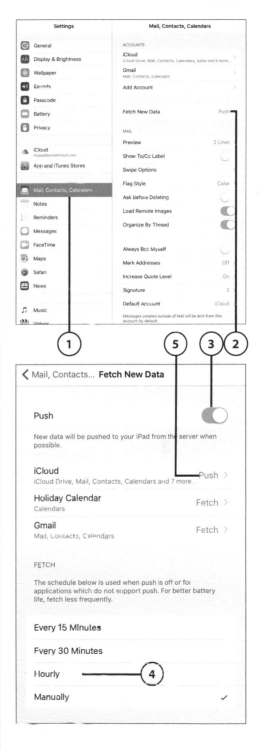

6. For each account you can set your preferences to Fetch, Manual, or Push if available for that email account. Note that more options exist for some accounts, such as specifying which folders are pushed.

‹ Fetch New Data	**iCloud**
SELECT SCHEDULE	
Push	✓
Fetch	
Manual	

If Push is not available, the Fetch schedule will be used.

PUSHED MAILBOXES	
✉ Inbox	✓
📄 Drafts	
✒ Sent	✓
🗑 Trash	
🗄 Archive	
☒ Junk	
📁 Notes	
📁 New Folder	
📁 To Do Items	
📁 Project Alpha	

Siri: Checking Email

You can ask Siri for a quick list of new email messages by saying "check my email." You'll get a list from within the Siri interface, and you can tap on a message to read it in the Mail app. If you say "read me my email," Siri will read your new messages out loud to you.

Creating a Signature

You can create a signature that appears below your messages automatically. You do this in the Settings app.

1. In the Settings app, choose Mail, Contacts, Calendars.

2. Tap Signature, which is way down in the list on the right.

3. If you have more than one email account set up, you can choose to have one signature for all accounts or a different signature for each account.

4. Type a signature in one of the signature text fields. You don't need to do anything to save the signature. You can tap the Home button on your iPad to exit Settings if you like.

Styles and Images in Signatures

You can make some text in your signature bold, italic, or underlined by selecting the text and tapping on the selection. In addition to Cut, Copy, and Paste options, you also see a "**B**/_U_" option. Tap that and you can style that selected text a bit. If you want to include an image in your signature, you can copy that image from another app and paste it in with the text. But try to refrain from pasting a photo or something large, as it may annoy your recipients to get a large image included with every message. A small company logo copied from your company's website might be more appropriate, although email etiquette points to keeping your signature simple and image-free.

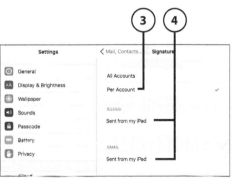

Case-By-Case Signatures

You can have only one signature, even if you have multiple email accounts on your iPad. But the signature is placed in the editable area of the message composition field, so you can edit it like the rest of your message.

More Email Settings

You can change even more email settings in the Settings app. Tap the Settings app on your Home screen, and then tap Mail, Contacts, Calendars so we can take a look at some of them.

1. Tap Preview to choose how many lines of message preview to show when stacking messages up in the list view.

2. Turn Show To/Cc Label on to view "To" or "Cc" in each email listed so that you know if you were the primary recipient or someone who was just copied on an email to someone else.

3. When viewing messages in your inbox, you can swipe left or right across the message in the list to take an action. You can set this up here. For instance, you can set a swipe to the right to mark an email as read, or you can set it to archive the message and remove it from the inbox.

4. Turn Ask Before Deleting on to require a confirmation when you tap the trash can button in Mail.

5. Turn Load Remote Images off so that images referenced in an mail, but stored on a remote server, are not shown in the message body.

6. To group replies to a message under the original message, select Organize By Thread. This is handy when you subscribe to email discussion lists.

7. Turn Always Bcc Myself on if you want to get a copy of every email you send so that later you can move your copies of emails to your Sent folder on your computer. This might be a good idea if you are using an older email system. Modern email systems like iCloud and Gmail should save your sent messages to the server just like other messages.

8. Choose whether to indent the quoted text from the original email when replying to a message.

9. Tap Default Account to determine which account is used to send email by default if you have more than one account set up on your iPad.

10. In most apps from which you send emails, you can type a message and also change the account you use to send the email. To do this, tap on the email address shown next to From: and you get a list of all your accounts, including alternate email addresses for each account.

MAIL	
Preview	2 Lines >
Show To/Cc Label	
Swipe Options	>
Flag Style	Color >
Ask Before Deleting	
Load Remote Images	
Organize By Thread	──6
Always Bcc Myself	──7
Mark Addresses	Off >
Increase Quote Level	On ──8
Signature	2 >
Default Account	iCloud ──9

Messages created outside of Mail will be sent from this account by default.

10

From: myipadbook@me.com

myipadbook@me.com   ✓

myipadbook@icloud.com

myipadbook@gmail.com

Why Not Show Remote Images?

The main reason to not show remote images is bandwidth. If you get an email that has 15 images referenced in it, you need to download a lot of data, and it takes a while for that email to show up completely. However, remote images are often used as ways to indicate whether you have opened and looked at messages. So, turning this off might break some statistics and receipt functionality expected from the sender (including from spammers).

Working with Messaging

Even though your iPad isn't a phone, you can send text messages. The catch is that you can only message others who are also using Apple's iMessage system. This would include anyone using iOS 5 or newer with an iPad, iPhone, or iPod touch, as long as they have signed up for the free service. Mac users can also send messages with the iMessage system.

Setting up Messaging

Settings

1. Tap the Settings app icon on your Home screen.

2. You need to be signed into iCloud with your Apple ID to use Messages. If you didn't do that when you set up your iPad, or when you set up iCloud email, you need to go to the iCloud settings and sign in or create an iCloud account.

3. Tap the Messages settings.

4. Make sure iMessage is turned on.

5. If you turn this option on, when someone sends you a message they will also get an indication when you have viewed the message.

6. You can use any valid email address that you own for Messages, even if it is not the same as your Apple ID email address. You can control which email addresses can be used to find you, adding more and removing others.

7. Apple's iMessage system can include a subject line along with the message, though most people don't use this.

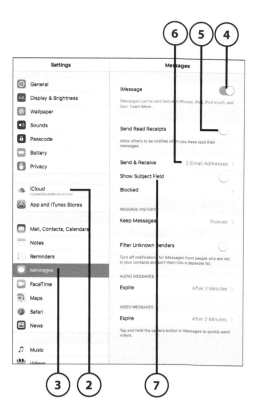

8. Tap Blocked to add email addresses to block so individuals cannot send you messages.

9. Most people prefer to keep old messages around forever, to refer to them later. Text messages are small, so you don't have to worry about them using up any noticeable space on your iPad. But your iPad allows you to send audio and video messages as well, which do take up some space. You can choose to have those automatically disappear after you have listened to or viewed them.

10. You can opt to have messages received from senders not in your contacts list to be put in a separate list in the Messages app. You also won't receive notifications when someone not in your contacts list sends you a message.

11. Set how long to keep audio and video messages you receive. Typically, you want these to expire soon after you view them so that they don't fill up your iPad's storage space.

Stop Contacting Me!

There is an even easier way to block unwanted messengers when using the Messages app. You can tap on a Details button at the upper-right corner of the screen while viewing the conversation in Messages. Then an info button appears. It looks like an i with a circle around it. Tap that and you get additional options. Scroll all the way down in these options and a Block this Caller option will appear. Use this and you'll never get another message from that account again. Better still, it will block audio and FaceTime calls from them as well.

Conversing with Messages

After you have set up an account with Messages, you can quickly and easily send messages to others. The next time you launch Messages, you will be taken directly to the main screen.

Messages

1. Tap the Messages app icon on your home screen.

2. Tap the New Message button at the top of the screen.

3. In a new message, tap in the To field and enter the email address of the recipient. Note that they should already be signed up for iMessage or you will not be able to send them anything. Some iPhone users may use their phone number as their iMessage ID instead of, or in addition to, their email address. As long as the phone number is tied to an iMessage account, you can still converse with them using Messages on your iPad.

4. Tap the text field above the keyboard to type your message.

5. If you want to include a picture or video with your message, tap the camera button. This allows you to choose a picture or video from your photo library, or take a new one with your iPad's camera.

6. To the right of the message field is a microphone. Before you type anything, you can tap this to record a short audio message to send instead of text. But as soon as you start typing text, the microphone button is replaced with the word Send. Tap this Send to send your message.

7. You will see the conversation as a series of talk bubbles. Yours will appear on the right.

8. When your friend responds, you will see their talk bubbles as well.

9. A list of conversations appears on the left. You can have many going on at the same time, or use this list to look at old conversations.

10. Tap Edit to access buttons to delete old conversations.

11. Tap on the Details button to do various tasks such as adding them to your contacts, or starting a FaceTime video chat. You can also send your current location to the people you are messaging, which saves you time if you want to tell someone to meet you at your current location.

12. If you see a small bubble with three dots, it means that the other party is typing. You see this with other people using Apple's iMessage system, but if they are using a mobile phone with SMS or if their connection is poor, you may not see these indicators.

13. Tap and hold on any message to bring up more options. You can also drag right to left across the messages to reveal time stamps for each message that was sent to you.

14. Use the More button to bring up options like selecting and deleting individual messages in the conversation.

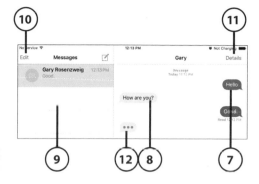

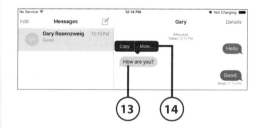

>>>Go Further

SMS ON YOUR iPAD

SMS, or Short Message Service, is the system of sending messages, sometimes called "texts," through your mobile carrier to other phone users. Unlike iMessage, SMS messages go through carriers like AT&T, Verizon, T-Mobile, and Sprint. So SMS is available on your iPhone, but not your iPad since your iPad isn't a phone and doesn't use these carriers for voice and messaging.

However, a feature called SMS Relay allows iPhone users to automatically forward SMS messages to their iPad and for their iPad to send SMS messages through the iPhone. This feature will appear if both your iPhone and iPad use the same iCloud account, and they are both connected to the same Wi-Fi network. You'll receive an initial prompt asking if you want to enable SMS Relay. After you confirm, you'll be able to converse using SMS on your iPad so long as your iPhone is connected to the same Wi-Fi network.

This enables you to send messages from your iPad to friends who have non-Apple devices and use SMS.

Siri: Sending Messages

You can use Siri to send messages. Simply tell Siri something like "Send a text message to Gary" and Siri will respond by asking you what you want to say in your message. Or, you can say something like "Send a message to Gary telling him I'll meet him after the movie," and Siri will create the whole message for you. You can review the message before it is sent for a truly hands-free operation. When you get a message, you can also ask Siri to "Read me that message" and you can listen to the message without ever glancing at your iPad's screen.

Browse your photos on the iPad's brilliant screen.

Take pictures with the iPad's cameras.

Take fun selfies with Photo Booth.

In this chapter, we use the Camera and Photo Booth apps to take pictures. Then we learn how to view, edit, and share photos.

→ Taking Photos

→ Editing and Adjusting Photos

→ Taking Panoramic Photos

→ Using Photo Booth

→ Photo Sources

→ Browsing Your Photos

→ Viewing Your Photos

→ Sharing Your Photos

→ Viewing Albums

→ Creating Albums

→ Creating a Slideshow

→ Capturing the Screen

Taking and Editing Photos

In addition to replacing books, the iPad replaces physical photo albums. You can literally carry thousands of photos with you on your iPad. Plus, your iPad's screen is a beautiful way to display these photos. It can also replace your camera, as long as you don't mind its size.

In addition to photos you take using your iPad, you can sync photos from your computer to your iPad, or use the iCloud Photo Library. Then you can use the Photos app to browse and view your photos.

Working with Photos

All IPads after the first generation include two cameras you can use to take a variety of photos that you can then edit and adjust as you need. One camera is located on the front, and one on the back. The primary app for doing this is through the Camera app. Let's take a look at the things you can do with this app.

Taking Photos

Camera

1. Tap the Camera app icon on the home screen. This brings up the Camera app, and you should immediately see the image from the camera.

2. The camera app has six modes: Time-Lapse, Slo-Mo, Video, Photo, Square, and Pano. The first three are for video filming mode, and the other three take rectangular, square, and panoramic photographs. To switch between modes, you can tap and drag up and down in this area. Or, you could tap the word representing the mode you want, and it will switch to it. The option in yellow with a dot next to it is the mode you are currently using. Switch to Photo mode if you are not in that mode already.

Mode Support

Not all iPad models support each mode. Pano requires at least an iPad with a Retina display (like the iPad Air). Slo-Mo requires an iPad Air 2 or newer model.

3. Tap the button at the top right to switch between front and rear cameras.

4. Tap anywhere on the image to specify that you want to use that portion of the image to determine the focus and exposure for the photo. A yellow box appears at that spot.

5. After you have tapped on the image, and if you are using the rear-facing camera, you can zoom in. To do that, use your fingers to pinch apart.

6. Tap the HDR button to turn on High Dynamic Range Imaging.

7. Tap the time delay button to set a timer for 3 or 10 seconds. This allows you to set your iPad down on a stand or lean it against something and get into the shot.

8. Tap the large camera button at the right side of the screen to take the picture. Alternatively, press one of the volume buttons on the side of your iPad to take the picture. If you hold either button down, your iPad will continue to take pictures in rapid succession.

9. Tap the button at the lower right to go to the Camera Roll and see the pictures you have taken. You can edit and adjust the photo you have just taken, as you'll learn in the next task.

The Focus and Exposure Area

When you tap the screen as in step 4, the yellow box will appear. This area is now used for both focus and exposure. After you tap the screen, you can now tap and drag your finger up and down to make further exposure adjustments. You'll see the little sun icon next to the box move up and down along the line as you do so.

If you hold your finger down for a few seconds, the box will pulse and the text AE/AF Lock will appear at the top of the screen. This means the focus and exposure are now locked and will not change as you move your iPad to point it at something different.

High Dynamic What?

High Dynamic Range Imaging is a process where multiple pictures are taken in quick succession, each using a different exposure. Then the multiple images are combined. For instance, if you are taking a picture of a person with a bright sky behind them, one picture will do better with the person, and the other with the sky. Combining the multiple images gives you a picture that shows them both better than a single shot would.

When you use HDR, be sure to hold your iPad steady so each shot captures the same image. They will be taken a fraction of a second apart. So, HDR does not work well with moving objects or a moving camera.

It's Not All Good

You're Holding It Wrong

It is natural to hold your iPad vertically. You may use a majority of apps that way, so when it comes time to take photos or video, it is easy to forget and to continue to hold it vertically. This drives professional and amateur photographers crazy when they see a good photo ruined because a phone or iPad user forgot to turn the device before shooting the picture.

Although portrait photos have their uses, most pictures are best taken in horizontal orientation. Cameras are usually held horizontally, and when you view your photos on a computer screen or television, a horizontal photo will fit nicely whereas a vertical photo will need to shrink to fit, with vertical space wasted on the left and right. Never shoot video in portrait orientation

Editing and Adjusting Photos

You can start editing photos by tapping on the photo icon, like in step 9 of the previous task. Or, you can enter the Photos app and edit photos from there. We'll look more at the Photos app later in this chapter.

1. If you don't see buttons at the top and bottom of the photo, tap the middle of the photo to bring up controls on the top and bottom of the screen.

2. Use the thumbnails at the bottom to select a specific picture to view your photos. Or just swipe left and right through the thumbnails to flip through all your photos.

3. If you are editing a photo you just took using the Camera app, you can tap Done to exit viewing this one image and jump back to the camera interface. Otherwise, continue on to step 4.

4. Tap the Trash icon to delete the photo. Deleted photos appear for 30 days in a special Recently Deleted photo album, where you can rescue them if the deletion was a mistake. You can also tap and hold in the middle of a photo and then select Hide to hide the photo from Years, Collections and Moments views, though it is still shown in any album you have added it to.

5. Tap the Share icon to send the photo to someone else via message, email, AirDrop, or a variety of other methods depending on which apps you have installed. This is also where you can copy the image so you can paste it into an email or another app.

6. Tap the Favorites button to mark this photo as one of your best. You'll be able to find it quickly in the Favorites album in the Photos app.

7. Tap Edit to enter Editing mode and bring up controls on the left side of the screen.

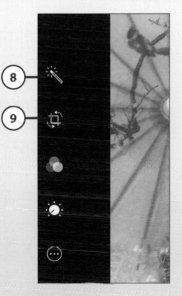

8. Tap Enhance to have the app examine the brightness and contrast in the photo and try to bring out the best image.

9. Tap the Crop button.

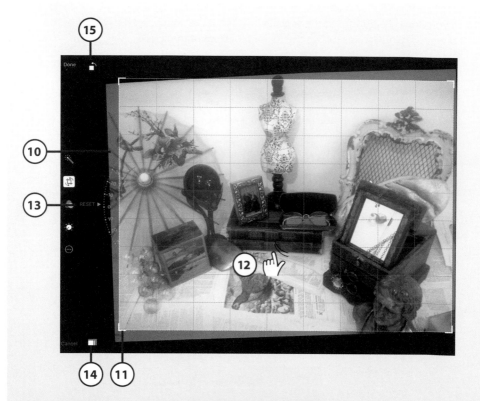

10. In this example, notice that the image automatically rotates slightly. The accelerometer in your iPad recorded the orientation of your iPad at the moment you took the photo, so it can now straighten the photo to be level. Now you can tap and drag this angle dial up or down to rotate the photo manually.

11. You can crop the photo by dragging any one of the four corners. Drag as many corners as you like to get the cropping just the way you want it.

12. You can pinch in or out to zoom, or drag the photo to reposition it within the crop frame.

13. Tap Reset to set the rotation to 0 degrees and the cropping back to the full image size. Tap here again to rotate the photo automatically as it first appeared after step 9.

14. Tap this button to set the cropping rectangle to a specific size, such as 3:2 or square.

15. Tap the Rotate button to rotate the photo by 90 degree increments. This is useful when a photo is upside down or the wrong orientation.

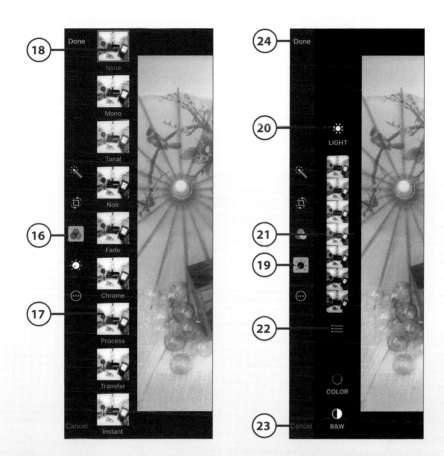

16. Tap the filters button to apply a color filter to the photo.

17. You can choose from one of the filters in the list and preview the changes immediately.

18. You can always tap None to remove the color filter.

19. Tap the color adjustments button.

20. Tap one of the three color adjustment types: Light, Color, or B&W.

21. Each type of adjustment has a filmstrip you can drag up and down to position the red line to indicate the level of adjustment you want. The main image on the screen shows you a preview of the result.

22. You can dig deeper into each adjustment with the list button and modify only one sub-setting. For instance, you can adjust the contrast, brightness, or exposure.

23. Tap Cancel to leave the cropping editor without saving the changes.

24. Tap Done to exit the cropping editor and apply the changes to the photo.

>>>Go Further
EXTENDING PHOTO EDITING

You can add extensions to the Photos app that allow you to edit photos without leaving the app. When you install third-party apps such as **Camera+**, **Afterlight**, and **Fragment Prismatic Effects**, they add more functionality to photo editing. Look for a small button with three dots on the Photo app edit screen. You can see it just below step 19 in the screenshots. Tap that button, and then tap the More button to switch on an extension.

After it is switched on, tap the small three-dot button when editing a photo to select the extended functionality and apply interesting effects to your photo. Dozens, if not hundreds, of third-party apps will soon be available to give you all sorts of photo-editing fun.

Taking Panoramic Photos

If you have an iPad Air or an iPad mini with a retina display, the Pano option is available in the Camera app. This option allows you to take wide panoramic shots, covering a larger area than you could normally fit into a photo.

1. In the Camera app, slide the available capture types up until Pano is yellow.

2. Hold your camera in vertical orientation. Look at the rectangle in the middle of the screen. You will be filling this rectangle with images from the camera. Position it so the left side of the rectangle contains the portion of the scene you want to be on the left side of the finished panoramic photo.

3. Tap the camera shutter button, or the physical volume buttons, on your iPad to start taking the photo.

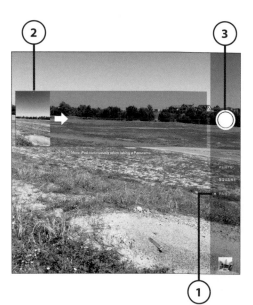

4. Slowly and steadily turn your body and your iPad from left to right to allow the camera to take in more of the image. As you move, the rectangle fills up with the scene. Small parts of the top and bottom may remain empty if you tilt the iPad a little up or down. Try to keep these areas to a minimum, but a little of this is typically unavoidable.

5. You don't need to fill the entire rectangle. Most panoramic photos don't need to use the full horizontal area. Just get as much as you need to make a good photograph.

6. Tap the shutter button again to finish.

7. The result is just like a regular photo in your photo library, except that it is wider. You view it and edit it just like in the previous task.

>>>Go Further
PANORAMIC TIPS

- Before you start taking the panoramic, you can tap the arrow on the screen to reverse direction and take the photo from right to left.

- You don't need to restrict yourself to horizontal panoramas. You can hold your iPad in horizontal orientation and take a vertical one. This could be used to capture a skyscraper, or to get both the ground and a plane in the same shot.

- Panoramas don't have to be of scenery. For instance, you can capture a wide painting in an art museum even if there is not enough space to back up and get it in one shot. Or you can capture everyone sitting around a dining table in one shot.

- If there are moving objects in your panorama, such as soccer players running on a field, you might not get a clean shot. Sometimes a player who is moving fast might appear twice in the same panorama.

Using Photo Booth

In addition to the basic picture-taking functionality of the Camera app, you can also use the included Photo Booth app to take more creative shots using one of eight special filters.

Photo Booth

1. Launch the Photo Booth app.

2. You'll start by seeing all the filters you can choose from. Tap one of the filters to select it.

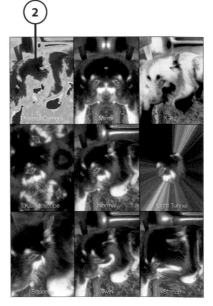

3. Now you'll see just that one filter. In addition, you have some buttons. Tap on the button at the bottom right to switch between the front and rear cameras.

4. Tap the button at the bottom left to return to the 9-filter preview.

5. Tap the camera button at the bottom to take a picture.

6. Some filters also allow you to tap the live video image to adjust the filter. For instance, the Light Tunnel filter enables you to set the position of the center of the tunnel.

A Kind of Flash

When you take a picture with the camera on the front of the iPad, you get a kind of flash effect from the screen. It simply turns all white for a second. This helps in low light situations.

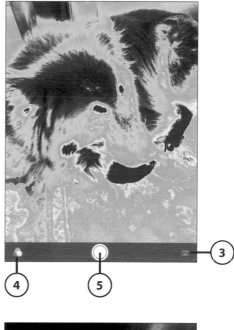

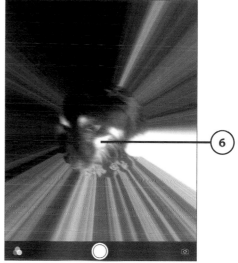

Photo Sources

Your iPad's Photos app can display photos from many different sources. You can then view them chronologically by Years, Collections, and Moments, as we'll look at in the next task. You can also organize them by albums that you create. Before we look at how to view your photos, it is important to understand where the photos come from. Here are all the possible sources:

- **Photos you take with your iPad's camera:** When you use the Camera app or the Photo Booth app to take a picture, it is added to your library with easy access through an album named Camera Roll.

- **Images from apps:** Many apps allow you to export images into your iPad's photo library. These will also be seen in the Photos app. Included in this category is when you take a screen shot. We'll look at that later in this chapter.

- **Synced from your computer:** iTunes on Mac and Windows computers can sync photos to your iPad. See "Syncing Photos" in Chapter 3. You can take pictures with a dedicated camera device, organize them on your computer, and then sync the ones you like to view on the iPad.

- **Transferred over a network:** You can use AirDrop on an iPod, iPhone, or Mac to send images to an iPad. You can also save images you see on the web (see, "Copying Images from Web Pages," in Chapter 7), or save images attached to emails or messages. Sometimes third-party apps allow you to access images stored on other photo services and transfer these to your photo library as well.

- **iCloud Photo Library:** You can choose to store all your photos on Apple's cloud server and access them from all your iOS devices and Macs. When you use this option, you can no longer sync with iTunes on a computer because the two methods are mutually exclusive. You can turn this on in the Settings app, under Photos & Camera.

- **Photo Stream:** If you enable Photo Stream, every picture you take is automatically sent to iCloud's Photo Stream where it also appears on your iPad, Mac, and even your Apple TV, if you have Photo Stream enabled on those devices. Think of this as a temporary email inbox for photos. Only the most recent 1,000 pictures from the last 30 days are stored in Photo Stream. You could take a picture on your iPhone and see it on your Mac and iPad, choosing to then move it to your main library if you want to keep it permanently. You can turn this on in the Settings app, under Photos & Camera.

- **iCloud Photo Sharing:** You can create iCloud photo albums and share them with others. Likewise, you can subscribe to someone else's shared album. Then you can view these shared album photos in the Photos app.

The big choice you need to make is whether to use iCloud Photo Library or sync photos using iTunes.

iCloud Photo Library is a great way to manage your photos as they will simply be available to you everywhere. But if you have a slow Internet connection at home, then you might want to stick with the old system of storing your photo library on your computer. Though this might be a good excuse to call your service provider and get a faster connection.

Browsing Your Photos

The Photos app on your iPad organizes your photos chronologically and breaks time into three levels: Years, Collections, and Moments. The photos taken on your iPad are combined with photos you synced from your computer or photos in your iCloud Photos Library. Let's take a tour of the Photos app to learn how to browse through your photos.

Photos

1. Launch the Photos app to view your photos.

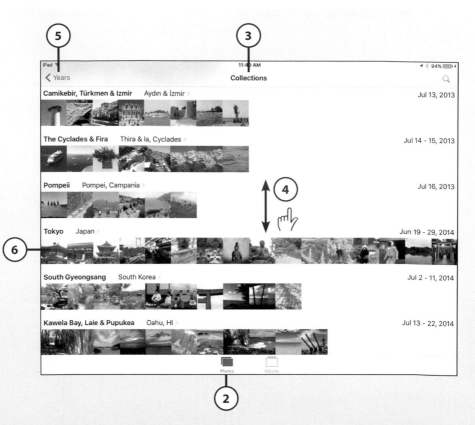

2. Tap Photos at the bottom to browse your photos.

3. You will resume viewing your photos at the same level you were viewing them the last time you looked. The three levels are: Years, Collections, and Moments. You can see which level you are at by looking at the top of the screen.

4. You can tap and drag vertically to scroll through your photos.

5. To move up a level, from Collections to Years, or Moments to Collections, tap the label in the upper-left corner. If you are viewing Collections, the label says Years to indicate that is the view you are moving back to.

6. Whichever level you are at, you can dig down to the next level by tapping one of the strips of photos. You can also tap and hold your finger over any photo until it pops out of the strip, and then release to jump right to viewing that photo.

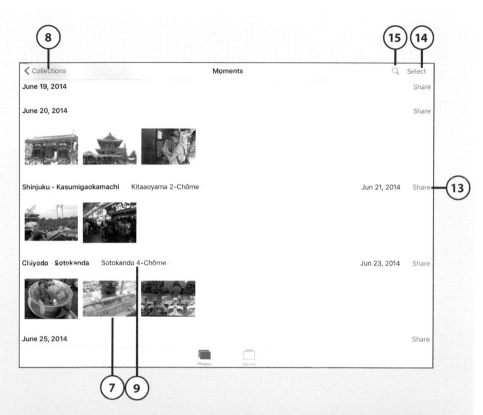

7. At the Moments level, you see the individual photos. Tap one to view it. We'll look more in depth at viewing photos in the next task. Note that Moment groupings are based both on time and location. So photos taken at a park in the afternoon and then at dinner later that day on the other side of town could be grouped into different Moments.

8. Tap Collections to go back up to the Collections level.

9. At the Moments or Collections level, you can tap any location name to go to a map where the photos are arranged by location.

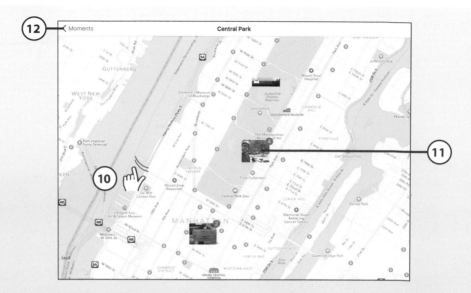

10. The map resizes to contain all the photos in the Moment or Collection you are viewing. If the photos are all taken in the same city, you may get a city map. If they are taken across the world, you may see the whole planet. You can pinch to zoom, or tap and drag to move the map.

11. Tap any single photo to view it, or tap a group of photos to see a screen that shows each one and allows you to scroll through them.

12. Tap at the top left to return to Moments or Collections.

13. At the Moments level, you can tap a Share button next to any Moment grouping and share some or all of the photos through email, iCloud, Messages, or Facebook.

14. You can also tap the Select button, and then you can select multiple Moments groups to share.

15. Tap the Search button, and you can search by typing location or date terms like "Hawaii" or "October."

It's Not All Good

Where in the World Are You?

When you take pictures with a mobile phone like the iPhone, the location is automatically added to the photo. But most dedicated digital cameras, even expensive ones, do not have any GPS feature, so they don't know your location. iPads without a live Wi-Fi connection won't know, either. So your photo collection may have a lot of photos with no location information. These photos will not appear on maps and can't be accurately divided into Moments by location.

Viewing Your Photos

Whether you are viewing a photo you tapped on at the Moments level, such as in step 7 of the previous task, or you are viewing a photo in an album or from the Camera app, the interface is basically the same.

1. Tap in the middle of the photo to remove the buttons and text at the top and bottom of the screen so you can enjoy the photo. Tap again to bring the interface elements back.

2. Pinch out to zoom in on the photo. Once zoomed, you can tap and drag to see different areas of the photo.

3. When zoomed out to view the entire photo, you can swipe left or right to view the previous or next photo in the Moment or album.

4. Alternatively, you can tap or drag in the strip of photos at the bottom to move through the photos in the Moment or album.

5. Tap Edit to edit or adjust the photo. See "Editing and Adjusting Photos," earlier in this chapter.

6. Tap Moments to exit viewing this photo and return to the Moments level. If you are viewing a photo from the Cameras after taking a picture, you'll have a Done button at the right to return to the Camera screen, plus an All Photos button to the left to open the Photos app.

7. Tap the Share button to share via AirDrop, email, social networks, and a variety of other methods. See the next section for more information about sharing.

>>>Go Further
ZOOM AND ROTATE

Here are a few tips on how to navigate your photos as you view them:

- Pinch or unpinch with two fingers to zoom out and in.

- Double-tap a photo to zoom back out to normal size.

- While a photo is at normal size, double-tap to zoom it to make it fit on the screen with the edges cropped.

- If you pinch in far enough, the picture closes, and you return to browsing mode.

Sharing Your Photos

You can share photos while viewing an individual photo, such as in step 7 of the previous task. You can also share from the Moments screen by tapping Share next to any moment.

Let's pick up from step 7 of the previous task, as if you have just tapped the Share button while viewing a photo.

1. At the top of the Sharing screen, you see your selected photo—plus you can choose others in the same Moment or album to share. Tap any photo to include it. You'll see a checkmark on photos that you have set to share.

2. You can share via AirDrop, sending the photo to another iOS or Mac user near you. See "Sharing with AirDrop" in Chapter 3.

3. You can send the photos using either the Message or Mail apps.

4. You can also post directly to Facebook, Twitter, or Flickr, so long as you have configured these services in your Settings app.

5. You can copy a photo to use it in another app. You can also tap and hold in the middle of a photo while editing it, and select Copy.

6. AirPlay lets you show the photo on an Apple TV connected to the same Wi-Fi network. See "AirPlay Mirroring with Apple TV" in Chapter 18.

7. You can send the photo to a printer on your network. See "Printing from Your iPad" in Chapter 18.

8. iCloud Photo Sharing lets you add the photo to an online shared album.

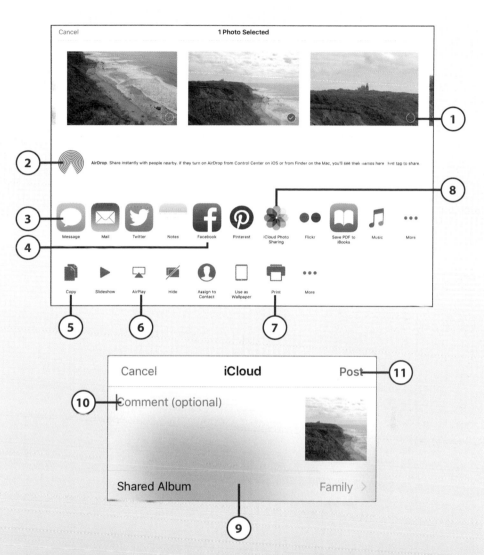

9. Set the online album where the photo should be placed. You'll also be given the chance to create a new album.

10. You can add a comment that will appear online with the photo.

11. Tap Post to send the photos to iCloud.

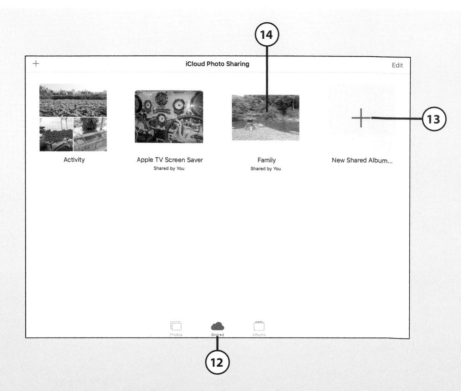

12. You can see these online albums in the Photos app by tapping on the Shared button at the bottom of the Years/Collections/Moments screen.

13. You can create a new shared album from this screen.

14. Tap on a shared album to view it.

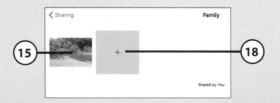

15. You see all the photos in that album. Tap a single photo to view it.

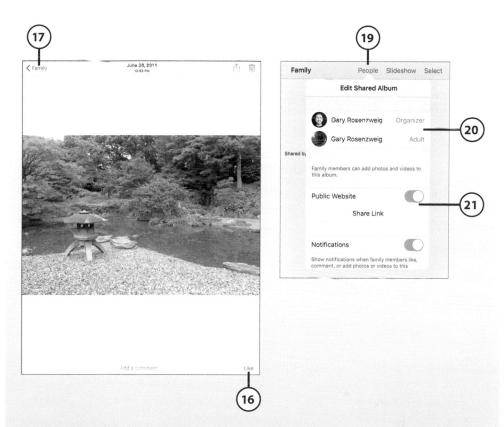

16. When looking at an individual photo, you can "like" the photo and add a comment.

17. Tap the name of the album in the upper-left corner to go back to the previous screen.

18. Tap the blank album with the + sign to create a new shared photo album. You'll be asked to give it a name and enter email addresses of people with whom you want to share the album.

19. While viewing a shared photo album that you have created, tap the People button to change the sharing options.

20. If this wasn't the Family album, then you'd see a list of people with whom the album is shared. Since this is a special Family photo album created by the Family Sharing feature, it is automatically shared by everyone in the family group. Other albums you create can be shared with anyone. An option here would be to allow you to invite more people to share it.

21. You can also turn on the Public Website option to let anyone view these photos. Then, tap the Share Link button to send people a link to the web page.

You can share your photos in many ways, and it is likely that more will be added in the future. What you can use depends on what you have set up on your iPad. For instance, if you have Messaging and Twitter set up, you can use the Message and Tweet buttons to share using those services.

Working with Albums

Using the chronological Years/Collections/Moments views of the Photos app is a great way to find the photos you want to view. But, if you would rather organize your photos yourself, you can do so by creating albums.

Albums can be made using the photo library software on your Mac, Photoshop Albums or Photoshop Elements on Windows, or by using file system folders on Mac and windows. When you sync to your iPad with iTunes, you'll see these albums using the steps that follow. Or, if you are using iCloud Photo Library, you can create the albums on any device, and the albums will also show up on all your other devices.

The important thing to realize about photo albums is that the photos aren't really *in* the album. Think of them as a list of references to photos, the same way a playlist in iTunes refers to songs stored in your music library.

A photo appears once in your photo library, and you can see it once in the Years/Collections/Moments views, but you can put a reference to that photo in multiple albums. For instance, you can have a photo appear in an album named "My Best Pictures" and also in an album named "Summer 2014." If you delete it from one or both, the photo is still in your library—it just doesn't happen to be in any album.

Viewing Albums

1. In the Photos app, tap the Albums button.

2. Tap on an album to expand it to see all the photos.

3. Tap any photo to view it.

4. Tap the album name to return from viewing the photo, and then tap the Albums button on the next screen to return to the list of albums.

Getting Back to the Album

After you finish digging down into an album, you can go back to the list of albums by tapping the Albums button, or a similarly named button, at the top left. But you can also pinch in all photos to group them in the middle of the screen and then release to move back to the albums list.

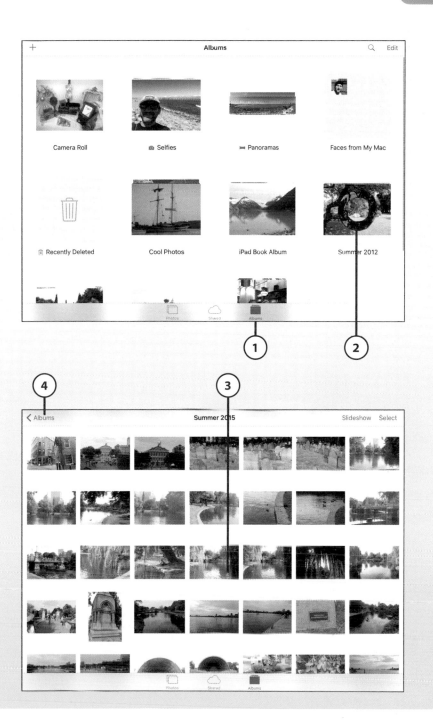

Creating Albums

You can create new albums on your iPad. If you are using iCloud Photo Library, these albums appear across all your devices. The process involves naming a new album and then selecting the photos to appear in the album.

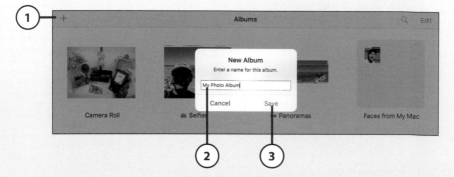

1. In the Photos app, tap Albums at the bottom to view your albums, and then tap the + button to create a new album.

2. Enter a name for the album.

3. Tap Save.

4. Now you can start adding some photos to this empty album. You see all your photos appear in the Moments view, just as they did in step 7 of the task "Browsing Your Photos," earlier in this chapter.

5. Tap and drag vertically to flip through your photos to locate the ones you want to include in this new album.

6. If you prefer Albums view, you can tap Albums to switch to that view.

7. Tap photos to add them to the album. Tap again to undo the selection.

8. You can also select an entire Moment group of photos.

9. When you have added all the photos you want to the album, tap Done. You can always add more by viewing that album, tapping the Select button at the top, and then tapping the Add button at the top.

Special Albums

Many special albums are created automatically by the Photos app—most notably is the Camera Roll album with images you have just taken. There might also be a Recently Deleted album acting as a trash can or recycling bin, where you can rescue recently deleted photos. The Photos app also groups other items into albums automatically, such as Panoramas and Videos.

Creating a Slideshow

Another way to look at your photos is as a slideshow with music and transitions. You can quickly and easily create a slideshow with any group of photos in the Photos app that shows a Slideshow button at the top—for example, an album synced to, or that you created on, your iPad.

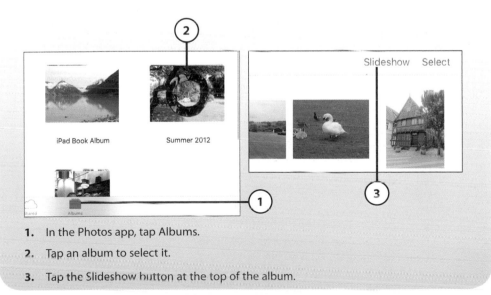

1. In the Photos app, tap Albums.

2. Tap an album to select it.

3. Tap the Slideshow button at the top of the album.

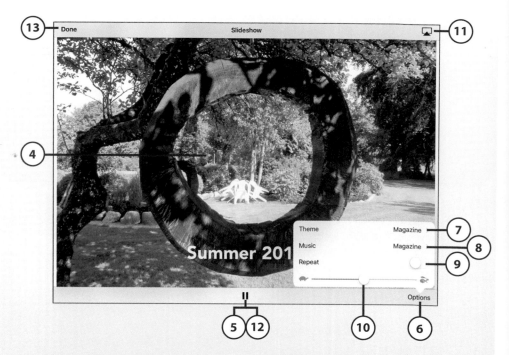

4. The slideshow immediately starts playing with default options. To customize it, first tap in the middle of the screen to bring up controls at the top and bottom.

5. Tap the pause button to stop playback while you adjust the settings.

6. Tap the Options button at the bottom right.

7. You can select from one of many themes for the slideshow.

8. You can change the music to one of many presets, or use a song from iTunes.

9. You can set the slideshow to loop.

10. Use this slider to change the speed.

11. Slideshows can be played on your iPad's screen, or on any connected AirPlay video devices, such as an Apple TV connected to the same Wi-Fi network.

12. Tap the Play button that took the place of the Pause button to start the slideshow.

13. Tap Done to exit the slideshow.

Stopping a Slideshow

Tap on the screen anywhere to stop a slideshow. This will take you into the album. Start with the current photo. Then you can continue to browse that album normally swiping left or right and using the strip of thumbnails at the bottom.

Capturing the Screen

You can capture the entire iPad screen and send it to your Photos app. This feature is useful if you want to save what you see to an image for later.

1. Make sure the screen shows what you want to capture. Try the Home screen, as an example.

2. Press and hold the Wake/Sleep button and Home button at the same time. The screen flashes and you hear a camera shutter sound, (unless you have the volume turned down).

3. Go to the Photos app.

4. Tap on Albums and then go to the Camera Roll album.

5. The last image in this album should be your new screen capture. Tap it to open it.

6. The screen shot will appear just like any other photo. You can edit it or delete it with the buttons on the top right and bottom right.

7. Tap the Share icon to email the photo or copy it to use in another application. Or you can leave the photo in your photo library for future use.

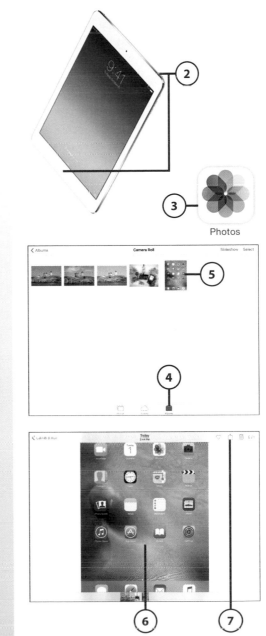

Photos

It's Not All Good

Sharing Slideshows

Want to share a slideshow via a social network or YouTube? You can, but not by using the Photos app's simple Slideshow feature. Instead, use iMovie. See "Adding Photos to Your Video in iMovie" in Chapter 10 to learn how to make a video that is a series of photos. See "Combining Clips in iMovie" in that same chapter to learn how to share a movie. You can also use one of many slideshow and photo-sharing apps you can get in the App Store.

Make video calls
with FaceTime.

Record video with your
iPad's cameras.

Put together movies from
your video clips and photos.

In this chapter, we use the Camera, Photo Booth, and iMovie apps to shoot and edit video with your iPad. We'll also use the FaceTime app to make a video call.

→ Shooting Video

→ Trimming Video Clips

→ Combining Clips in iMovie

→ Editing Transitions in iMovie

→ Adding Photos to Your Video in iMovie

→ Adding Video Titles in iMovie

→ Setting Up FaceTime

→ Placing Video Calls with FaceTime

→ Receiving Video Calls with FaceTime

Recording Video

You can record video using either of the two cameras on your iPad. The primary app for doing this is the Camera app.

In addition, you can edit video with the iMovie app. This app, which you can download from Apple in the App Store, lets you combine clips and add transitions, titles, and audio.

The cameras on your iPad can also be used to video chat with someone on another iPad, an iPhone, iPod Touch, or a Mac using the FaceTime app.

Shooting Video

If you simply want to record something that is happening using the cameras, you can do it with the Camera app.

Camera

1. Launch the Camera app. Also, turn your iPad sideways so you are shooting horizontal video, like you are used to seeing on TV and in movies. Your iPad can shoot in both vertical and horizontal orientations, but horizontal is better for playback on most screens.

2. Switch the camera mode to video by tapping this area and sliding the words "Time-Lapse, Slo-Mo, Video, Photo, Square, and Pano" so that "Video" is next to the yellow dot.

3. If needed, you can toggle between the rear and front cameras. Remember that the rear camera is much better quality than the front camera, so use the rear one whenever possible.

4. Optionally, tap in the image to set the best point for the exposure setting.

5. Tap the record button to start recording. While you are recording, the red dot will flash and the length of the recording will show on the right side above the button. Tap the same button to stop recording.

6. Tap the image in the lower-right corner to see your video when you are done. You can then tap the play button to watch it.

7. You are now viewing an item in your photo library, the same place as you were in Chapter 9, "Taking and Editing Photos." But the interface looks different when you have a video instead of a still photo. Tap the play button to watch the video.

8. Tap the Share button to email the video, send via a text message, or upload it directly to a service like YouTube, Facebook, or Vimeo. You can also stream it to an AirPlay device on your network such as an Apple TV.

9. Tap the trashcan to delete the video.

10. When you are done viewing your video, tap Done to shoot another.

>>>Go Further

TIME-LAPSE PHOTOGRAPHY AND SLO-MO VIDEO New!

A second video mode is Time-Lapse. Instead of filming video at a fast rate of 30 frames per second, your iPad will take video at a much slower rate, starting at around 1 frame per second. This allows you to capture slow-moving events like a sunset or a flower opening its petals.

To make a good time-lapse video, you need to find a way to keep your iPad completely stationary. Alternatively, you could take a moving time-lapse by having a passenger hold the iPad pointed out the front window of your car while driving.

With time-lapse, a 10-minute period of time unfolds in 30 seconds. If you want more control over the exact rate of the time-lapse, search for "time lapse" in the App Store—you'll find all sorts of third-party time-lapse photography apps that allow you to control the frame rate and much more.

Slo-Mo is the opposite of time-lapse and is only available on more recent iPad models. It takes video at a high frame rate, and then shows the start and end of the video at normal speed, and the middle of the video in slow motion. You can adjust the portion of the video that is shown in slow motion using a slider control that appears just above the trimming control, which is discussed in the next section.

It's Not All Good

Emailing Compresses the Video

Video with the rear camera is shot at 1280x720 on the iPad 2 and 1920x1080 on newer iPads. But when you email a video, it's usually compressed to a much smaller size. This is good because you won't be sending a massive video file, using your bandwidth and the bandwidth of the recipient. But don't use email to save your videos to your computer. Instead, connect to your computer with a cable and transfer, as you would with photos. If you use iCloud Photo Library, your video will be stored there.

Trimming Video Clips

While viewing a video in your photo library, you can also trim it to cut some unneeded footage from the start and end of the video.

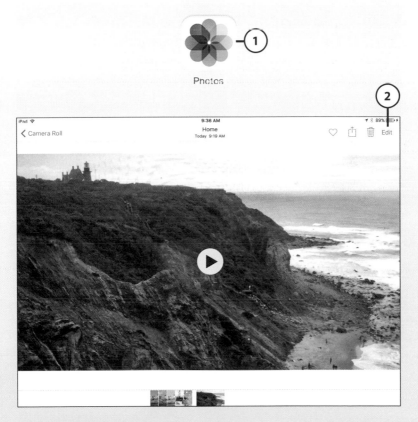

1. Launch the Photos app.

2. Find a video you want to trim and view it. Then tap the Edit button at the upper right. Notice that in the previous task, after initially taking the video with the Camera app, you also get an Edit button you can tap to start trimming.

3. You will see a timeline of sorts at the top of the screen.

4. Drag the left side of the timeline to the right to trim from the start of the video.

5. Drag the right side of the timeline to the left to trim from the end of the video.

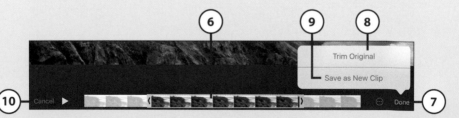

6. The section you have selected is now outlined in yellow. Areas to the left and right of this area will be removed.

7. Tap the Trim button.

8. Tap Trim Original to replace the video with the trimmed version.

9. Tap Save as New Clip to keep the original, and also save your trimmed version as a separate clip.

10. You can tap Cancel to quit without trimming if you want.

Editing in iMovie

The trimming functionality of the Camera and Photos apps gives you the basic ability to edit a video clip, but you can go a lot further if you purchase the iMovie app from Apple. Although it's not a full-featured editor like you might have on your computer, you can combine clips, add titles and transitions, and produce a short video from your clips.

>>>Go Further
iMOVIE EDITING WITHOUT LEAVING THE PHOTOS APP

You can add extensions to the Photos app that allow you to edit videos without leaving the app. Extensions come with apps like iMovie when you install them. After you have iMovie, you get a small button with three dots on the Photo app video edit screen. Tap that button, and then tap the More button to switch on the extension.

After it is switched on, you can tap the small, three-dot button when editing a video to enter a special iMovie editing screen. This screen allows you to trim, apply filters, add music, and add titles. So, if you just want to do something quick to a single video clip, using the extension is the way to go.

Movie

1. Launch the IMovie app. Turn your iPad to look at the screen horizontally. iMovie is a little easier to use in that orientation.

2. You can view your video clips by tapping Video at the top.

3. Projects allow you to combine clips into longer movies with transitions and titles. Tap Projects to see a list of your projects.

4. Tap the + button to create a new project.

5. Tap Movie.

6. You can choose from many themes, each with their own set of transitions and titles. Tap Simple to create a basic project without anything fancy.

7. Tap Create.

8. You can record a new video clip right here and now by tapping the camera button.

9. You can use a video clip you have already recorded by selecting it in this area. First, you are shown a list of albums where videos are located. Tap on an album to dig down into it.

10. Select a video.

11. Tap the down-arrow button to place this video in the timeline.

12. Continue to add more clips. Each one will be appended to the end of the project.

13. The line indicates the current position of the video.

14. The preview area shows you the image at the current position.

15. You can drag the project timeline left and right to scroll through it.

16. You can pinch in and out to shrink or enlarge the timeline.

17. Press play to play the video in the preview area. If the line is at the end of the video, it will jump back to the start of the video first.

18. Tap and hold a clip until it "pops" off the timeline, and you can drag it to a different part of the project timeline.

19. Tap the back button when you are done editing. There is no need to "save" your project—the current state of the project is always saved.

20. Tap the name of the project to edit the name.

21. Tap the play button to view the finished project.

22. Tap the Share button to save the video to your photo library, send it via email or Messages, or upload it to YouTube, Vimeo, Facebook, and a variety of other video services.

Best Way to Share with Friends?

While it may seem to be a good idea to simply email a video to your friends, remember that video files are usually very large. Even if you have the bandwidth to upload them, your friends need the bandwidth to download them. Some may have restrictions on how large email attachments can be.

So, the video sharing options in iMovie are better for all concerned. You can upload to your Facebook or YouTube account and even set the video to "private" or "unlisted." Then just let a few friends know about it with the link in an email instead of a huge file attachment.

Editing Transitions

Between each clip in your iMovie project is a transition. You can choose between a direct cut (no transition), a cross-dissolve transition, or a special theme transition. But first, you must select a theme.

1. Open up the project you created in the previous task.

2. Tap the settings button at the lower right to select a theme.

3. Swipe through the themes and choose one.

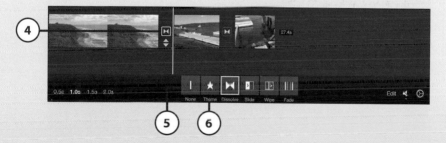

4. Tap one of the transition icons that appear between each clip. This should bring up the Transition Settings menu along the bottom of the screen.

5. Along the bottom will be a set of icons representing different transitions. Choose the first one if you want no transition at all, but just want one clip to cut right into the other.

6. Choose the star icon to use the special theme transition. These vary depending on which theme you choose.

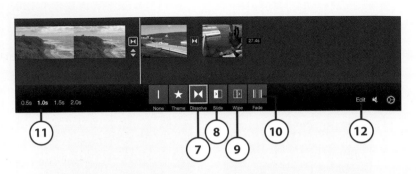

7. Choose the dissolve transition if you want one clip to fade into the other. This is the most common transition for most purposes.

8. The slide transition moves the next clip over the current one. You'll see some other icons appear above it when you first tap this transition. This allows you to pick the direction of the slide.

9. The wipe transition wipes and replaces one clip with the other, starting at one edge. You can pick the direction here as well.

10. This transition will fade out and then fade in the next clip. You can choose to fade to black or white.

11. Choose a duration for the transition.

12. Tap the triangles below the transition button, or the Edit button at the bottom right, to expand into a precision editor.

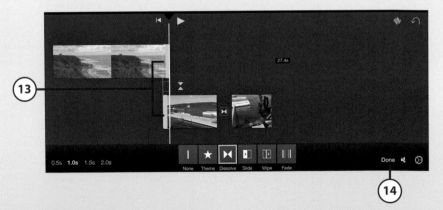

13. Move the transition area to select how you want the two clips to overlap during the transition. To make it easier to move the yellow bars, you may want to pinch out to zoom in for a closer look at the area.

14. Tap the triangles or the Done button to leave the precision edit mode.

Adding Photos to Your Video

You can also add photos from your Camera Roll or any album on your iPad. You can just use a series of photos in a video, or mix photos and video clips.

1. Continuing with the previous example, scroll the timeline all the way to the left.

2. Tap the photos button.

3. Tap the name of the album that contains your photo.

4. Tap the photo you want to use.

5. It now appears in the timeline at the current position. Tap it to select it.

6. Tap and drag the yellow bars to change the duration of the photo in the timeline. It starts with a default of 5 seconds. But, for example, you could increase it to 10 seconds.

7. Tap the Start button that appears in the preview area. Then adjust the photo by pinching, zooming, and dragging to get it just as you like. For instance, pinch in so the photo fits into the frame.

8. Tap the End button to set the end position for the picture. For instance, unpinch to zoom in on a specific area.

9. Tap Done when you finish adjusting both the start and end positions.

10. Slide the timeline back and forth to preview how the movement in the picture will work.

You can continue to add pictures just as you would add video clips. Add as many as you like. You can even create a slideshow of just photos without ever shooting a single second of video footage.

>>>*Go Further*
GETTING CREATIVE WITH PICTURES

You can even create a video slideshow without any photos. For example, you could use one of the drawing programs mentioned in Chapter 16, such as SketchBook Pro, Brushes, ArtStudio, or Adobe Ideas, to create images with text and drawings on them. Create a series to illustrate an idea or story. Then bring them together as a series of pictures in an iMovie project. Add music and a voiceover to make something very interesting.

Adding Video Titles

You can also add titles that overlay clips or photos in iMovie. Like the transitions, the style of the titles depends on the theme you are using.

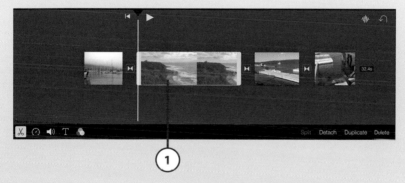

1. Continue with the example we have been building. Tap on a clip to select it.

2. Tap the title style button.

3. Select a title style. As you do so, a preview appears in the preview area.

4. Tap one of the text field areas in the preview to bring up the keyboard, and enter text.

>>>Go Further
MUSIC AND VOICEOVERS

You can also do a lot with the audio in iMovie. You can add any song from your iPad's iTunes collection to the video as the background track. There are also a number of theme music tracks included that you can use.

You can also add from a collection of sound effects the same way. However, sound effects can appear at any point in your movie, whereas music covers the entire span of the video.

You can also record a voiceover so you can narrate your video. This means you can have four audio tracks: the audio attached to the video, background music, sound effects, and a voiceover.

To learn how to use all the additional features of iMovie, look for the help button at the bottom-left corner of the projects screen. This brings up complete documentation for the app.

Making Video Calls with FaceTime

Another major use of the video cameras is FaceTime. This is Apple's video calling service. You can make video phone calls between any devices that have FaceTime, including recent iPhones, iPod touches, iPads, and Macs. As the number of people with FaceTime increases, this app will become more useful.

All that's required to make a FaceTime call is a free account. You can use your existing Apple ID or create a new one. You can also assign alternate email addresses to be used as FaceTime "phone numbers" that people can use to contact you via FaceTime.

Wi-Fi Preferred

You still need to be connected to the Internet with a Wi-Fi connection. Some mobile carriers do support FaceTime calls with their iPad data plans. If you have an iPad data plan with a wireless carrier, contact your provider for details.

Setting Up FaceTime

Settings

1. Launch the Settings app.

Settings	FaceTime
iCloud myipadbook@icloud.com	**FaceTime** ⬤③ Your phone number and/or email address will be shared with people you call.
App and iTunes Stores	
	Calls from iPhone ⬤ Use your iPhone cellular connection to make and receive calls when your iPhone is nearby and on Wi-Fi.
Mail, Contacts, Calendars	
Notes	
Reminders	Apple ID: myipadbook@icloud.com ④
Messages	
② FaceTime	Respond with Text ›
Maps	YOU CAN BE REACHED BY FACETIME AT
Safari	✓ myipadbook@icloud.com ⓘ ⑤
News	✓ myipadbook@me.com ⓘ
	Add Another Email...
Music	CALLER ID
Videos	✓ myipadbook@icloud.com ⑥
Photos & Camera	myipadbook@me.com
iBooks	
Podcasts	Blocked ›
Game Center	
Twitter	
Facebook	

2. Tap FaceTime on the left.

3. Turn on FaceTime if it isn't already.

4. An Apple ID is needed for FaceTime even if you don't plan to use that same email address with FaceTime calls. If you haven't used FaceTime before, you will be prompted to enter your Apple ID and password.

5. This list contains email addresses others can use to reach you via a FaceTime call. By default, your Apple ID email address will be here. But you can add another one and even remove your Apple ID email address if you never want to use that for FaceTime.

6. The Caller ID represents your default email address used to place FaceTime calls. It is what others will see when you call them. You'll see this if you have two or more email addresses assigned to your Apple ID account.

Multiple Email Addresses

By using different email addresses for different iOS devices, you can more easily specify which device you are calling. For instance, if you and your spouse both have iPhones, and you share an iPad, you can give the iPad a different email address (maybe a free email account). That way you can specify which device you want to call.

Placing Video Calls with FaceTime

FaceTime

After you have your account set up in FaceTime, you can place and receive calls.

1. Launch the FaceTime app.

2. Start typing the name, email address, or iPhone phone number of whom you want to reach.

3. Alternatively, you can use your contacts list by tapping the + button and choosing from the list of contacts.

4. Tap FaceTime to start a video call with that person.

5. Tap FaceTime Audio to start an audio-only call. This might make more sense if you know bandwidth at either end is tight, or you are having a bad hair day.

6. Wait while the call is placed. You'll hear a ringing. You can tap the End button to cancel the call before you connect.

7. After the other party has answered the call, you can see both her image filling the whole screen and your image in the bottom right. You can drag your image to any of the four corners.

8. Tap the mute button to mute your microphone.

9. Tap the switch cameras button to show the view from the rear camera.

10. Tap End to finish the call.

Two-Way Street

In order for you to place a FaceTime call, of course, the recipient also needs to have FaceTime set up. If you try to place a call and they do not have FaceTime, you'll get a message telling you so. It may be that they have simply not given you the correct email address to use for them for FaceTime calls.

myipadbook@icloud.com
FaceTime...

6

Video stream showing the other person

Video stream showing you

9   10   8   7

Receiving Video Calls with FaceTime

After you have a FaceTime account, you can receive calls as well. Make sure you have set up FaceTime by following the steps in the "Setting Up FaceTime" task earlier in this chapter. Then it is a matter of just waiting to receive a call from a friend.

1. If you aren't currently using your iPad, it will ring using the ringtone you choose in Settings, Sounds. When you pick up your iPad, you'll see something similar to the lock screen, but with a live feed from your camera (so you can see if you look good enough to video chat) and the caller's name at the top.

2. Slide the Slide to Answer button to the right to wake up your iPad and go immediately into the call. If you are using your iPad at the time the call comes in, FaceTime launches and you get a screen with two buttons. The screen will still show your camera's image and the name of the caller.

3. You also have the option to dismiss the call. You can do this by simply pressing the wake/sleep button at the top of your iPad. Or, you can tap the Remind Me button, which will dismiss the call and set a reminder for one hour later so you can call the person back.

4. You can also tap the Message button to dismiss the call and send a polite text message to the caller.

5. You can choose a message from the list.

6. Or, you can tap Custom to type a message.

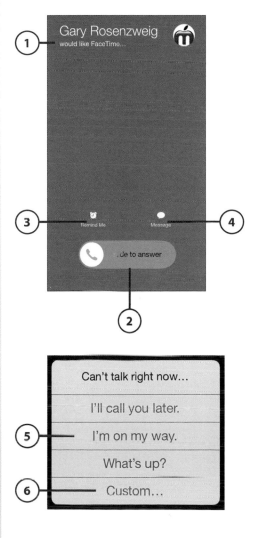

7. After the conversation starts, you can mute your microphone.

8. You can switch to the rear camera.

9. Tap End to end the call.

Ring Ring

Remember that you can set your ringtone in the Settings app under Sounds. You can even set the volume for rings to be unaffected by the volume controls on the side of your iPad. That way you don't miss a call because you left the volume turned down.

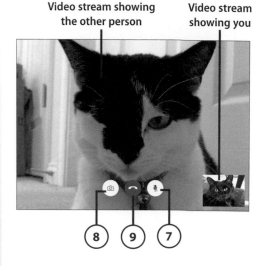

Video stream showing the other person

Video stream showing you

>>>Go Further

SO WHAT IF IT DOESN'T WORK?

FaceTime is set up to be simple. It just works. Except when it doesn't. There are no network settings to fiddle with. So the problem usually lies in the Wi-Fi router at either end of the call. If someone has security on their modem or Wi-Fi router, then it could be interfering with the call. See this document at Apple's site for some FaceTime troubleshooting tips:

http://support.apple.com/kb/HT4319.

Create and edit word
processing documents
with Pages.

In this chapter, we begin to get work done on the iPad by using Pages to create and format documents.

11

Writing with Pages

The iPad is great as a personal media device, with your music, pictures, and videos. But it can also be used to get some work done. If you write for work or leisure, you'll want to download the Pages app from the App Store. Pages is a basic word processor, which you can use to write anything from short essays to long novels. You can also use images and formatting tools to build simple reports and newsletters.

Creating a New Document

Let's start off simple. The most basic use of Pages is to create a new document and enter some text.

1. Tap the Pages app icon on the Home screen.

Pages

2. If this is the first time you have run Pages, you will go through a series of screens welcoming you to Pages and asking if you want to set up iCloud as the storage space for Pages documents. This is the best way to use Pages, Numbers, Keynote, and other apps. All of your documents will sync with all of your iOS and Mac devices, so you will have one collection of documents available everywhere.

3. The next screen asks if you want to create a new document right away. Instead, tap Use Pages to go to the documents screen that will list all your iCloud documents. If this is your first time using Pages with iCloud, then it will show that you have no documents.

4. Tap the + button at the top-left corner of the screen to start a new document.

5. Tap Create Document.

6. You are then faced with the template choices display. You can scroll vertically to see more. Tap the Blank template to go into the main editing view.

7. Type some sample text in the document just to get the feel for entering text.

8. Return to your documents list by tapping Documents.

9. You can now see the new document. Tap the name of the document, Blank, to then assign a proper name to it.

10. Tap the document to open it later to continue working with it.

11. Tap Edit to move into Edit mode where you can delete or duplicate any selected document.

A Real Keyboard

If you plan on using Pages on your iPad often, you might want to invest in a physical keyboard for your iPad. You can use the Apple Wireless keyboard or almost any Bluetooth keyboard. Apple also has a version of the iPad dock that includes a keyboard. See Chapter 18, "iPad Accessories," for details.

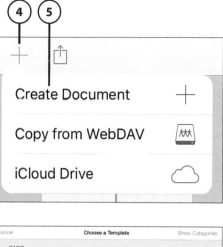

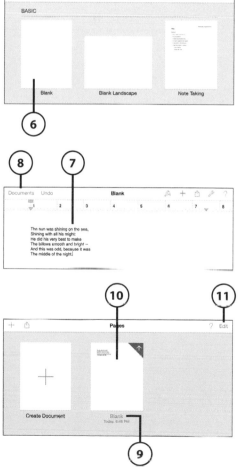

Styling and Formatting Text

One of the most basic things you'll need to do in a word processor is to change the style and format of text. This example shows how to use the built-in paragraph styles of Pages, how to set the font and style of text, and how to set text alignment.

1. Create a new document and type some text. In this example, the first line is the title of a poem, the second is the author's name, and the rest is the body of the poem.

2. Tap in the first line of text to place the blinking cursor there. It doesn't matter where in the line of text the cursor appears—we are about to set the paragraph style, which applies to an entire line of text.

3. Tap the paintbrush button. This brings up controls to adjust the appearance of text.

4. Make sure the Style controls are selected. If not, tap Style to select them.

5. Tap Title under Paragraph Style to assign this style to the line of text.

6. Tap outside the controls to dismiss them.

7. Place the cursor in the second line of text and repeat steps 3–6, but this time apply the Subtitle style to the second line.

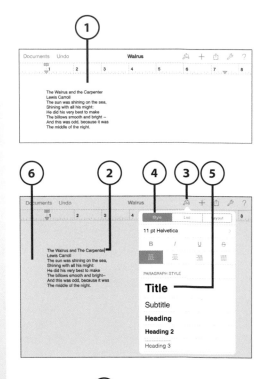

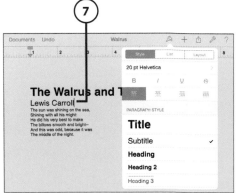

8. To style the remaining text, you need to select it. Double-tap any word in the text so the word is highlighted in blue and has selection markers on the side. Then drag the selection markers so the entire set of lines is selected.

9. The highlighted area should now encompass all the lines.

10. Tap the paintbrush button.

11. Tap the size and name of the font.

12. Increase the size of the font.

13. Tap Color.

14. Since the text is currently black, you'll see black, white, and gray text colors. The current color has a checkmark.

15. Notice that the dots at the bottom indicate there are four pages of colors. Swipe left to right to move to the first page.

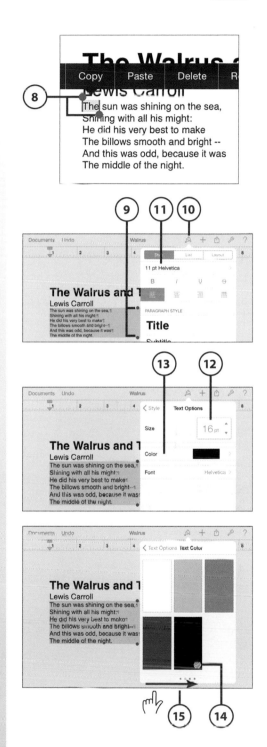

16. Select a color.

17. Tap Text Options to return to the previous set of controls.

18. Tap the font name.

19. Select a different font for this text. You can drag the list up and down to see all of the available fonts.

20. Tap outside the controls to dismiss them.

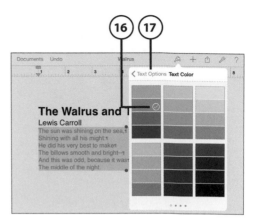

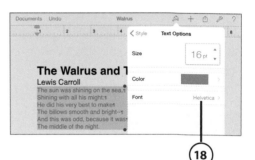

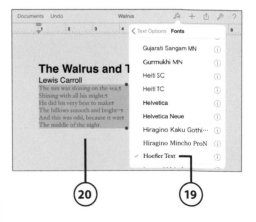

21. Select all the text, including the title and author lines. We're going to center all this text.

22. We could use the alignment buttons in the style tools, but instead let's use the handy buttons that appear right above the keyboard at the bottom of the screen. Tap the Alignment button there.

23. A menu of alignment settings appears. Tap Center to center all the text.

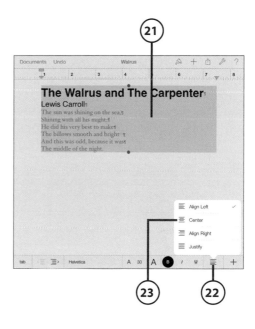

Notice that there are two ways to access most style and alignment settings in Pages. The first way is to tap the paintbrush button at the top of the screen and then go to the Styles section of those controls. The second is to use the toolbar that appears above the keyboard.

You can also access the basic text styles of bold, italic, and underline from either of these.

Undo Mistakes

At the top of the Pages screen, there is an Undo button. Use that to undo the last action you took—whether it is typing some text or changing styles. You can use Undo multiple times to go back several steps.

Creating Lists

You can easily create lists in Pages, just like in a normal word processor.

1. Create a new document in Pages using the Blank template.

2. Type a word that could be the first item in a list. Don't tap return on the keyboard.

3. Tap the paintbrush button on the toolbar.

4. Tap List.

5. Tap the Bullet option to turn the text you just typed into the first item in a bulleted list.

6. Tap outside the controls to dismiss them.

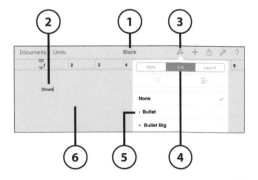

7. Use the on-screen keyboard to tap return and type several more lines. Tapping return always creates a new line in the list. Tapping return a second time ends the list formatting.

8. Select the entire list.

9. Tap the paintbrush button.

10. Tap List, if it isn't already selected.

11. Tap Numbered to change the list to a numbered list.

12. Tap outside the controls to dismiss them.

13. Tap one line of the list to place the cursor in it.

14. Tap paintbrush again.

15. Tap the move right button in the List menu to indent the line and create a sublist. You can create sublists as you type or by selecting lines and using the arrow buttons to format after you type.

16. Alternatively, you can use these buttons in the toolbar above the keyboard to indent items in the list without bringing up the paintbrush controls.

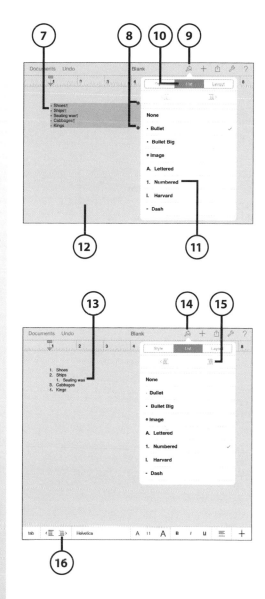

Inserting Images

You can place images into your Pages documents. You can even wrap text around the images.

1. We'll start with a document that already has some text in it. Tap to place the cursor where you want to insert the image.

2. Tap the + button.

3. Select the Pictures icon to insert a picture, and give Pages permission to access your media (if this is the first time you've inserted a picture).

4. You'll see your photo albums. Tap to select the album that contains the image you want to insert, and find the image in that album and tap it. Then tap outside the controls to dismiss them.

But I Don't Want To Use a Photo

You can insert any image that lives in your photo library. But, it doesn't have to be a photograph you took. You can import images and clipart from the web, email messages, and other apps. For instance, in Safari if you tap and hold an image, you get the option to Save Image. This puts it in your photo library, and you can now insert it into a Pages document. You can also use AirDrop to send images from other iOS devices or Macs.

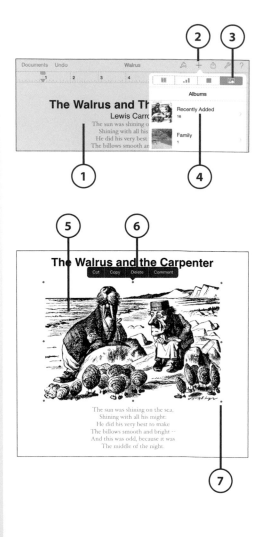

5. Tap the image to select it.

6. You can delete the image with the context menu that appears.

7. You can drag any of the blue dots around the edges of the image to resize it.

8. Double-tap the image to scale and mask it.

9. Use the slider to resize the image. Notice that as you enlarge the image, the parts outside the visible area are dimmed. This gives you an idea of which parts of the image will be visible after you are done scaling.

10. You can drag and position the image so a different area is visible.

11. Tap Done when you are finished.

12. With the image selected, tap the paintbrush button.

13. Tap Style.

14. Choose a frame style.

15. Tap Style Options if you want more control over the border style, color, and width. You can also choose from effects such as shadows and reflections.

16. Tap Arrange.

17. Tap Wrap.

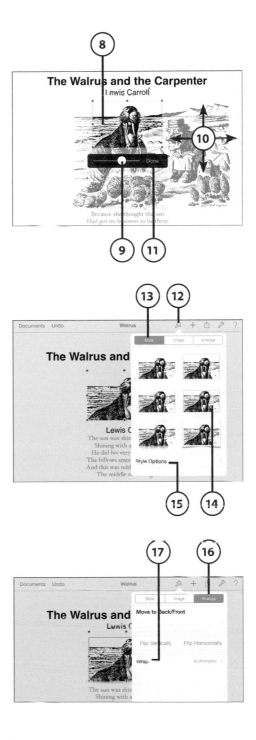

18. Here you can determine how you want the text to wrap around the image. Tap Around to make sure the text wraps around it.

19. You can add an extra margin around the image so text stays further away or comes closer to the image.

20. Tap outside the controls to dismiss them.

21. Wrapping text around images works well with multiple columns of text. So, let's make the text layout two columns so the text wraps around the image. Select all the text except the title and author line.

22. Tap the paintbrush button.

23. Tap Layout.

24. Increase the number of columns to two.

25. Notice that the text now wraps around the image on both sides. Also notice that we only converted the paragraphs of the poem to two columns. We left the title and author line as a single column.

Rearranging Images

After you place an image in your document, you can drag it around and resize it as much as you want. Pages automatically snaps the edges of the image to the margins and center lines of the page as you drag it around.

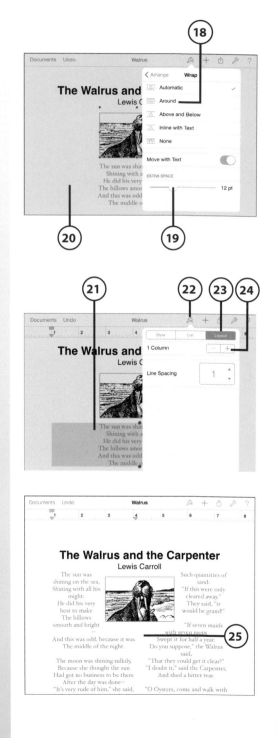

SHAPES, TABLES, AND CHARTS

In addition to inserting images, you can also add three other types of graphic elements: shapes, tables, and charts. With Shapes, you can choose from a variety of types, such as rectangles, circles, arrows, and stars. Each shape can have a different border and fill color. You can also put content inside of shapes, such as text or images.

Tables are like little spreadsheets inside your documents. You can fill up cells with information or numbers, and even perform basic calculations with formulas. You can also represent numbers as charts, selecting from line, bar, or pie charts of many different types and styles.

Create a sample document and try adding each one of these elements by tapping the + button. Play around with all the different styles by selecting the element and tapping the paintbrush just as you did with images.

Document Setup

You can change a variety of your document's properties in Pages.

1. Open a document or create a new one.

2. Tap the Wrench button.

3. Choose Document Setup.

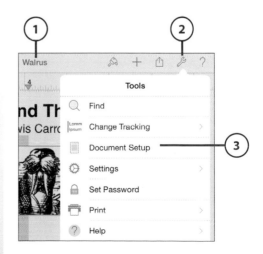

4. Drag the arrows at the four edges of the page to adjust the width and height of the page.

5. You can change the paper size from Letter to A4.

6. Tap the + button to add content that will appear in the background of every page in the document. For instance, you could add a rectangle shape, fill it with a texture, and stretch it to fill the entire page to add a textured background. Or, you could use an image as the background.

7. Tap in the header or footer to add text to the top or bottom of every page in the document.

8. You can add text to the left, center, or right portions of the header or footer by tapping one of these boxed areas.

9. You can add any text to these boxes. For instance, you can put the name of your document or your name in one of these sections. You can also tap to reveal a context menu that allows you to add a page number that automatically increments for each additional page.

10. Tap one of the page number options to add that element. Tap Done when you are finished.

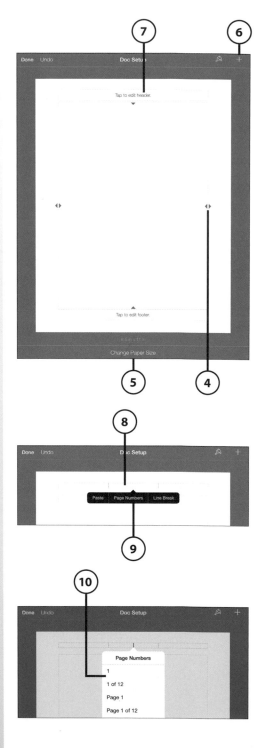

Sharing and Printing Documents

Thanks to iCloud, sharing documents with Pages, Numbers, and Keynote among your own devices is very easy. Any document you create on any device will simply be available to the others. But you can also share your document with another person by emailing it, printing it, or sending it to a network server.

1. Tap the Share button.

2. You can send a link to a copy of your document stored with iCloud. Anyone with that link can have access to your document, so you might want to avoid doing this if security is a concern with this document.

3. You can export your Pages document to third-party apps that can accept PDF or ePub-formats.

4. Tap Send a Copy to share via other methods.

5. Choose a format. Using PDF, Word, or ePub will export the document in that format. Choose Pages to send the original document.

6. You can send the document to another device using AirDrop.

7. Tap Mail or Message to send the document as an attachment using those methods.

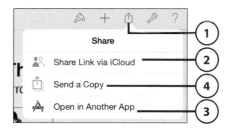

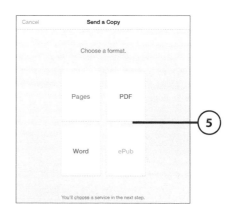

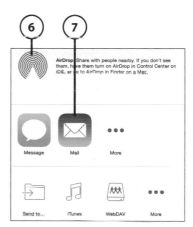

8. Tap the wrench button to open the Tools menu.

9. Tap Print.

10. Tap to select a printer. The name of the printer will now appear here and should be selected by default the next time you print. AirPrint is used to print wirelessly from your iPad. See "Printing from Your iPad" in Chapter 18 to set up AirPrint.

11. You can select a range of pages to print.

12. You can also select the number of copies.

13. Tap Print to send the document to the printer.

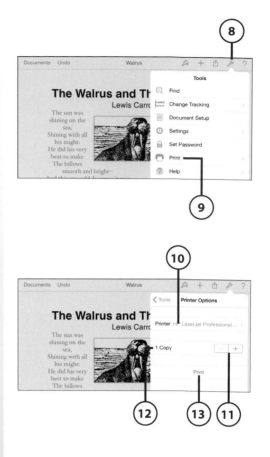

Pages Does Word

You can put more than just Pages documents into the iTunes list to import. Pages can also take Microsoft Word .doc and even .docx files.

Pages Is Not Pages

The Pages on your iPad and the Pages on your Mac are not the same. You can do a lot more with Pages on your Mac. So, sometimes you might receive a Document Import Warning message telling you what didn't work as you import your file to your iPad.

>>>Go Further

WORD PROCESSING ALTERNATIVES

 Microsoft Word: Although many apps will display Word documents, and a few will allow you to edit Word documents, it is worth getting the official Microsoft Word app if you are already an Office 360 user. However, if you don't subscribe to Microsoft's Office 360 cloud service, then you won't be able to really use the app.

 Google Docs: Google also has a suite of office tools that are usually accessed in a web browser. But they have an iPad app that lets you access and work on your documents directly.

iA Writer: This is a word processor focused on writing, not styles and formatting. Its simplicity is designed to let you focus on writing.

Create and
enter data into
spreadsheets.

With Numbers, you can create data spreadsheets, perform calculations, and create forms and charts.

Spreadsheets with Numbers

Numbers is a versatile program that enables you to create the most boring table of numbers ever (feel free to try for the world record on that one) or an elegant chart that illustrates a point like no paragraph of text ever could.

Creating a New Spreadsheet

The way you manage documents in Numbers is exactly the same as you do in Pages, so if you need a refresher, refer to Chapter 11, "Writing with Pages." Let's jump right in to creating a simple spreadsheet.

1. Tap the Numbers icon on your Home screen to start.

2. Tap + and then Create Spreadsheet to see all the template choices.

3. Tap Blank to choose the most basic template.

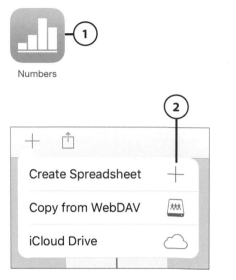

Numbers

Numbers Terminology

A grid of numbers is called a *table*. A page of tables, often just a single table taking up the whole page, is a *sheet*. You can have multiple sheets in a document, all represented by tabs. The first tab in this case represents "Sheet 1." Tap the + to add a new sheet.

---

4. Tap in one of the cells to select the sheet. An outline appears around the cell.

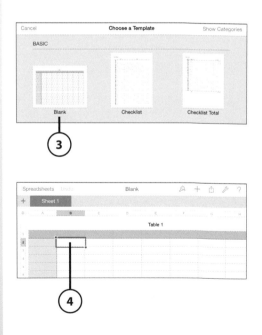

5. Double-tap the cell this time. An on-screen keypad appears.

6. Use the keypad to type a number. The number appears in both the cell and a text field above the keypad. Use this text field to edit the text, tapping inside it to reposition the cursor if necessary.

7. Tap the upper next button, the one with the arrow pointing right.

Switching Keyboard Options

The four buttons just above and to the left of the keypad represent number, time, text, and formula formats for cells. If you select the number, you get a keypad to enter a number. If you select the clock, you get a special keypad to enter dates and times. If you select the T, you get a regular keyboard. Finally, if you select the equal sign (=) , you get a keypad and special buttons to enter formulas.

8. The cursor moves to the column in the next cell. Type a number here, too.

9. Tap the next button again and enter a third number.

10. Tap the space just above the first number you entered. The keypad changes to a standard keyboard to type text instead of numbers.

11. Type a label for this first column.

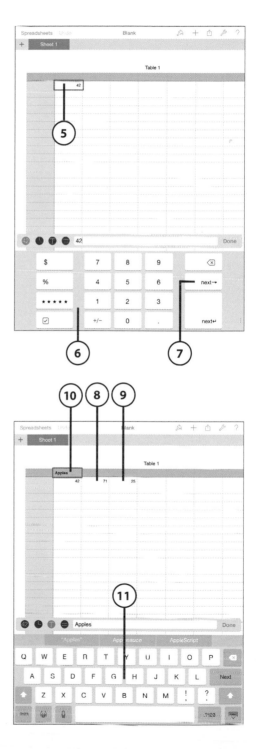

12. Tap in each of the other two column heads to enter titles for them as well.

13. Tap to the left of the first number you entered. Type a row title.

14. Now enter a few more rows of data.

15. Tap the Done button or tap outside of the table to dismiss the keyboard.

16. Tap any cell in the table to select the table.

17. Tap and drag the circle with two lines in it to the right of the bar above the table. Drag it to the left to remove the unneeded columns. To do this, you might need to drag the whole screen to bring the right side of the table into view.

18. Tap and drag the same circle at the bottom of the vertical bar to the left of the table. Drag it up to remove most of the extra rows, leaving two at the bottom for future use.

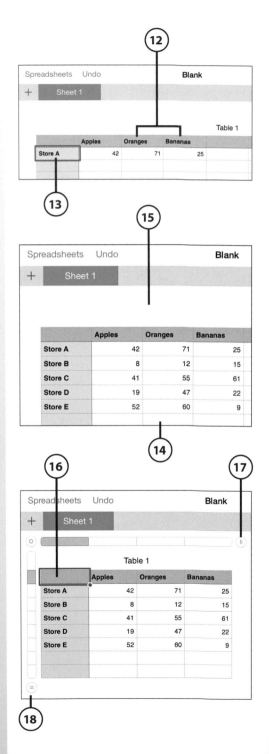

19. Double-tap the title of the table and give it a name.

Inventory Sold			
	Apples	**Oranges**	**Bananas**
Store A	42	71	25
Store B	8	12	15
Store C	41	55	61
Store D	19	47	22
Store E	52	60	9

Calculating Totals and Averages

One of the most basic formula types is a sum. In the previous example, for instance, you might want to total each column. You might also want to find the average of the numbers in the columns.

With tables, you typically put these kinds of calculations in footer rows. So, your table has header rows with the title of each column and footer rows with things like sums and averages.

1. Start with the result of the previous example. Select any cell in the table. Then tap the paintbrush to bring up the controls.

2. Tap the Headers tools.

3. Increase the number of Footer Rows to 2. This will turn the last two rows in the table to footer rows.

The Advantage of Footer Rows

You can put a formula to perform calculations in any cell of a table. So why bother with footer rows? They give you two nice features. First, you can now ask for the sum or average of an entire column, and Numbers knows to not include values in header and footer rows. Second, if you are entering values in the last cell of the last row above a footer row, and you tap the New key on the keyboard, Numbers will insert a new row and automatically move the footer rows down.

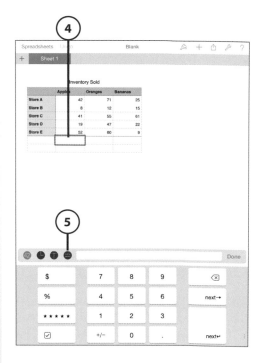

4. Double-tap in the cell just below the bottom number in the first column.

5. Tap the = button to switch to the formula keypad.

6. Tap the SUM button on the keypad.

7. The formula for the cell appears in the text field. Because we are using a footer row, Number automatically assumes we want the sum of this column, so it puts the name of the column into the formula. Otherwise, we would have to tap the column letter at the top of the column, manually enter "B," or select a range of cells such as "B2:B6" for the formula.

8. The result of the formula instantly appears in the spreadsheet.

9. Tap the green check mark button to dismiss the keyboard.

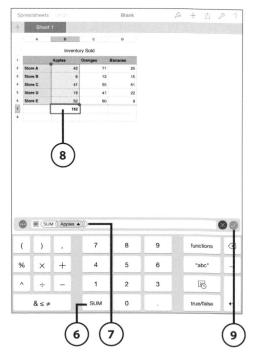

10. Repeat steps 2 through 4 for the other columns in the table.

11. Double-tap the last cell in the first column.

12. Tap the = button like you did in step 5, but this time tap the functions button instead of SUM. This brings up the functions menu.

13. Tap Categories at the top of the functions menu.

14. Tap Statistical to dig down into those functions, and then tap AVERAGE in the list that appears.

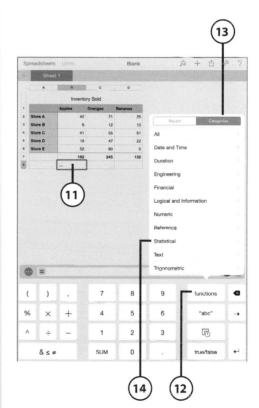

15. This time we need to give the AVERAGE function a range to work with, as it doesn't do it automatically like SUM did. Tap the B at the top of the column. This should fill in the function with "Apples," as that is the name of column B.

16. Tap the checkmark to dismiss the keyboard and complete the formula.

17. Do the same for the next two columns. Or, you can select the first cell, copy it, then paste it into the second and third. When you do, select Paste Formula so the formula and not the value will be pasted. The references to the columns will shift automatically so each averages the appropriate column.

18. You can also enter labels for these two footer rows.

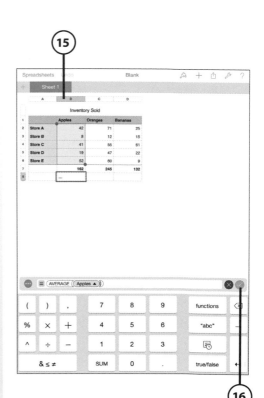

Automatic Updates

If you are not familiar with spreadsheets, the best thing about them is that formulas like this automatically update. So if you change the number of Apples in Store C in the table, the sum in the last row automatically changes to show the new total.

Inventory Sold			
	Apples	**Oranges**	**Bananas**
Store A	42	71	25
Store B	8	12	15
Store C	41	55	61
Store D	19	47	22
Store E	52	60	9
Total	162	245	132
Average	32.4	49	26.4

Styling Tables and Cells

When working with tables, you can assign many different style options. It is easy to set the style for an entire table, but you can also make design choices for a single cell or group of cells.

1. Start with a table like the one we have been working with in the previous tasks. Select any cell in it.

2. Tap the paintbrush button.

3. Select Table.

4. Select a style. You see it reflected in the table immediately.

5. Tap Table Options to customize the table design.

6. You can switch off the table name so it is no longer visible.

7. You can switch off the thin outline that surrounds the entire table.

8. Rows in the table normally alternate between light and dark background shades to make it easier to read. You can turn this off as well.

9. Grid Options lets you decide where lines appear between cells.

10. You can change the font used by the table.

11. You can easily make the text larger or smaller.

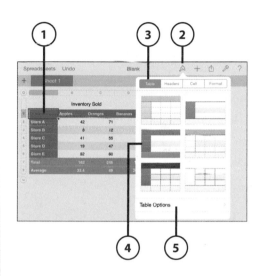

12. Select a single cell or group of cells. In this case, we'll select a cell to highlight to point out something in the table.

13. Tap the paintbrush button.

14. Tap Cell.

15. Tap any of the style buttons at the top to apply a style, such as italic.

16. Tap Text Options to change the size, color, and font.

17. Tap the Fill Color to change the background color of the cell.

18. Tap Format.

19. This menu allows you to set a format for the cell. For instance, you could choose Currency, and a currency symbol, such as $, would be placed before the number. There are a wide variety of different formats to choose from.

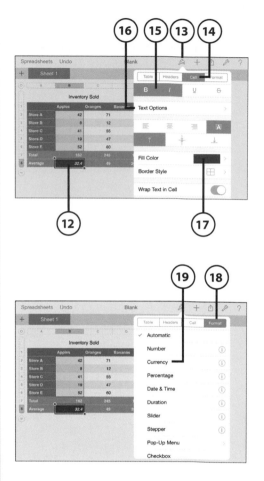

Creating Forms

Forms are an alternative way to enter data in a spreadsheet. A form contains many pages, each page representing a row in a table. Let's continue with the previous example and use it to make a form.

1. Tap the + button in the upper-left corner.

2. Tap New Form. Note that in order to get the option to make a form, you need to have at least one column with a value in its header row.

3. Choose a table. We have only one, so the choice is simple. Tap Table 1 to see the first page in the form, which represents the first row of data from our table.

4. The form appears. It shows one record, or row of the table, at a time. You can see which row it is showing and the total number of rows. Note that header and footer rows are not included—only the rows in the main body of the table.

5. You can tap any value and change it.

6. Tap the right arrow at the bottom of the screen to move through the five existing rows (pages) of data.

7. If you want to delete any row, tap the trash can button.

8. Tap the + button at the bottom of the screen to enter a new row of data. This row will be inserted after the one you are currently viewing. So if you want to add to the bottom of the table, go to the last page of the form first.

9. Tap at the top of the screen to enter a row heading.

10. Tap in each of the three fields to enter data.

11. When you finish, tap the first tab, Sheet 1, to return to the original spreadsheet. You should see the new data in a new row. The totals and averages have updated as well.

	Apples	Oranges	Bananas
Store A	42	71	25
Store B	8	12	15
Store C	41	55	61
Store D	19	47	22
Store E	52	60	9
Store F	74	25	68
Total	236	270	200
Average	39.3333333333	45	33.3333333333

Inventory Sold

Using Multiple Tables

The primary way Numbers differs from spreadsheet programs such as Excel is that Numbers emphasizes page design. A Numbers sheet is not meant to contain just one grid of numbers. In Numbers, you can use multiple tables. By using multiple tables, you can track data more efficiently. Let's look at an example.

1. Continuing with the example we have been building, keep the current table and move it down to make space for another. Tap the + button to add a second table.

Selecting a Table

It can be difficult to select an entire table without selecting a cell. Tap in a cell to select it. Then tap the circle that appears in the upper-left corner of the table to change your selection to the entire table.

2. Using what you have learned in this chapter so far, create a small second table with prices as shown.

3. Expand the original table by adding one more column.

4. Name this column Revenue. Notice that when you expand the table, the total and average formulas in the footer columns are automatically added. The average now gives an error because it is attempting to find the average of an empty column.

5. Double-tap the first empty cell in the new column to bring up the keyboard.

6. Tap the = button to start entering a formula.

7. We want to multiply the number of items in each cell by the price that matches it. Tap the cell that represents Apples from Store A, tap the X symbol on the keyboard, and then tap the cell that represents the price of Apples in the upper table. Tap + in the keyboard and do the same for Oranges and Bananas.

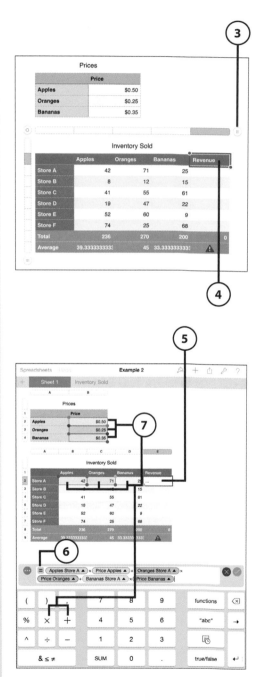

8. We plan to copy and paste this formula into all rows. When we do that, the references in the formula change to match the relative position of the cell it is being pasted into. We want that for the Inventory numbers, but we don't want that for the prices. We want those to stay fixed. So tap the Price Apples item in the formula to bring up a menu.

9. Switch on all Preserve options for this item. This ensures that as we paste the formula elsewhere, it will always point to the price of apples in the upper table.

10. Do the same for Price Oranges and Price Bananas.

11. The formula should now look like this. Notice the $ symbol is used to indicate that a reference is absolute and not relative to the position of the formula. Tap the green checkmark to finish the formula.

12. Tap to select this cell and then tap Copy from the context menu.

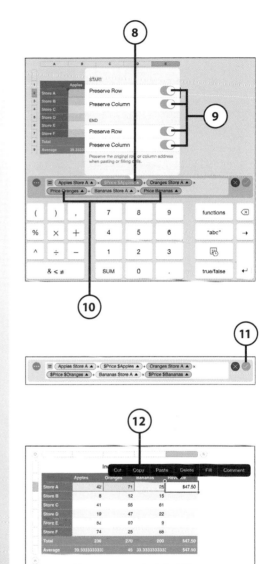

13. Tap the next cell, and then expand the selection to include all the empty cells in that column.

14. Tap Paste in the context menu that should appear.

15. Tap Paste Formulas.

16. The values for all the rows are calculated.

17. Note that the total and averages are calculated as well.

18. If you change one of the prices in the upper table, all the values for revenue will change instantly to reflect it.

Enhance the Sheet

Another thing you can do is add more titles, text, and images to the sheet—even shapes and arrows. These not only make the sheet look nice, but can also act as documentation as a reminder of what you need to do each month—or instruct someone else what to do to update the sheet.

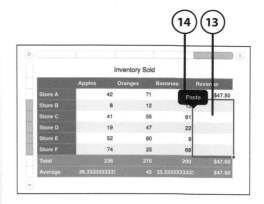

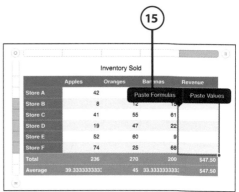

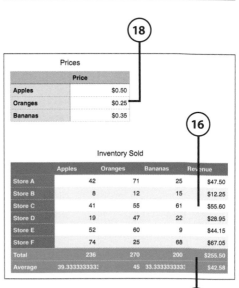

Creating Charts

Representing numbers visually is one of the primary functions of a modern spreadsheet program. With Numbers, you can create bar, line, and pie charts and many variations of each.

1. Start with a table similar to the one we have been working with in this chapter. Select the whole table. Numbers uses the header column and header row, along with the numbers in the body of the table, to build the chart.

2. Tap the + button.

3. Select charts.

4. You can select 2D, 3D, or Interactive charts. For this example, we'll stick with a simple 2D chart. But take the time to explore the others as well.

5. You can swipe horizontally to see different chart styles. There are several pages of them.

6. Tap a chart to insert it into your sheet.

7. A chart is created using the data from your table. In this case, each store is represented along the horizontal axis, with a bar for each product. The vertical axis shows you the number sold.

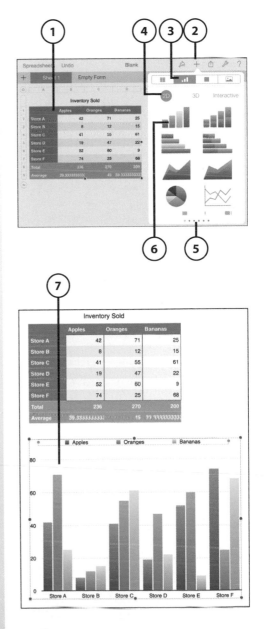

8. With the chart selected, tap the paintbrush button.

9. Tap Chart.

10. You can select a different style for the chart.

11. Tap Chart Options.

12. In the Chart Options controls, you can turn various elements on or off.

13. You can also customize the text in the chart.

14. You can even switch chart types.

15. Tap Chart to return to the previous set of controls.

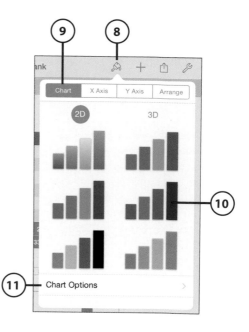

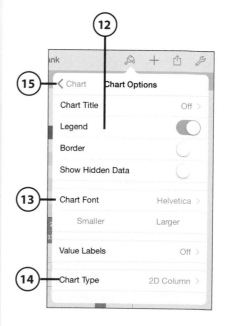

16. Tap X-Axis or Y-Axis.

17. You can turn off various portions of the chart related to the selected axis.

18. So what happens if you choose a different type of chart? Numbers tries its best to match the data to the chart. If you choose a pie chart, only one column of data is used. You can see when the chart is selected that the table above it uses colors to show which cell matches which slice of the pie.

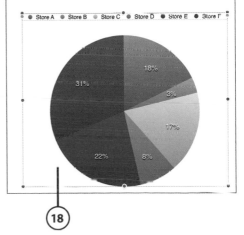

Create and
display business
and educational
presentations.

In this chapter, we use Keynote to build and display presentations.

→ Building a Simple Presentation
→ Building Your Own Slide
→ Adding Transitions
→ Organizing Slides
→ Playing Your Presentation

Presentations with Keynote

You can't have a suite of business apps without having a Presentation tool, and Keynote is that tool on the iPad. The basics of using Keynote are the same as for Pages and Numbers. So let's get right to making presentations.

Building a Simple Presentation

Keynote works only in horizontal screen orientation. So after you launch Keynote, turn your iPad on its side. The way you manage documents in Keynote is exactly the same as you do in Pages and Numbers, including the ability to use iCloud to store your documents. If you need a refresher, refer to Chapter 11, "Writing with Pages."

1. Tap the Keynote icon on the Home screen. If this is the first time you are using Keynote, you'll get a series of introduction screens. Continue until you are viewing an empty list of your presentations.

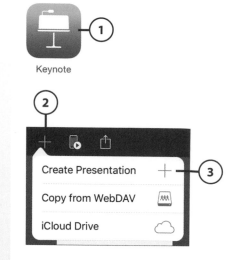

Keynote

2. Tap the + button to create a new presentation.

3. Tap Create Presentation.

4. Choose a theme. We use Gradient for the task.

5. Double-tap the first line of text that reads Double-tap to edit.

6. Type a title using the on-screen keyboard.

7. Double-tap the subtitle area and type a subtitle.

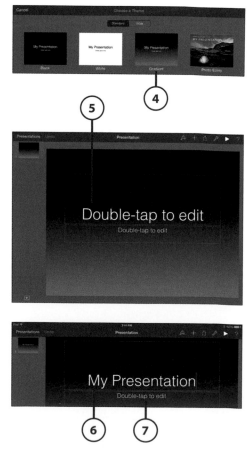

8. Tap the + button at the top of the screen.

9. Tap the media tab. You are asked to allow permission to access your media, if this is the first time you've used it.

10. Choose a photo.

11. Tap on the photo and use the blue dots at the corners and on the sides to resize the photo. Tap and drag in the middle of the photo to position it.

12. Tap the + button at the bottom-left corner to bring up a list of slides.

13. Tap any of the slides templates to add a slide. You now have two slides in your presentation.

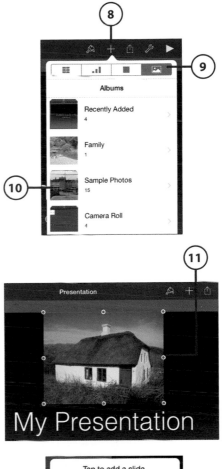

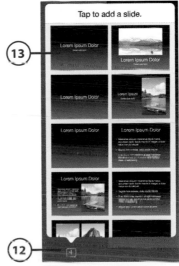

Building Your Own Slide

You can remove items and add your own to any template. You can practice adding your own elements to a slide by using the blank template.

1. Start a new document or continue from the previous example. Tap + to add a new slide.

2. Scroll down in this list and choose the blank slide to the lower right.

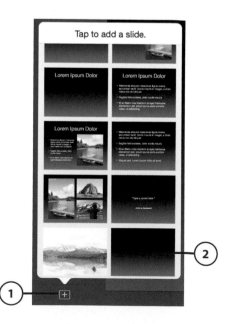

3. Tap the + button at the top to add an element.

4. Tap the media button.

5. Select an album, and then select a photo from that album.

6. With the photo selected, grab one of the blue dots and shrink the image.

7. With the image selected, tap the paintbrush button and then tap Style.

8. Tap the bottom right of the six basic image styles or tap Style Options to customize the look of the photo even more.

Select All

To select all objects, tap a space with no objects. After a short delay, tap there again, and then you can choose Select All.

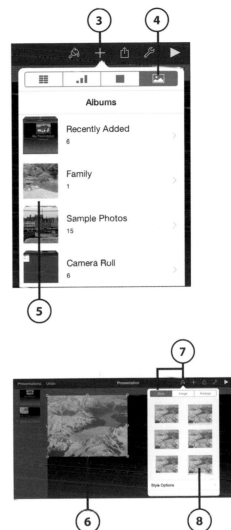

9. Add two more images using steps 3 through 8.

10. To select multiple items, use two fingers. Tap the first image with one finger and hold it. Use a second figure to tap the other two images to add them to the selection. Then drag all three images into a better position.

11. Tap the + button to add another element.

Tables and Charts Anyone?

You can also add tables and charts, even basic shapes, in the same way you would do it in Pages. There are a lot of similarities between using Pages and using Keynote.

12. Tap the shapes and text button.

13. Tap the first element, a plain text box.

14. Tap outside the menu to dismiss it.

15. Tap the text box to select it.

16. Drag it to a new position and expand it.

17. Double-tap in the text box to enter some text.

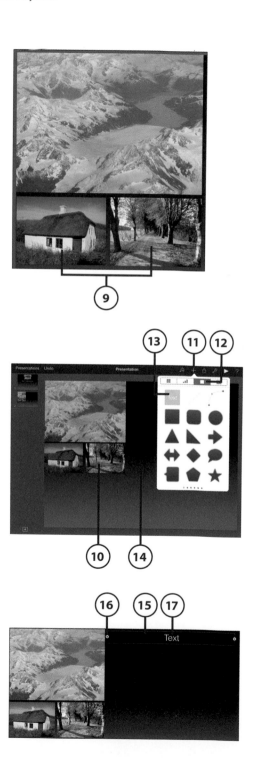

18. Close the keyboard and select the text box. With the text box selected, tap the paintbrush button.

19. Tap Text, and then change the font style and size.

20. Make the text bold by tapping B.

21. Tap outside the menu to dismiss it.

22. Your text is now bold. You now have a custom slide with three pictures and some text.

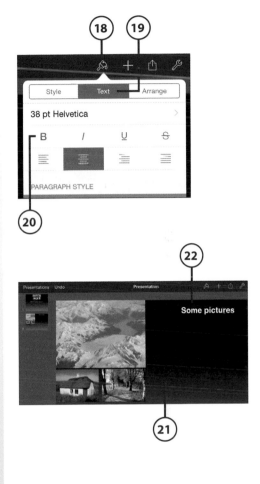

Adding Transitions

Just like other presentation programs, Keynote on iPad has a number of transition options. To practice working with transitions, start with a sample presentation, such as the one we have been working on, or create a new document with some sample slides.

1. Select the first slide on the left and then tap it again.

2. Tap the Transition button that appears.

3. Scroll through the transitions and pick one. Try Cube. The slide animates to show you the transition. It then returns.

4. Tap Options.

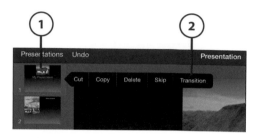

5. Select any options associated with the transition. For example, the Cube transition has a duration setting. If you don't want to change any options, tap elsewhere to dismiss the menu.

6. Tap Done in the upper-right corner of the screen.

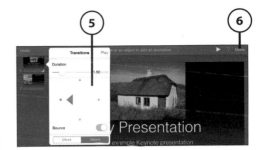

Magic Move

Another type of transition is the Magic Move. This is where objects on one slide are the same as the objects on the next, but they are in different positions. The transition between the slides moves these objects from the first position to the second.

1. Select a slide with several objects on it, such as three images. Tap it.

2. Tap Transition.

3. Choose Magic Move.

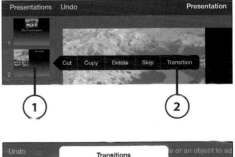

Unique Effects with Magic Move

The great thing about the Magic Move transition is that you can create some unique effects. For instance, in the example, I could bunch all the photos into a tiny space on the first slide and then spread them out in the second slide. The transition would make it seem like the photos are bursting out and falling into place.

4. Tap Yes to duplicate the current slide so that you have two identical slides from which to create the Magic Move transition.

5. Slides 2 and 3 are identical, and slide 3 is the current slide. Move the objects around to reposition them or resize them. The stars indicate which elements are taking part in the Magic Move. In this example, the images will be swapping places. The Magic Move transition causes them all to flow from one position and size to the other.

6. Tap the second frame.

7. Tap the arrow next to Magic Move and then tap play to preview the transition from slide 2 to slide 3. You will need to tap the screen then to proceed from the 2nd slide to the 3rd one and see the transition.

8. Tap Done in the upper-right corner of the screen.

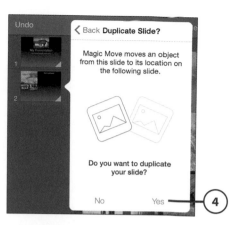

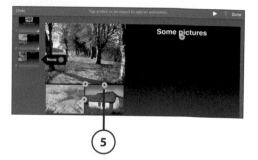

Object Transitions

In addition to the entire screen transforming from one slide to the next, you can also define how you want individual elements on the slide to appear.

1. Start off with a slide that includes a title and a bullet list. Tap the slide's title text.

2. Tap Animate.

3. Tap the build in button.

4. Tap Blast to see a preview of the animation.

5. Tap the bullet list.

6. Tap build in.

7. Scroll down to Move In and tap it.

8. Tap Delivery. You can also explore the Options and Order parts of the menu, but for this task we leave those settings alone.

Don't Build the First Object

A common mistake is to set every object to build, as we have in this example. Because the first object, the title, builds in, it means that nothing appears on the slide at first. You start off blank. Then the title appears and then the bullet items. Sometimes, though, you should start a slide with the title already on it.

9. Tap By Bullet and then tap Done in the upper-right corner of the screen. The effect works by first showing you a blank screen, and then when you tap the screen, the title appears with the Blast transition. Each of your next three taps makes a bullet appear.

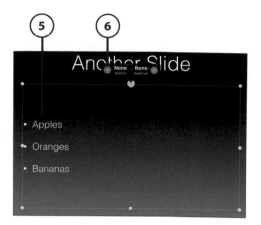

Organizing Slides

As you create presentations on your iPad, you might discover you need to re-order your slides, but that's no problem with Keynote. To practice, use a presentation that has several slides.

1. Create a presentation that includes several slides.

2. Tap and hold the third slide. It grows slightly larger and begins to follow your finger so that you can drag it down into another position.

Grouping Slides

There are two options when you drag a slide and place it back in the list. The first is to place it flush left, where it inserts normally. If you move the slide slightly to the right, though, you are grouping the slide with the one above it. Groups are a great way to put slides that belong together as a single element. That way, you can move them as one unit if you need to. To move them as a group, you close the group by tapping the triangle next to the parent slide. Then move the parent slide around, and all children come with it.

3. Drag slide 3 to the right so it inserts in a group owned by slide 2.

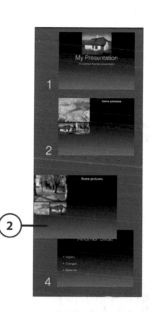

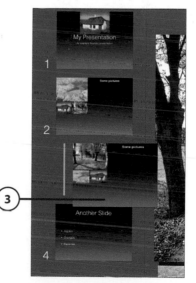

4. Tap the triangle on the left of slide 2 to close the group.

5. Tap slide 3 with your finger and continue to hold.

6. Use your other hand to tap slide 4 and then release your finger. You can now move this group of two slides as one unit.

7. Tap once to select a slide. Then tap a second time after a short delay to bring up a menu.

8. Use Cut, Copy, and Paste as you would while editing text. You can duplicate slides using Copy.

9. Tap Delete to remove a slide.

10. Tap Skip to mark a slide as one to skip during the presentation. This comes in handy when you want to remove a slide from a presentation temporarily, perhaps while presenting to a specific audience.

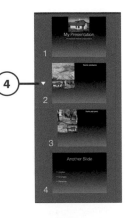

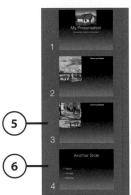

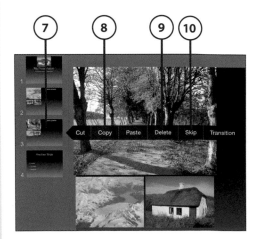

Playing Your Presentation

After you create your presentation, or if you want to preview what you've done, you can play your presentation.

1. With a presentation open in Keynote, tap the Play button.

2. The presentation fills the screen. Tap on the center or right side of the screen to advance to the next slide. You can also tap and drag from left to right.

3. To go back to the previous slide, drag right to left.

4. Tap on the left edge of the screen to bring up a list of slides.

5. Tap one of the items in the list to go directly to that slide.

6. Tap outside of the list of slides to dismiss the list.

7. Pinch in at the center of the screen to end the presentation and return to editing mode.

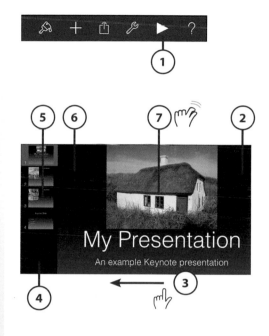

>>>Go Further
WHICH VIDEO ADAPTER?

One way to get Keynote's presentation out to an external screen is to use an adapter. There are two main choices: the VGA adapter or the HDMI adapter. Get the VGA adapter if you plan to present over a traditional meeting room projector. However, newer televisions and maybe some advanced projectors would use an HDMI connection. You can also convert VGA to fit other video connections. For instance, if you need to connect to a TV using a component or s-video, you should find some VGA adapters that work. See if you can find one that has been verified to work with an iPad before buying.

8. Tap and hold in the middle of the slide to bring up special pointer controls.

9. A row of tools appears at the bottom. Select a color of pen.

10. Now you can use your finger to draw on the slide.

11. You can undo drawing.

12. You can use the laser pointer dot instead of drawing.

13. While in this mode, you can use the arrow buttons to navigate between slides.

14. Tap Done to return to normal presentation mode.

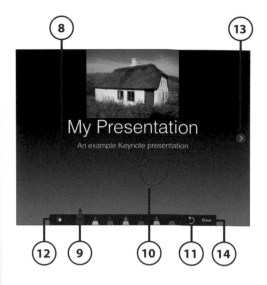

>>>Go Further
PRESENTING ON AN EXTERNAL DISPLAY

Presenting on your iPad with people looking over your shoulder probably isn't your goal. You want to present on a large monitor or a projector, which you can do with a Lightning to VGA Adapter (see Chapter 18, "iPad Accessories," for more information).

You can also use the AirPlay ability of an Apple TV (2nd generation or newer) to send your presentation wirelessly to a TV. See "Using AirPlay to Play Music and Video on Other Devices" in Chapter 4 to set up AirPlay mirroring. When you tap the Play button to play your presentation, mirroring goes into a special mode, with the actual presentation on the TV and your presenter layout on your iPad's screen, so you can control the slides.

Presenting with an external display works slightly differently than without one. Your iPad's screen shows the time and some buttons at the top. You can bring up the list of slides on the left, but it only appears on your iPad's screen, not the external display.

One of the buttons at the top, Layouts Options, lets you choose to show both
the current slide and the next slide on your iPad's screen, while the projector
or TV shows only the current slide. You can also choose to see your notes on
your iPad's screen.

Search for locations or get
directions with Maps.

In this chapter, you learn to use the Maps app to find locations and get directions.

→ Finding a Location

→ Searching for Places and Things

→ Getting Directions

→ Using Views

→ Getting Traffic Reports

14

Navigating with Maps

The Maps app is a great way to plan a trip—whether you're going across the country or to the grocery store. You can search for locations on the map, view satellite images, see optimized driving routes, and even get information and reviews of local businesses.

Finding a Location

The simplest thing you can probably do with Maps is to find a location.

1. Tap the Maps app on your Home screen.

2. Type an address or the name of a place in the search field.

3. As you type, you get a list of suggestions. You can tap one of these if you notice it matches your search closely enough.

4. Otherwise, finish typing the address or name and tap the Search button on the on-screen keyboard.

What Can You Search For?

You can search for a specific address. You can also use a general area or the name of a place or person, and Maps does the best it can to locate it. For example, you can try three-letter airport codes, landmark names, street intersections, and building names. The search keeps in mind your current Maps view, so if you search for a general area first, such as Denver, CO, and then for a building name, it attempts to find the building in Denver before looking elsewhere in the world.

5. The map shifts to that location and zooms in.

6. Tap the location name to get more information.

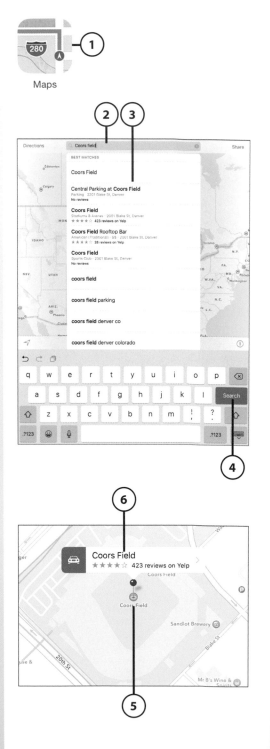

Maps

7. You see information about the location, such as the telephone number and website. You can click on these to call the location or visit the web page.

8. Tap Directions to get directions to the address.

9. Drag up to reveal more information below.

8 **7**

Coors Field

★★★★☆ 423 reviews on Yelp

Directions

Phone
+1 (303) 292-0200

Homepage
http://www.rockies.com

Address
2001 Blake St
Denver, CO 80205-2060
United States

Category
Stadiums & Arenas **9**

Kids
Yes

Wikipedia   Open Wikipedia

Coors Field is a baseball venue located in Denver, Colorado. It is the home field of Major League Baseball's Colorado Rockies. It is named for the Coors Brewing Company of Golden, Colorado, which purchased the naming rights to the park prior to its completion in 1995. The Rockies played their first two seasons, 1993 and 1994, in Mile High Stadium before moving to Coors Field, two blocks from Union Station in Denver's Lower Downtown (or LoDo) neighborhood.

Photos   Open Yelp

10. You can see a few reviews from Yelp, or tap the See More button (not shown) to jump to the Yelp app. You are directed to its listing in the App Store, if you don't have it installed.

11. Tap Create New Contact or Add to Existing Contact to add the name, address, phone number, and other information to your Contacts app.

12. You'll also see apps that are related to this location, or are popularly downloaded by people near the location.

13. You can help Apple improve its map database with the Report a Issue button. If the location happens to be a business you are associated with, and you want to correct some missing or inaccurate information, this is the place to start.

Where Am I?

Want to quickly center the map on your current location? Tap the GPS button (it looks like a small arrow) at the bottom-left corner of the screen. Even if your iPad doesn't have a GPS receiver, it takes a good guess as to your current location based on the local Wi-Fi networks it can see.

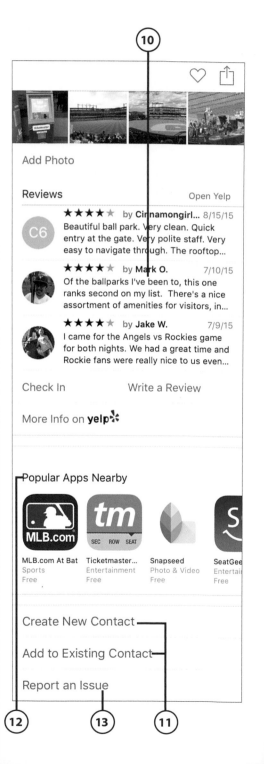

Searching for Places and Things

You can also use Maps to search for something that has more than one location. For instance, you could search for the location of your favorite computer store.

1. Start in Maps. You should see the last area you were viewing. If it is not your current location, search for that location or tap the GPS button to go there.

2. Tap the search field and enter the name of a store. Don't always restrict yourself to specific names such as "Apple store." You can type in general terms such as "coffee" or "restaurant" to get a broader selection of results.

3. Red pins appear on the map for all locations matching the search term in the general area. If more than one location is found on the map, the closest one should already display the name above it or next to it. If that is not the location you want, tap another red pin to focus on that location instead.

4. Tap the name for more information about that location.

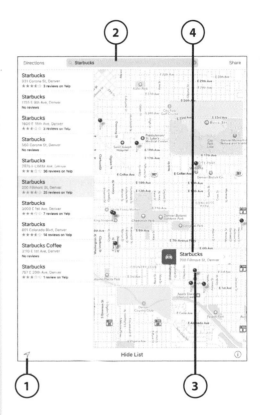

Sometimes It Gets It Wrong

The maps database is huge, which means it also contains errors. Sometimes an address is wrong or the information is out of date, so you find yourself in front of a shoe shop instead of your favorite restaurant.

Siri: Finding Map Locations

You can ask Siri to find locations without even being in the Maps app. A small map will appear in the Siri interface, and you can tap on it to open up the Maps app, centered on that location. Try commands like:

"Where is Coors Field?"
"Show me Broadway and First Avenue on the map."
"Map 6th and Colorado Boulevard."

Getting Directions

Say you want to do more than just look at a location on a map—you actually want to go there. Apple Maps can help you with that by giving you turn-by-turn directions you can follow while you drive. Your iPad can even speak them out loud. However, if your iPad is Wi-Fi only, you most likely won't have a connection while driving. In that case, you can still bring up a list of directions on your iPad before you leave home.

1. In Maps, tap the Directions button. At this point, you may be asked to confirm whether the Maps app is allowed to use your current location.

2. Two fields appear at the top. The first field is already filled in with Current Location. Change the location by tapping in the field to clear it and typing a new address. If you happen to have been searching for a location just before tapping the directions button, it automatically give you directions from your current location to the place you were looking at before. Tap the Clear button at the top left to clear the search and start again.

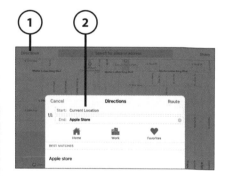

3. Tap in the second field and type the destination location. Suggestions appear underneath in a list. You can tap a suggestion to fill that into the destination box.

4. Tap the Route button.

5. The directions show up as a blue line on the map. You might need to pinch to zoom out to see the whole route.

6. Alternate routes may also appear in a lighter shade of blue. Tap any route label to switch to that route.

7. You can switch modes of transportation to get a different set of directions. Walking is always an option, and Transit appears if you are located in some major cities.

8. You see the directions in list form on the left, and shown on the map on the right.

9. Tap the Start button to go through the route turn-by-turn.

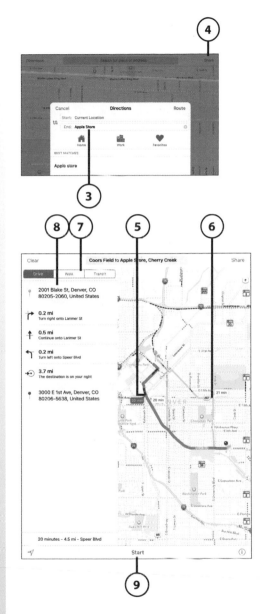

10. The current instruction appears at the top of the screen.

11. Tap on the next instruction to jump to it, or it will automatically shift over to the left as you accomplish the previous instruction. You can also swipe left to right to view future instructions.

12. When you are done using the directions feature, tap End to exit back into normal map mode.

Spoken Turn-By-Turn Directions

For those who have a wireless mobile connection on their iPad, directions become much more useful. You can use your mobile connection as you drive and the Maps app will follow along, updating the steps in your route as you make progress. You even get spoken directions as you approach each turn, so you don't need to take your eyes off the road.

Siri: Getting Directions

The easiest way to get the Maps app to show you directions is to ask Siri. With or without the Maps app open, try phrases like:

"How do I get to Denver International Airport?"
"Take me to the nearest coffee shop."
"Plot a course to Colfax Avenue and Colorado Boulevard."
"Take me home."

Using Views

One of the coolest things about online maps are the satellite and street views. Both are fun and helpful and a lot more interesting than a traditional map.

Using Satellite View

Satellite view is like the standard Map view in that you can search for places and get directions. But you can also get a better sense of what is at a location.

1. In Maps, tap the i button in the bottom-right corner.

2. Tap Satellite to see a satellite view of your location.

3. Unpinch in the center of the map to zoom in.

4. The closer view helps show you what the streets actually look like.

Using 3D View

The popular Google Maps app has street view, a way to view images taken at street level. However, the Apple Maps app uses 3D aerial views—images taken from airplanes that include all sides of buildings in major downtown areas.

1. Start by looking in Maps using the standard view. Tap the i button.

2. Tap the 3D Map button.

3. The flat top-down view is replaced by a perspective view. Pinch to zoom in closer.

4. Larger buildings in downtown areas are now 3D objects. Use two fingers to rotate the image, and you can see the buildings from all angles.

5. Tap the Info button in the bottom-right corner.

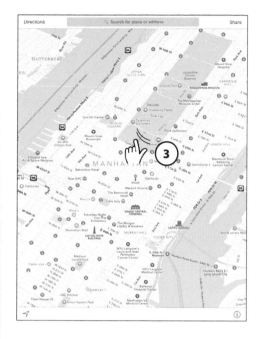

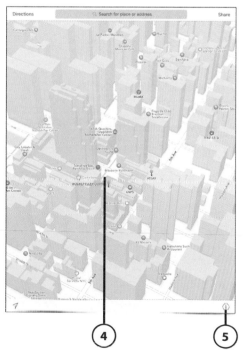

6. Select Satellite view. You can still zoom and rotate in satellite view, even getting so close to the ground that you can virtually move between buildings.

7. Use two fingers and swipe up. This will tilt the 3D effect for a more horizontal view.

8. Tap to turn off 3D mode and return to standard top-down flat mode.

Not in My Town

Although 3D view is great for those of us who live in big cities, it isn't available for every location. For there to be 3D models and textures, an Apple-hired airplane has to take pictures of your city. They have gotten a lot of the world's major cities, but not everywhere yet.

Getting Traffic Reports

The Maps app includes a way for you to see up-to-date traffic flow and information.

1. Bring up a Map view that shows some highways and major boulevards.

2. Tap the i button.

3. Tap Show Traffic. If you cannot use this button, it means no traffic information is available for your area.

4. The map shows red or yellow dashed lines where traffic is slow.

5. You can also see the locations of accidents that are affecting traffic. Tap for details. Other symbols you see represent road closures, police activity, or other things that might affect traffic. You can tap on them to see more information.

Siri: Traffic Reports

You can quickly bring up the map with traffic reports turned on by asking Siri:

"What's the traffic like?"
"What's the traffic like in San Francisco?"

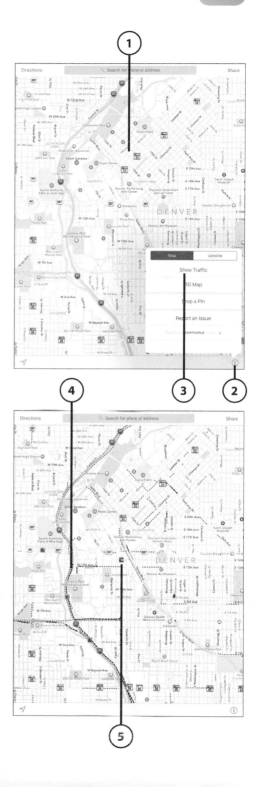

>>>*Go Further*

GET MORE WITH GOOGLE MAPS

There are many other map apps in the App Store, but Google Maps stands out as almost a must-have for anyone who uses maps. It has similar functionality to the built-in Apple Maps app, but uses different map data and information about locations. It comes in handy to have two maps in case one doesn't list or have enough details about a location.

Google Maps has also been around for a lot longer than Apple Maps, so it has some features you can't find in the latter, such as biking trails. It also has something called Street View, where you can view 360-degree pictures taken right on the streets.

See Chapter 15, "The World of Apps," to learn how to use the App Store to find and install new apps like Google Maps.

Search Apple's App
Store for thousands of
useful, educational, and
entertaining apps.

In this chapter, you learn how to go beyond the basic functionality of your iPad, and add more apps using the App Store.

→ Purchasing an App

→ Arranging Apps on Your iPad

→ Creating App Folders

→ Viewing Currently Running Apps

→ Quitting Apps

→ Viewing a Second App with Slide Over

→ Interacting with Two Apps At Once with Split View

→ Viewing Video with Picture-In-Picture

→ Finding Good Apps

→ Using iPhone/iPod touch Apps

→ Getting Help with Apps

→ Monitoring and Managing Your Apps

The World of Apps

Apps that come with your iPad and Apple's office apps, Pages, Numbers, and Keynote are just the tip of the iceberg. The App Store contains hundreds of thousands of apps from third-party developers, with more added each day.

You use the App Store app to shop for and purchase new apps—although many are free. You can also rearrange the app icons on your Home screen pages to organize them.

Purchasing an App

Adding a new app to your iPad requires that you visit the App Store. You do that, not surprisingly, with the App Store app on your Home screen.

1. Tap the App Store icon on your Home screen.

2. If this is the first time you have used the App Store, you see the featured apps at the top of the screen. Otherwise, tap the Featured button at the bottom.

3. Swipe left or right to view more featured apps. You can do the same for the sections below, which often change to feature different types of apps.

4. Swipe up to scroll down and see more featured apps.

5. Tap Top Charts to see the top paid apps and top free apps.

6. Tap Categories to see a list of app categories. Another way to see apps by category is to tap the Explore button at the bottom of the screen.

7. Tap any category to go to the page of featured apps in that category.

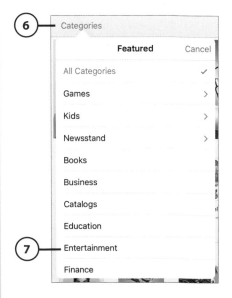

App Store

8. Use the search box to search for an app by keyword.

9. The button at the top lets you filter between iPad apps and iPhone apps. Apps that are optimized to work well with both screen sizes will appear in both.

10. Select whether you want to see apps that are free or both free and paid.

11. Select a category to narrow down the search results.

12. Choose how you want the results to be ordered: relevance, popularity, ratings, or release date.

13. Tap here to see the apps you have saved to your wish list.

14. Tap an app to read more about it and see screenshots, other apps by the same company, and user reviews.

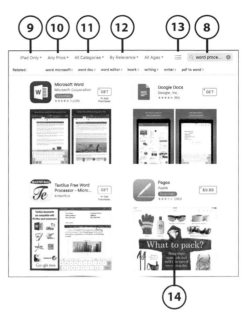

Redeem Codes

If you go to the bottom of the Featured page in the App Store, you will see a button marked Redeem. Use this to enter any redemption code you get for a free app. You may get a code because someone sends you an app as a gift. Developers also send out a handful of these codes when they release a new app or app version.

Automatically Download New Apps

If you go to the Settings app, look for the iTunes & App Store category. There you can turn on automatic downloads for apps, as well as music and books. Once you turn this on, purchasing an app on your Mac or PC in iTunes, or on another iOS device with the same Apple ID, will automatically send this app to your iPad as well.

15. Tap on the price on the left under the large icon to purchase an app. It changes to a Buy App button. Tap it again. If you have already purchased the app, the button will say Open, and you can launch the app by tapping the button.

Purchased Apps

If you have purchased the app in the past, but don't currently have it on your iPad, you will see a cloud/download button that lets you download the app again. You do not pay again for an app you have already purchased.

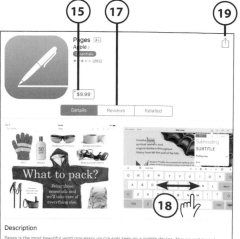

16. Swipe up to read the description of the app.

17. Tap Reviews to look at reviews for the app.

18. Scroll left and right to flip through the screenshots for the app.

19. Tap the Share button to send a link to the app to friends via email, Messages, and so on. You can also pay for and send a non-free app to a friend as a gift, or add a non-free app to your wish list to remember it for future consideration.

20. When you purchase an app, it starts installing, and you can watch the progress from the app's information page in the App Store app or from the location of the app's icon on your Home screen.

Redownloading an App You Already Purchased

Once you buy an app, you own it forever—at least as long as you keep using the same Apple ID. At the bottom of the App Store app, you see a button marked Purchased. Tap that to see a list of all apps you have bought, even if you have removed them from this iPad, or maybe never even downloaded them in the first place. Perhaps you previously bought an app on your iPhone or iPod Touch. You can quickly jump to any of these apps and download them to your iPad without paying for it a second time.

>>>Go Further
FREE, PAID, AND FREEMIUM

Some apps in the App Store are free, and others you need to pay for before downloading and installing. But some apps are free for the basic version, and then you need to make in-app purchases to use advanced functions or buy more content. These are called "freemium" apps.

It is up to the developer of the app to design the method of making purchases. Most apps show you a preview of the function or content and then include a purchase or buy button. Before any app can charge your iTunes account for an in-app purchase, you will see a standard Confirm Your In-App Purchase prompt.

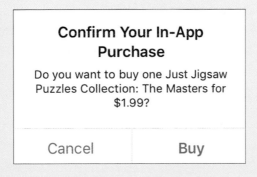

Confirm Your In-App Purchase

Do you want to buy one Just Jigsaw Puzzles Collection: The Masters for $1.99?

Cancel	Buy

Photo apps may use in-app purchases to charge you for additional filters or effects. Drawing apps may charge for new brushes or tools. Some free apps have advertising and allow you to make an in-app purchase to be able to use the app ad-free.

Often games will have a variety of items you can purchase to alter gameplay. But instead of a long list of in-app purchases, they simply charge you for in-game currency such as tokens, gems, or gold. Then you can use these to purchase items inside the game.

There's no risk in trying free apps that offer in-app purchases. If you find that the purchases in the app are not worth it for you, simply do not purchase anything. If the app isn't useful, you can delete it without spending a penny.

Organizing Apps on Your iPad

It doesn't take long to have several pages of apps. Fortunately, you can rearrange your app icons in two ways. The first is to do it on the iPad Home screen and allow apps to appear on multiple pages of the screen as each page fills up. In addition to spreading your apps across multiple pages, you can also group them together in folders so that several apps take up only one icon position on a screen.

Arranging Apps on the Home Screen

1. Tap and hold an icon until all the icons start to jiggle.

2. The icon you are holding is a little larger than the others. Drag it and drop it in a new location. To carry the icon to the next page of apps, drag it to the right side of the screen.

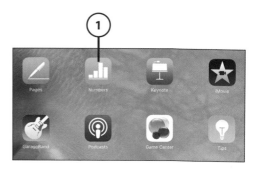

3. Delete an app from your iPad by tapping the X at the upper left of the icon. Note that the X does not appear over all apps, as the default set of apps that come with your iPad cannot be removed.

4. When finished, press the Home button (not shown).

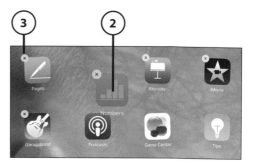

Deleting Is Not Forever

If you sync your iPad to iTunes on a computer, you do not delete apps forever. All apps remain in your iTunes library on your computer unless you remove them. So, you can get rid of the app from your iPad and find it is still on your computer if you want to select it to sync back to your iPad. You can always re-download an app from the app store that you purchased previously, without paying again. If you don't think you'll need an app for a while, you can delete it and then add it back again later.

>>>*Go Further*

WHAT ELSE CAN I DO?

Here are a few more tips that might make your app housekeeping easier:

- You can release an app and then grab another to move it. If the apps still jiggle, you can keep moving app icons.

- You can drag apps into and out of the dock along the bottom where you can fit up to six apps. Apps in the dock appear on all pages of your Home screen.

- You can drag an app to the right on the last page of apps to create a new page of your Home screen.

Creating App Folders

Grouping apps in a folder enables you to de-clutter your Home screen if you find you have too many apps competing for space on the screen.

1. Identify several apps that you want to group together. Tap and hold one of those apps until the icons start to jiggle.

2. Continue to hold your finger down, and drag the icon over another one you wish to group it with.

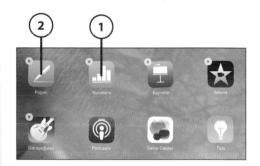

3. An app folder appears and enlarges to fill the center of the screen.

4. Change the name of the app folder.

5. Press the Home button once to dismiss the name editor, and again to return to your home screen (not shown).

6. You now see the app folder on your home screen. You can drag other apps to this folder using steps 1 and 2.

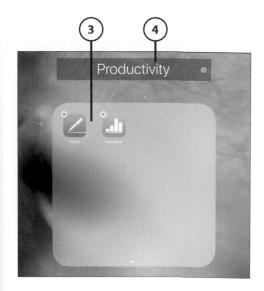

Working with Folders

After you have created an app folder, you can access the apps in it by first tapping on the folder and then tapping the app you want to launch. Tapping and holding any app in the folder gives you the opportunity to rename the folder, rearrange the icons in the folder, or drag an app out of the folder.

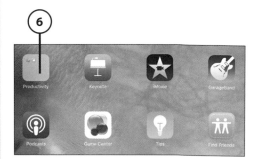

>>>Go Further

WORKING WITH APP FOLDERS

Here are a few more things you can do inside app folders:

- To remove an app from a folder and put it back into a position on the Home screen, tap and hold the icon until it jiggles. Then drag it out to the surrounding area outside of the folder.

- Inside app folders, you can have more than one page if you have more than nine apps stored in it. You can swipe left and right to move between pages while the folder is open.

- While apps in the app folder are jiggling, you can move them around inside the folder and off to the left or right to move them between pages inside the folder.

- You can move app folders around your Home screen and between Home screen pages just as you can with an app icon.

Working with Apps

You can have many apps running at once on your iPad. In fact, after you launch an app, it remains running by default even if you switch back to the home screen and run another app. With iOS 9, you can even view a second app at the same time you're running another one, or set up video to run picture-in-picture with another app.

Viewing Currently Running Apps

Apps running in the background use little or no resources. You can think of them as paused apps. You can switch back to them at any time, and most apps resume right where you left off.

1. Double-press the Home button (not shown).

2. This gives you a new view, called the Recents list, that shows all your currently running apps in a 3D series of pages. The app you currently are using appears to the right, and the previous app that you used is in the middle. This lets you easily switch between the current app and the previous app.

3. Swipe left and right to see more items in the list. The further to the right in the list the app is located, the longer it has been since you last used it.

4. Icons for each app also appear at the top. You can tap on these icons just as you can tap on the screens.

Moving from App to App with a Gesture

If you have several apps running, you can quickly move between them by using four-finger gestures. Just swipe left or right with four fingers at the same time. This will move you from app to app without needing to go back to the Home screen, or use the list of recent apps.

Quitting Apps

Although it is rarely necessary to completely quit an app, you can do it in one of two ways. This forces the app to shut down if it has frozen, or if you simply want to start the app fresh to see an introduction sequence or work around problems the app may be having.

1. Press the home button twice to see the list of your currently running apps (not shown).

2. Swipe to the left or right so the app you want to force to quit is in the center of the screen.

3. Tap the preview of the app and swipe upward quickly until your finger is almost at the top of the screen; then let go. The app will quit and be removed from the list.

>>>Go Further

DELETING ACTIVE APPS

A second method works when the app is the one currently onscreen.

Press and hold the wake/sleep button on the top of your iPad for about three seconds. You will see the "Slide to power off" control appear.

Don't use the "Slide to power off" control or press the Cancel button. Instead, hold the Home button down for several seconds. This quits the app and returns you to your Home Screen; or for some apps, it restarts the app.

The app also remains in the list you see when you double-press the Home button since it is one you recently used, even though it is not currently running.

Viewing a Second App with Slide Over **New!**

Ever wish you could check your email while surfing the web? Or write something in the Notes app while reading the News app? New in iOS 9 is the ability to view more than one app at a time on the iPad. The first of three methods for doing this is called Slide Over. As an example, start in Safari.

1. Tap and swipe in from the right side of the screen. It may be easier to touch just outside of the visible area of the screen so your finger moves from off the screen to on the screen. Then continue moving, and you will see the Slide Over screen appear. Stop when you are about a third of the way across the screen.

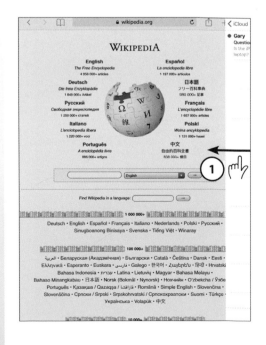

2. An app appears on the right side of the screen, taking up about a third of the space.

3. The app you were previously using remains on the other part of the screen, but is inactive. If you tap it, you dismiss the Slide Over app and return to your original app.

4. You can also tap and slide the handle on the left side of the Slide Over portion of the screen to go back to your original app.

5. To switch which app is shown in Slide Over, tap and drag down from the top of the screen on the right side. Start your finger just outside the screen for this to work.

6. You get a list of app icons. Only apps currently running and compatible with Slide Over are shown. Tap and slide vertically to see all the items in the list.

7. Tap an icon to have that app fill the Slide Over portion of the screen.

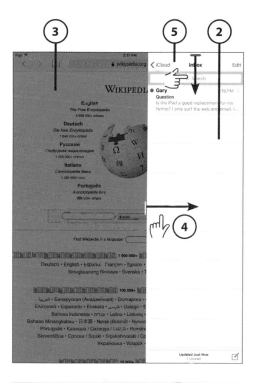

Limitations

Apps running in the Slide Over portion of the screen look and act differently from when they are running full screen, naturally. For instance, Mail shows you the list of messages in an inbox or the contents of a single message. But there is no room for both.

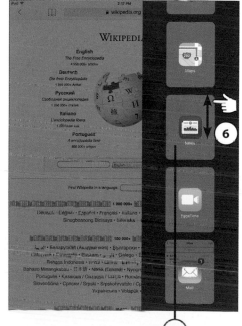

>>>*Go Further*
SLIDE OVER REQUIREMENTS

Slide Over requires a fairly new iPad model: The iPad Air or newer, the iPad mini 2 or newer, or an iPad Pro. In addition, for an app to work in Slide Over, it must be designed with that feature in mind. So many Apple-created apps like Mail, Calendar, Notes, News, and so on, work with it. However, most third-party apps do not.

Interacting with Two Apps at Once with Split View New!

Another way to interact with more than one app at a time is to use Split View. This mode seems to be similar to Slide Over, but there are two important differences. The first is that you can interact with both apps, not just the one brought over from the right. The second is that both apps take up equal space on the screen.

Split View works best when you are in horizontal orientation. So start by holding your iPad horizontally and bring up Safari.

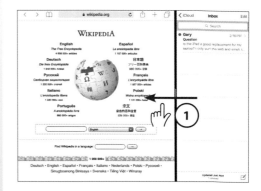

1. Start Split View the same way you start Slide Over, by dragging from outside the right side of the screen to the left. Stop about a third of the way to leave the app in Slide Over mode. But this time, tap and drag the handle again until you get to the middle of the screen.

Best on a Pro
This works particularly well if you have an iPad Pro. The Pro was designed to be about twice the screen size of an iPad Air. So using Split View is like having two iPads.

2. The new app appears on the right. You can interact with it the same way as with Slide Over. In vertical orientation many apps on the right still only use about a third of the screen, while in horizontal mode they use half of it. This may change in future versions of iOS 9.

3. The original app is now on the left, and you can interact with it as well.

4. You can drag from the top of the right side down to view other apps to replace this one, just like with Slide Over.

5. You can drag the center handle to the right or left to allow one of the two apps to take over the whole screen.

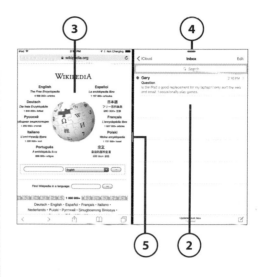

>>>Go Further
SPLIT VIEW REQUIREMENTS

Split View requires an even newer model of iPad than Slide Over. You need an iPad Air 2, iPad mini 4, iPad Pro, or newer models for this.

In addition, both apps must be compatible with Split View in order for it to work. This is because both apps need to know how to behave when they only have half a screen to work with. Most third-party apps won't work with Split View, but many Apple-created apps will.

Viewing Video with Picture-In-Picture New!

A third method for multitasking is specific to video. While you are watching video in some apps, like Safari, you can keep the video playing on the screen while you move to another app. As an example, we look at a video on a web page.

1. Start on a web page that has an embedded video.

2. Sometimes you need to start the video to see the controls.

3. Look for this Picture-in-Picture control. If you don't see it, it means that the video isn't being presented in a format that is compatible with picture-in-picture on your iPad. Tap this button.

4. The video is replaced with a "This video is playing in Picture in Picture" message.

5. The video moves to a corner of the screen.

6. Now you can leave this app. For instance, tap the Home button to go to your iPad's Home screen.

7. The video remains. You can tap and drag it now to move it elsewhere on the screen. You can also pinch it in or out to resize it.

8. Tap the Close button to remove the video from the screen.

9. Tap the Play/Pause button to toggle playback.

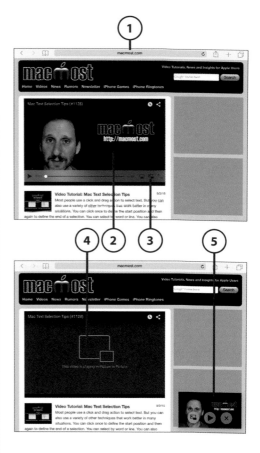

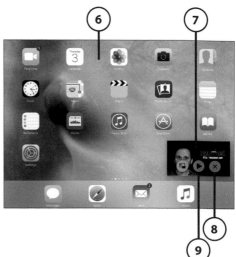

10. Tap the Return button to return to the app where the video originated. You can continue to move from app to app, and the video remains on the screen until you dismiss it. You can also drag it off to the left or right side to reduce the video to only a small "tab" that can be tapped to bring the video back onto the screen.

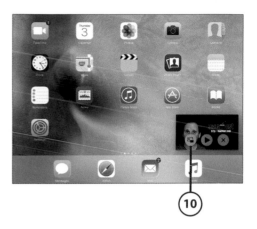

10

Finding Good Apps

Finding good apps might be the biggest problem that iPad users have. With more than a million apps in the App Store, it can be hard to find what you want, so here are some tips.

1. Check out the featured apps in the App Store (not shown). Be wary because they tend to be heavy on apps by large companies with well-established brands.

2. In the App Store app, find an app close to what you want and then check out the Related section.

3. Look for trial versions, which often have names with "Lite" or "Free" at the end. Search for the name of the app and see if other versions turn up. Use free versions of apps to determine if it is worth paying for the full or enhanced version.

4. Tap on Reviews.

5. Read reviews, but don't trust them completely. Casual users are not always the best at providing balanced reviews.

>>>Go Further
USING RESOURCES OUTSIDE THE APP STORE

Many good resources for finding apps aren't part of the App Store. Following are a few suggestions:

- Search using Google. For example, if you want another spreadsheet app, search "iPad App Spreadsheet."

- After you find an app that you want, try another Google search using the name of the app followed by the word "review."

- Find sites that feature and review apps. Many are out there, but be aware that some sites are paid by developers to review an app, so the review might not be the most objective.

- The author provides a list of recommended apps at http://macmost.com/featurediphoneapps.

Using iPhone/iPod touch Apps

Most apps in Apple's App Store are built for both the iPhone (and iPod touch) and iPad. Both devices run iOS, but the iPhone has a much smaller screen than the iPad. If a developer has created an app specifically for the iPhone's screen, and not the iPad, you can use a special feature of the iPad to enlarge the app to make it fill most of your display.

1. To enlarge the app, tap the 2x button at the upper-left corner.

2. If the app looks blurry when it's enlarged, tap the 1x button to return to normal size.

Getting Help with Apps

Apps are developed rapidly by both large and small companies. And apps are difficult to test because of Apple's restrictions on app distribution. So it is common to find bugs, have problems, or simply need to ask a question.

1. Check in the app to see if you can contact the developer. For example, in the Word Spell game app, there is a FAQ/Feedback button that takes you to a page of frequently asked questions and contact information.

2. If you don't find a way to contact support in the app, launch the App Store app and search for the app there.

3. Select the app to view its information.

4. Go to the Reviews section.

5. Tap the App Support button.

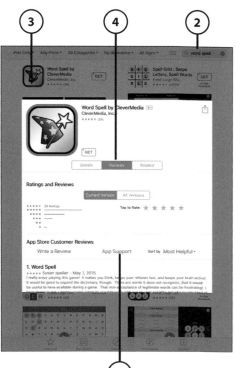

REVIEWS VS. DIRECT CONTACT

You may be tempted to leave a review for an app and ask questions there, or ask the developer for new features or bug fixes. However, the developer does not have any way to respond to reviews in the App Store. In fact, the developer cannot even tell who is writing the review, so it would be impossible for them to ask more questions or communicate in any way. Be sure to contact the developer directly and not use reviews as a way to send a message. Only use reviews as a way to leave honest, helpful information for others who may be looking to purchase an app.

SHARING APPS

When you buy an app, it can be put on any iPad (or iPhone/iPod touch if it works there, too) registered to your iTunes account. So if you have an iPad and an iPhone, you can buy the app on one and put it on the other at no extra charge. You can use the Family Sharing feature of iOS to also share that app purchase with other members of your family. See "Sharing Purchases with Your Family" in Chapter 4 to learn more about Family Sharing.

Monitoring and Managing Your Apps

For most users, you don't need to do anything extra to keep your apps running smoothly. However, you do have a variety of tools that let you see how much storage space and battery power your apps are using, and whether they are accessing your location and other information.

Viewing App Storage Information

To see how much storage space each app is using on your iPad, go to the Settings app.

1. Tap the Settings app icon.

2. Tap General settings.

3. Tap Storage & iCloud Usage.

4. Tap Manage Storage under the Storage heading, not the iCloud heading.

Settings

5. You see a list of all your apps sorted by how much storage they are using. Tap any app for more details.

6. For the majority of apps, you will simply see another screen with the app size, version number, and total storage being used.

7. You always have the option to delete the app from your iPad, too, without needing to go back to the Home screen to do it.

‹ Storage & Cloud Usage **Storage**

Used	5.1 GB
Available	7.2 GB

Videos	3.2 GB	›
Music	212 MB	›
Just Jigsaw	67.3 MB	›
Mah Jongg	25.6 MB	›
Photos & Camera	17.0 MB	›
Safari	13.4 MB	›
Podcasts	8.8 MB	›
Free Games 2	7.9 MB	›
Mail	3.5 MB	›
Contacts	2.2 MB	›
Messages	1.0 MB	›
Calendars & Reminders	816 KB	›
iBooks	168 KB	›

8. For some apps, you get a list of content and a breakdown of how much space each item is using.

9. You can often swipe right-to-left to reveal a delete button for each item.

10. Another way to delete content is to use the Edit button, and then select items to be deleted.

⟨ Storage	**Videos**		Edit
MOVIES			3.2 GB
	The Big Lebowski		1.7 GB
HE_BIG_SLEEP		1.5 GB	Delete

Viewing Battery Usage

If you notice your iPad's battery life isn't as long as you think it should be, it could be because an app is using more than its share. You can check the battery usage for each app in the Settings app.

1. From the Settings app, tap on Battery.

2. Tap either Last 24 Hours or Last X Days to get an idea of how much battery each app has been using. If you haven't been using your iPad unplugged from power for a while, you might not see any apps listed at all.

Days Vary

The number of days you see in Last X Days can vary based on your usage.

3. The list gives you an idea of which app may be an energy hog. Keep in mind that it is relative. In this example, the Marvel Unlimited app had just recently consumed the most battery power because I'd used it the most. However, I actually used the Pinball Arcade app for much less time, and it still consumed a significant chunk of battery power.

4. Tap the clock icon to see a list of how much time you've recently spent using each app.

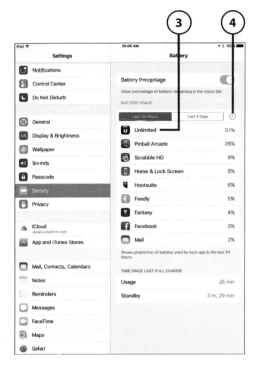

Viewing Location Usage

Another thing apps use is information. Of particular use is your location. This helps mapping and information apps to give you relevant results, for instance. You can see which apps use your location and how often they access it in the Settings app.

Locating Wi-Fi

Remember that your iPad can get your location even if you do not have a mobile wireless data plan. It looks at which Wi-Fi hotspots are near, and figures out your location from a database that knows where these hotspots are located.

1. In the Settings app, go to the Privacy settings.

2. Tap Location Services.

3. Here you see a list of apps that access your location. Some apps access your location only while they are the app you are currently using. Other apps access that information even while they are running in the background. Keep in mind that this is about permissions, not usage. Just because an app has been given permission to access your location in the background doesn't mean it is always doing so.

4. The little compass needle icons are color-coded to let you know how often your location is used by the apps. For instance, three apps show a gray icon, which means that they have used your location in the last 24 hours, but not recently.

5. You can tap any item to revoke location access, or in some cases change it from Always to While Using the App.

What Is a Geofence?

The Location Services screen in the Settings app shows a hollow purple arrow next to an app that is using a Geofence. This simply means the app checks to see whether you are in a certain area. For instance, a shopping app may check to see if you are in the store. The MLB At the Ballpark app uses this to see if you are in the stadium, and will customize the information based on that fact.

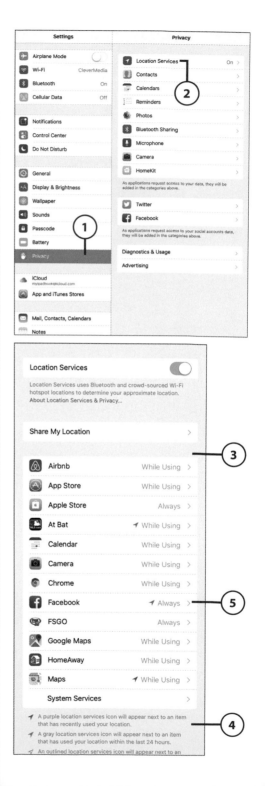

Viewing Information Sharing Permissions

Some apps communicate with each other. For instance, Keynote might have access to your photo library, or Skype may have access to your Contacts database. You are usually asked for permission when this first happens. For instance, the first time you insert an image into a Keynote presentation, a dialog pops up asking for you to grant permission for Keynote to access your photos.

You can view these connections between apps in the Settings app. You can also revoke these permissions.

1. In the Settings app, tap Privacy.

2. You see a list of apps that share information. Tap one of them.

3. In this case, four apps have asked for permission to access the photo library. Some built-in apps that are part of iOS, like Contacts or Camera, won't be listed.

4. You can switch off access to any app. Keep in mind that this could have consequences and the app might no longer be able to get the information it needs to operate.

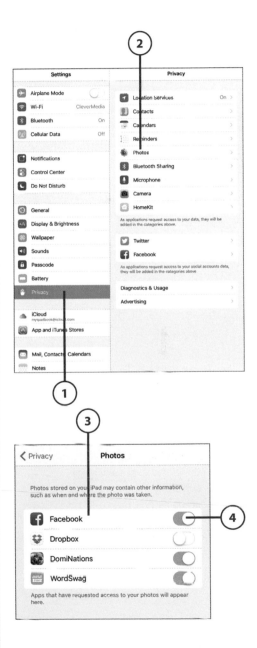

Modifying Notifications Settings

When you start using an app, it might ask you if it is okay for it to send you notifications. These are little alert boxes in the middle of your screen, or messages at the top of your screen, that appear when something happens that the app wants you to know about. Apps need your permission to show you these notifications, which is why they ask. You can change your decision later by using the Settings app.

1. Open the Settings app and tap Notifications.

2. You see a list of all apps that send notifications. You can sort this list by most recent, or set a specific order by switching this to manual.

3. Tap an app to view its specific notifications settings.

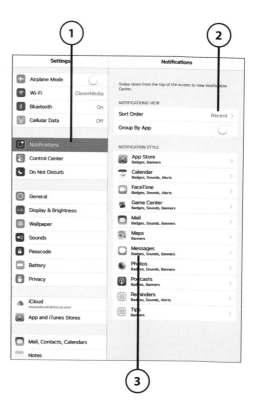

4. Choosing the None alert style means that neither a banner nor alert will appear.

5. Choosing Banners means that a drop-down banner appears when the app has a message, and it will go away on its own after a few seconds. These do not interrupt your work when they appear.

6. Choosing Alerts means that a box pops up in the middle of the screen when the app has a message, and you must dismiss it to continue.

7. Turning on Badge App Icon means that the app's icon shows a number over it when there is a message.

8. Many apps let you set the specific sound used. Tap Sounds to specify the sound the app uses.

9. Tap Show in Notification Center to choose how many alerts appear in the list in Notifications Center. You can also choose No Recent Items to indicate that you don't want to see them in the Notifications Center at all.

10. Show on Lock Screen means that alerts from this app appear, even when the iPad is locked.

11. Turn off Show Preview if you prefer that the small preview of the message does not appear with the alert.

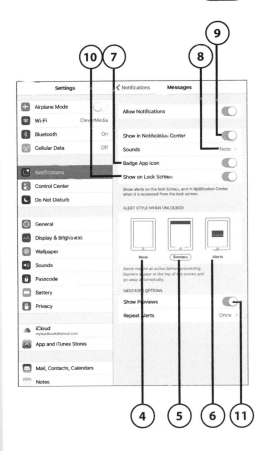

12. Tap Repeat Alerts to configure whether the alert repeats after a few minutes, and how many times. It is useful to have an alert repeat in case you missed it the first time.

13. If you want to completely disable an app's ability to send you notifications, you can do this quickly by just switching off Allow Notifications.

Apps Vary

Each app has its own set of settings, so take a few minutes to go through them all and see what options are offered. As you add new apps to your iPad, any that use the Notifications Center are added to this list, so it is a good idea to occasionally review your settings.

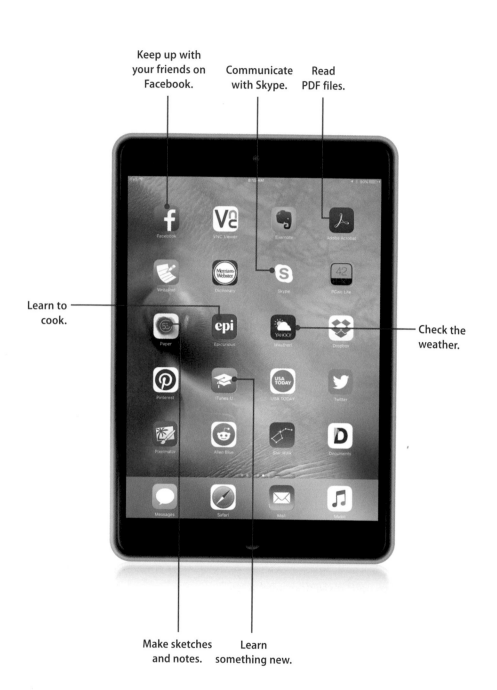

Keep up with
your friends on
Facebook.

Communicate
with Skype.

Read
PDF files.

Learn to
cook.

Check the
weather.

Make sketches
and notes.

Learn
something new.

In this chapter, we take a look at various apps that you should add to your iPad to make it even more useful.

→ Connecting with Friends on Facebook

→ Reading the News

→ Reading and Collecting Documents

→ Adding a Dictionary

→ Making Phone Calls with Skype

→ Creating Multimedia Cloud Notes with Evernote

→ Handwriting Notes with WritePad

→ Sketching Ideas with Paper

→ Adding a Calculator with PCalc Lite

→ Finding Recipes with Epicurious

→ Checking the Weather

→ Learning New Things with iTunes U

→ Other Useful Apps

Must-Have Apps

Ask almost anyone what the best feature of the iPad is and you'll get the same answer: all the apps! The App Store is not only a source of hundreds of thousands of useful, interesting, and fun apps, but it grows each day as third-party developers and Apple add more. Here's a look at how to use some of the most popular apps for the iPad to perform various useful tasks.

Connecting with Friends on Facebook

Many people now spend more time on Facebook than the rest of the Internet combined. If you are one of those people, the official Facebook app is probably the first third-party app you should put on your iPad.

With it you can browse your wall, post status updates, send messages, post photos, and do most things that you can do on the Facebook website, but inside an environment designed for iPad users.

1. Search the App Store for the Facebook app. Tap GET to download and install it.

2. Instead of going to the app to log in, go to the Settings app and look for Facebook on the left. Facebook is somewhat integrated into iOS so you can upload photos directly from the Photos app and perform other tasks. Logging in with the Settings app enables more of this than just logging in with the Facebook app.

3. Tap here to log in. After you have done so, you see your account name appear here.

4. Now launch the Facebook app (not shown).

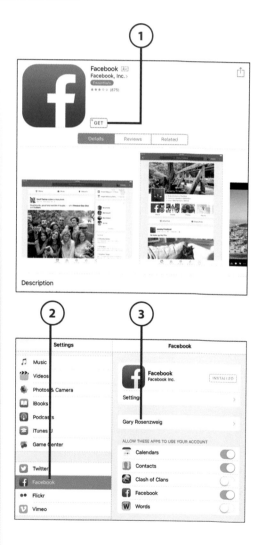

5. Scroll up and down to view your news feed.

6. You can Like posts just as you would on the Facebook website.

7. You can also tap Comment to add a comment to a post.

8. View and handle friend requests.

9. This button shows you if you have any direct messages. However, you cannot use the Facebook app to view or respond to Facebook messages. Frustrating, right? Facebook insists that you use their Messenger app for that. Search the App Store for "Facebook Messenger," which you can install for free.

10. See your list of Facebook notifications.

11. Tap the More button to access different parts of Facebook.

12. Tap your name to examine your own wall and edit your profile.

13. Tap Most Recent to see recent items in your Facebook feed instead of just what Facebook deems important.

14. See a list of your friends and view their information and their wall.

15. You can also post to walls of Facebook pages you manage.

16. Or, post just to a Facebook group you belong to.

17. To post to Facebook, use the Status, Photo, or Check In buttons, depending on the type of post you want to make. If you don't see these three buttons here, drag the screen downward until they appear.

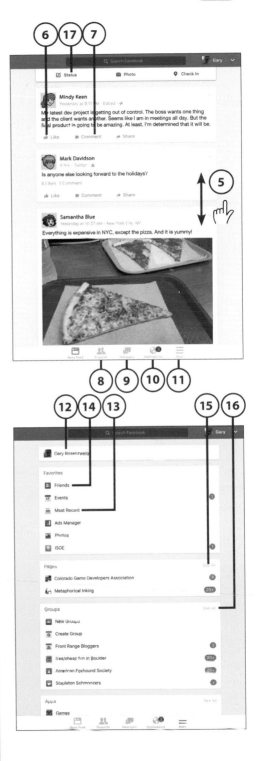

18. Type the text of your update.

19. Add friends who are with you to the update.

20. Add a photo from your Photos library, or take a new photo using your iPad's cameras.

21. If you want to include your location in the post, tap this button.

22. Post the update to Facebook.

It All Looks Different

If there is one consistent thing about Facebook, it is change. Facebook loves to change how its website and apps look. So if the Facebook app looks different than what you see here, it could simply be that Facebook has, once again, decided to redesign the interface.

Post from Outside

You don't need to use the Facebook app to post pictures. You can do it right from the Photos app and other image-handling apps. But you first need to go to the Settings app, then the Facebook section, and enter your email and password again. This gives iOS permission to use your Facebook account for posting. Then you can do things like post pictures from the Photos app, post links from Safari, and ask Siri to "update my Facebook status."

>>>*Go Further*

MORE SOCIAL MEDIA APPS

Facebook is undoubtedly the primary social media platform for most people. Others do exist, and they also have apps you might want to try as well. If you use any of these services, the app is worth adding to your iPad.

 Twitter: Twitter is a hugely popular app for sharing short messages with others and following the tweets of friends and other public figures.

 LinkedIn: For many business professionals and job-seekers, LinkedIn is even more important than Facebook.

 Pinterest: A fun way to visually share your interests with others.

 Google+: Google's social network is similar to Facebook, but part of the Google ecosystem.

 Instagram: A very popular way to share photos with friends. Unfortunately, this app is still just optimized for iPhone screens, though you can use it on your iPad as well.

Reading the News New!

With iOS 9, Apple introduced its own News app. This app isn't unlike many of the third-party news apps that have been available in the past, such as Flipboard. But with the News app being standard on your iPad, it will quickly become the most popular app of this kind.

With News, you can read news stories from hundreds of newspapers, magazines, blogs, and other sources, all in one place. The articles are presented in a nice design that makes it easy to browse through stories and bookmark some for later reading. Better still, you can pick which news sources you see and which interests you have, so you are essentially getting a newspaper customized for you.

1. Launch the News app. It is a default app that comes with your iPad and iOS 9.

2. If this is the first time you are running News, you are shown a series of welcome screens. Tap Get Started on the first screen.

3. You are asked to pick three news sources or topics of interest to get started. Don't worry, you can customize your sources later on.

4. Tap Continue. You may see more welcome screens and information. The News app is sure to evolve over time, so the setup process may change.

News

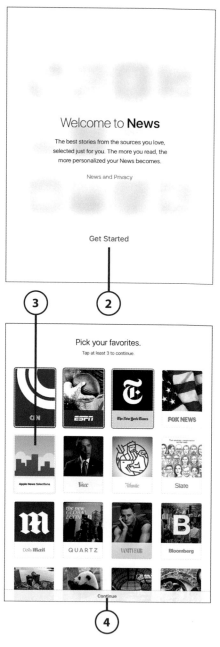

5. A good place to start is the Explore screen. If you find yourself elsewhere in the app, tap Explore at the bottom to go to this screen.

6. With News, you scan tap and drag to scroll vertically to see more stories.

7. Tap any story to read it.

8. How a story looks depends on the source. Some are just text, while others have pictures and even video. If there is more text than can fit on the screen, tap and drag to scroll.

9. You can share a news story in a message, email, social network, or open Safari and display the web page with the original news article.

10. If you want to read a story later, or just want to save it, you can tap this button.

11. Tap here to return to the previous screen.

12. Tap Favorites to see which news sources and topics you have chosen as your favorites and change them.

13. You can tap a source to view only news articles from that one source.

14. Tap Edit to be able to select and delete news sources.

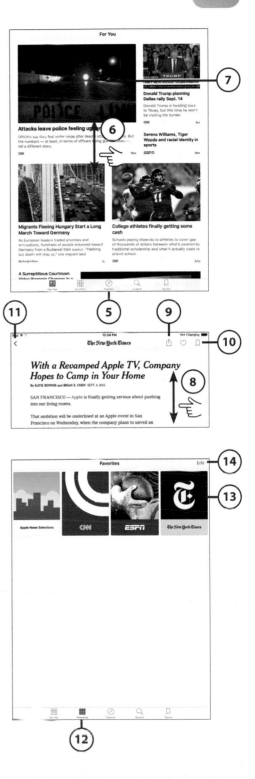

15. Tap Explore to find new news sources to add to your favorites. Even if you are satisfied with your selections, it could be useful to see occasionally what is new.

16. Tap any source to view news from that one source.

17. The suggested channels and suggested topics can be scrolled horizontally to view more.

18. You can also dig down into topics and subtopics to view more sources.

19. Tap Saved to see your saved news stories and history.

20. You can switch between which articles you have saved and your complete viewing history. Under History there is an option to clear your history.

21. Tap any story to go back and read it again.

22. To remove an item from your Saved screen, tap and swipe to the left.

23. You can also use the Search button to search news for articles on a specific topic or from a source.

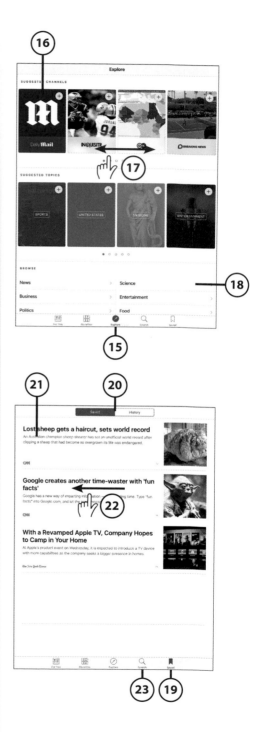

>>>Go Further
LOCAL NEWS AND MORE

Using search in step 23 enables you to quickly find sources that don't show up easily when browsing. For instance, you can search for the name of your city, state, or country to see if any local news sources present. Sometimes there are topics that pertain to your location, such as a sports team.

Next to the Save button at the top of a news article you also see a heart-shaped "Love" button. Tap that if you would like to see more news stories like the current one. The app notes your preference and gives a higher priority to those stories.

>>>Go Further
MORE NEWS READING APPS

For reading news, you have two types of apps: ones like News that aggregate news from many sources, and apps from a single news source.

USA Today: This daily newspaper features concise news stories and other articles in an easy-to-browse format.

Flipboard: This third-party app is very similar to Apple's News app, but it has been around a lot longer.

Zite: Another like Flipboard, but with more of a magazine feel. It will fine-tune which stories you see based on which ones you have liked or disliked in the past.

Pulse: This news site from LinkedIn lets you build a custom news feed.

Feedly: This news reader lets you subscribe to any syndicated (RSS) content.

Zinio: Although some magazines have their own apps, many others can be found inside the app called Zinio. It is kind of a clearinghouse for hundreds of magazines that publish with a standard format. Browse sample articles for free, and then look for magazines you can purchase either as a single issue or as a subscription. You can even get European and Asian magazines that are hard to find in the U.S.

Reading and Collecting Documents

Although iBooks is great for basic document viewing, and iCloud Drive can be used to view some documents if they are saved to iCloud, those more serious about collecting documents to read on their iPad have looked to apps that have even more features. Mac users are familiar with the Preview app, but no equivalent built-in viewer exists for iOS.

So, it is useful to get an app such as Documents by Readdle. It enables you to create a library of viewable files such as PDFs, Word, images, text, and so on. You can then access these documents any time.

1. Search the App Store for Documents by Readdle. Tap GET to download and install it.

2. In order to see how the app works, let's take a look at a simple way to bring a PDF into it. Open Safari and go to a page that contains a PDF file. Tap on that PDF file and it loads in Safari. You can read it there if you want, but we're going to add it to our Documents 5 collection.

3. Tap once in the center of the document to reveal a small toolbar at the top. It contains a button to open in iBooks, and another labeled Open in….

4. Tap Open in… to bring up a set of sharing controls.

5. Tap Copy to Documents. When you installed the Documents app, this button was added to appropriate sharing controls such as this one. You'll also find it if you are viewing a PDF or other document in Mail, for instance.

6. Now open the Documents app you downloaded in step 1. You might see some introductory screens. After those, you'll have a sidebar on the left. Tap Documents.

7. You see your imported document. You also see a number of example documents. Documents of all different types, such as PDF, Pages, Word, text, images, and audio files, can be viewed.

8. You can tap the Edit button to select and delete documents.

9. On the left, there are other ways to import documents into the app. Tap Network and you get a list of services that include Dropbox, Google Drive, or even a plain FTP server.

10. Tap a document to read it.

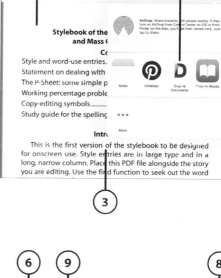

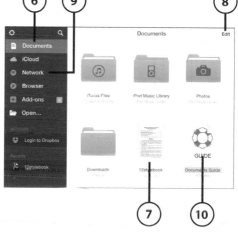

11. While reading, you can tap the text button to highlight passages.

12. Tap the magnifying glass to search the text.

13. Tap the book icon to add bookmarks.

14. You can export, print, or open in another app. Tap the Sharing button to access those options.

15. Tap Document to exit and return to your list of documents.

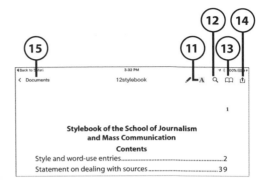

>>>Go Further
MORE DOCUMENT VIEWING APPS

DropBox: This is a very popular cloud storage service. The iPad app not only allows you to see what files you have stored in your account, but is a very good document viewer as well, allowing you to view a wide variety of file types.

GoodReader: Very similar to Documents by Readdle, but not free. However, it has even more features and has been the gold standard for these kinds of apps.

Adobe Reader: The official PDF-viewing app from the company that is behind the format. It also allows you to fill out PDF forms on your iPad.

Adding a Dictionary

It would be a crime to have to carry a dictionary with you in addition to your iPad. Of course, the solution is to get a dictionary app for your iPad. The Merriam-Webster Dictionary HD app is a free download from the App Store. There is also a premium version that removes the ads and adds illustrations and other features for a few dollars.

1. Find the Merriam-Webster Dictionary HD app in the App Store. Tap GET to download and install it.

Use Any Online Dictionary

Of course, if you prefer another dictionary that doesn't have an iPad app, you can always just bookmark that site in Safari. You can also create a Home screen bookmark as we did in Chapter 7.

2. Tap in the search box and enter a word to look up.

3. You can also tap the microphone button and speak the word to look it up. Handy if you don't know how to spell the word.

4. The word and definition appear.

5. Tap the speaker icon to have the word spoken so you can hear its pronunciation.

6. The app can also be used as a thesaurus. A list of synonyms appears at the bottom. Tap any one to jump to that word. In fact, any blue word in the definition can also be tapped to jump to that word for further clarification.

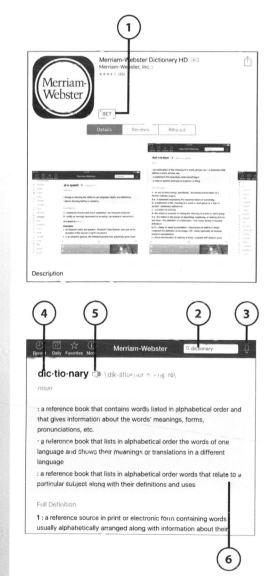

>>>Go Further

MORE DICTIONARY APPS

 Dictionary.com: This is an app, despite the .com name. It is a solid alternative to Merriam-Webster. There is a free version with ads, as well as a paid version.

 Urban Dictionary: Sometimes a standard dictionary isn't enough. If you want definitions for slang words and text message abbreviations, this app can help.

 Wikipedia Mobile: If you want an encyclopedia instead, you can use Wikipedia's official app for access to entries in their huge user-created database.

Don't forget about using a Google search as another alternative to a dictionary. Google can often take the oddest misspelling and come up with the correct word. Then, the search results will include definitions, as well as Wikipedia entries and links to articles about the subject that might help even more.

Making Phone Calls with Skype

Your iPad works quite well as a phone when you use a VoIP (voice over IP) app. Skype is probably the most well-known. Of course, you can use Face-Time to make both video and audio calls, but that only works if the other person is part of the Apple ecosystem using an iOS or Mac device. If they are on an Android, Windows, or Linux device, Skype is a good alternative.

1. Search for Skype in the App Store. Make sure you look for the iPad app, not the iPhone/iPod touch app of the same name. Tap GET to download and install it.

2. Tap Skype Name to sign in using your Skype account. You can also sign in with a Microsoft account. If you have neither, you can tap Create account, which appears at the very bottom of the screen. Complete the sign-in process by entering your ID and password.

Get a Skype Account

You need a Skype account to use the Skype app. You can get a free one at http://www.skype.com/. If you find the service useful, you might want to upgrade to a paid account, which lets you call landlines and other phones. The free account lets you call only other Skype users.

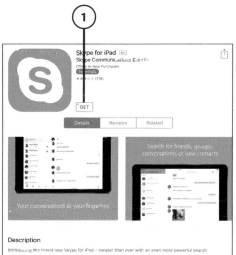

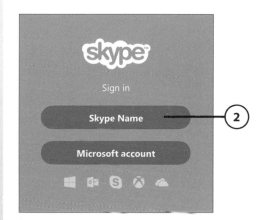

3. On the main Skype screen, you can view recent calls, your contacts list, and your Skype info. Tap Call phones.

4. Tap the keypad button at the top of the screen.

5. Use the on-screen keypad to enter a phone number. You need a country code, too, which means using a 1 for U.S. calls. It should be there by default.

6. Tap Call.

7. While placing a call, you see the status, and eventually the elapsed time.

8. Additional buttons are available across the bottom for things like mute, volume, voice call, recent chats, and accessing your profile.

9. Tap the end call button to hang up.

How Do You Hold Your iPad to Talk?

The microphone is at the top of your iPad. The speaker is at the bottom on the back. The best way may be to just put the iPad in front of you and ignore the locations of both. Or, you can get a set of iPhone EarPods, which include the speakers and the microphone.

How About Skype Video?

You can also make video calls with Skype using your iPad's cameras. But you must be connecting to another Skype user who also has a video camera connected to their computer, or perhaps they are using an iPad as well.

>>>Go Further

MORE COMMUNICATIONS APPS

FaceTime is the primary competitor to Skype on the iPad. See Chapter 10, "Recording Video," for several sections dealing with FaceTime. There are many other audio and messaging apps, and just a few are listed here.

 Fring: This app allows you to make voice and video calls to other iOS and Android users. You can also upgrade your account to allow you to make calls to regular phones.

 Google Voice: While not exactly a phone service, this app does allow Google Voice phone number users to access their voicemail and text messages on their iPad.

 HeyTell: Instead of making phone calls, HeyTell lets you send quick voice messages to others.

Creating Multimedia Cloud Notes with Evernote

One of the most popular productivity apps on the iPad and iPhone, as well as Macs and PCs, is Evernote. At its heart, it is like the built-in Notes app on your iPad. You can create text notes, and they will sync across your devices.

But Evernote has several advanced features that endear it to users. First, you can easily record audio and take photos and add them to your notes. Second, it is independent of an email service like iCloud or Gmail. Third, there are Evernote clients for almost every computer and device. You can even view your notes in a web-based interface if you need to.

1. Search for Evernote in the App Store. Tap GET to download and install it.

2. Next, you go through a series of questions that allow you to either set up an account or sign in to an existing one. All your notes are available to you through Evernote apps on other iOS devices, Macs, PCs, or Android devices.

3. The main screen shows your notes. Tap a note to view it.

4. To create a new text note, tap the text button on the left.

5. Tap in the title area to type a name for the note.

6. Tap in the body area to type text into the note.

7. Tap the attachment button to take a photo, add a photo from your library, or add audio to a note.

8. You can also use a note as a reminder, with a set alarm time.

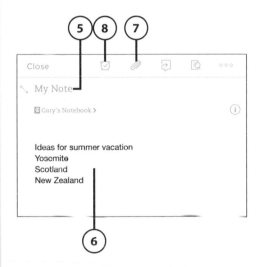

9. Tap the info button to get info on a note.

10. You can add tags to notes as one way to organize them.

11. If you allow it, notes will include location information about where you were when you created the note. You can tap here to change the location.

12. Use the … button to get to more functions, such as sharing your note. You can share the note on Messages, Twitter, via Email, or print it.

13. Tap the search button to search the content of notes.

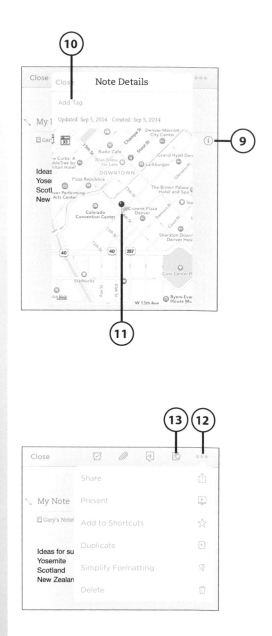

Empowering Evernote

The real power of Evernote involves how it syncs quickly and wirelessly over the Internet. For instance, you can use it to write notes, record audio, and take pictures with your iPad while out of the office, and then find them all on your Mac or PC when you get back to your desk. Often, the picture-taking ability is used to grab snapshots of sketches on napkins or product information on the back of a box.

>>>*Go Further*

MORE NOTE-TAKING APPS

 SoundNote: You can take notes and record audio at the same time. It matches the audio stream so you can hear what sound was recorded for each word of notes you took. So, tap a word to hear the audio at that moment.

 Circus Ponies NoteBook: You can type text, draw, take photos, and so on. You can turn on audio recording, and then each line in your note matches up with a portion of a recording. So, you can sit in a lecture or meeting and take notes, and then refer back to the audio that matches each portion of your notes.

 Penultimate: You create notebooks and write in them by drawing with your finger. You can also mark up PDF documents and enter text using the on-screen keyboard. Penultimate syncs with an Evernote account.

 Wunderlist: This is a popular list-making tool that offers some features that Reminders does not, such as attaching photos and PDFs to items.

Handwriting Notes with WritePad

You'd think with a touch screen that the iPad could recognize your handwriting instead of making you type on an on-screen keyboard. The WritePad app enables you to take notes by typing or by using the touch screen to write with your finger.

1. Search for WritePad in the App Store. Tap the price (currently it's $7.99) to download and install it.

2. The first time you use WritePad, you are guided through some setup screens.

3. After setup, you are taken right to an empty document. Instead of typing to add text, draw the text with your finger. Note that the cursor is at the upper left, but you don't need to write there. Write anywhere on the screen.

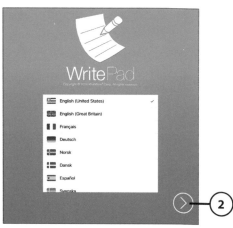

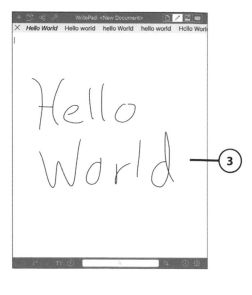

4. The text appears at the cursor.

5. Tap the documents button to see all of your WritePad notes.

6. You can tap on a note document to open it.

7. Tap the + button to add a new note.

>>>*Go Further*

MORE ALTERNATIVES TO TYPING

MyScript Memo: This app keeps your notes in handwritten form, but lets you convert them to text later. It works well when you need to combine text and drawings.

Dragon Dictation: iOS does a good job understanding speech and converting it to text using the built-in speech recognition (see "Dictating Text" in Chapter 1). But to take things to the next level, you can use this app from the leader in dictation software. It responds to dictation commands and spelling-out words for a completely hands-free solution.

Sketching Ideas with Paper

Perhaps you don't want your handwriting converted to text, but instead want to sketch out ideas or doodle on your iPad. Probably the most popular app for that is the simple Paper by FiftyThree.

1. Search the App Store for Paper by FiftyThree. Tap GET to download and install it.

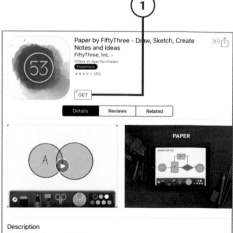

2. When you first run Paper, you go through a series of introductory messages. After that, you can create a new notebook to sketch in, but there are already several empty notebooks waiting for you when you first install the app.

3. Tap a notebook to open it.

4. Anything you may have sketched previously appears on the first page.

5. You can swipe left to flip through the pages in the book.

6. Tap in the middle or pinch out to zoom in on a page so you can sketch.

7. Tap the pen tool to draw.

8. Tap and drag your finger to draw lines.

9. Tap a color to change colors.

10. Tap the eraser tool and drag your finger on the page to erase.

11. Pinch in to zoom back out to view the whole notebook. Pinch in again to zoom out to see all your notebooks.

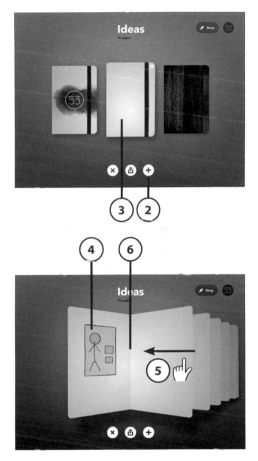

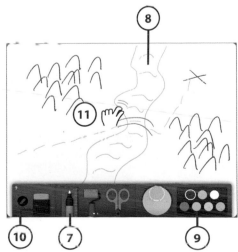

>>>*Go Further*

WHAT ELSE CAN I DO?

Here are some more things you can do with Paper by FiftyThree:

- The blank spots next to the eraser and pen are more drawing tools such as pencil, marker, more pens, and a color mixer. The basic Paper is free, but you need to pay with in-app purchases to get these tools.

- You can undo by tapping with two fingers and making a counter-clockwise circle. The more you circle, the further back in time you will go. You can reverse the direction of the circle to redo.

- When flipping through the pages of a notebook, you can use the Share button below the notebook to send the currently visible page to your Camera Roll for use in other apps, or even as your lock screen or home screen.

- You can also send a page to Tumblr, Facebook, Twitter, or to a friend via email.

>>>*Go Further*

MORE SKETCHING APPS

 SketchBook: Unlike Paper by FiftyThree, SketchBook is specifically for illustration. Professional artists have used it to create some amazing pieces.

 Adobe Illustrator: This sketching app uses vector-based tools, so it can be a good starting point for artists who need to take their sketches into other Adobe software later. It also has some interesting color tools.

 **Brushes 3** and **ArtStudio:** Two other excellent drawing tools with layers, and lots of brush and color options.

Adding a Calculator with PCalc Lite

Your iPad is a powerful computer, capable of processing data and performing calculations. So, how do you calculate a simple restaurant tip? There's no calculator built in to your iPad, but you can easily add one with a third-party app. Let's look at using the free PCalc Lite app. If you search for "calculator" in the app store, you'll also come up with dozens of other different free and paid calculator apps.

1. Find the PCalc Lite app in the App Store and tap GET.

2. You can enter numbers just like with a real calculator. For instance, enter 68.52, the cost of dinner for two at a nice restaurant. No wine, but desserts.

3. Tap X to multiply by the next number.

4. Tap 20 to indicate 20 percent. Good service with a smile. And then tap % to indicate that 20 is a percent (0.20).

5. The answer appears in the display. By all means, round up to $14. The waiter refilled your water three times without being asked.

6. Tap AC (all clear) to begin your next calculation.

7. In many ways, an app Calculator is better than the real thing. For instance, there is an Undo button.

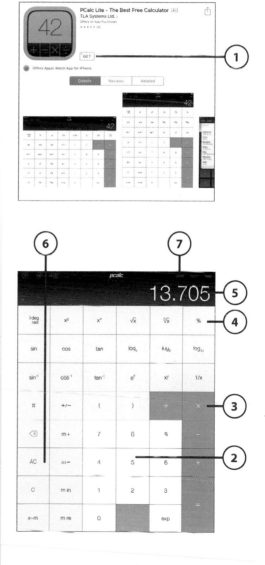

8. Tap the settings button.

9. You can choose to customize the look of the calculator by changing the theme and the look of the digits. Some calculator apps feature tons of options.

10. If you are a scientist, mathematician, or engineer, you might want to use the calculator in reverse polish notation mode. If you don't know what reverse polish notation is, then you don't want to use reverse polish notation mode.

8

Settings

To purchase extra features from the full version of PCalc, tap here.

RPN **10**

Theme   Samurai > **9**

Digits   Thin >

Key Click   System >

Reset to Defaults

>>>Go Further

MORE CALCULATOR APPS

MyScript Calculator: This app allows you to actually write your numbers as you would on a sheet of paper. You can use operations and mathematical symbols and it calculates what you are asking and gives you an answer. It will even find the value of variables in short algebraic equations.

Calculator: This alternative to PCalc includes both standard and scientific calculator modes.

Calculator HD: This other alternative lets you see your results history in a list.

Finding Recipes with Epicurious

One application for early personal computers was to store and recall recipes. With the Internet, we can also share those recipes. And now with the iPad, there is finally a way to easily have these recipes with you in the kitchen while cooking. The Epicurious app is a favorite for such tasks.

1. Search for Epicurious in the App Store. Tap GET to download and install it.

2. Creating an account lets you store your favorites.

3. You can tour the app without creating an account.

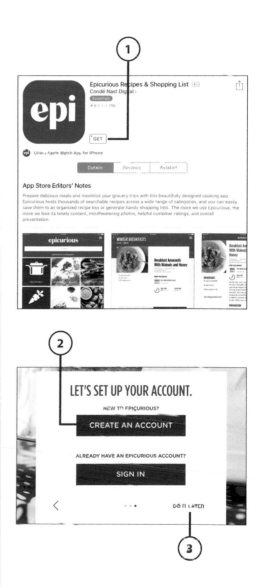

4. You can start by searching for a specific recipe, if you like.

5. You can also browse using categories. For instance, you can list recipes by their main ingredient or dietary considerations.

6. Tap one of the pictures to go right to a featured recipe.

7. First, you see the ingredients list. There is also other information like user ratings.

8. Tap View Recipe to see the instructions.

9. Tap View All to view a list of other recipes in this category.

10. Return to the main screen.

>>>*Go Further*

MORE COOKING APPS

Food Network In the Kitchen: This app gives you more than just recipes. You get videos featuring the TV network's stars showing you how to make the dishes.

Yummly: An alternative recipe database to Epicurious.

All Recipes Video Cookbook: Another alternative, this one includes videos as well.

Checking the Weather

The iPhone comes with a Weather app preinstalled, but the iPad does not. However, you can find many good weather apps in the App Store. Download any one of those to add this important information to your iPad. As an example, let's look at the Yahoo Weather app.

1. Search the App Store for Yahoo Weather. Tap GET to download and install it.

2. If this is the first time you have used the app, you might be asked if you want to enable daily weather notifications. You are also asked if you want to allow the app to use your location, which allows it to focus on your local weather without requiring you to enter your location. After that, the first screen you see shows you the current conditions for your location.

3. Tap and slide up to reveal more weather information.

4. You can view the hourly forecast for the rest of the day.

5. You also see a 10-day forecast.

6. Swipe up again to reveal more information.

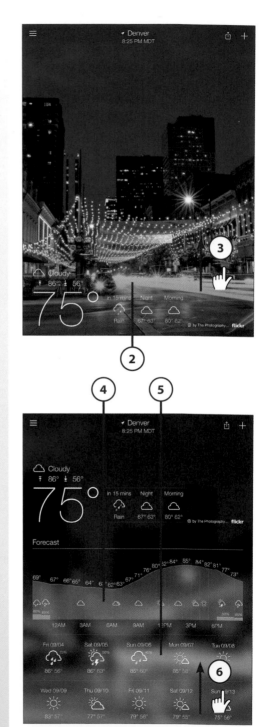

7. You can find more detailed information about the current conditions.

8. You can see basic information like sunrise, sunset, and moon phase.

9. At the bottom, you can see the current radar map. To the right of the map, you can use buttons to switch between satellite, heat, wind, and radar maps.

10. Tap the + button to add another location. When you have more than one location, you can swipe left and right to switch between locations, and check the weather in different places.

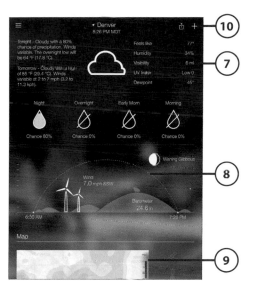

>>>Go Further
MORE WEATHER APPS

Weather+: This weather app features a customizable screen so you can change what you see when you first bring it up.

The Weather Channel: This is a comprehensive weather app from the cable network.

Weather Underground: This app from one of the most well-respected weather sites predicts the weather based on numerous sources and user reporting.

WeatherBug: Another good alternative weather app.

Living Earth: View a 3D globe showing conditions and forecasts.

Learning New Things with iTunes U

You have an entire school in your iPad—many universities, in fact. Apple's iTunes U app is your gateway to free educational content provided by many of the world's top colleges.

1. Search the App Store for the iTunes U app. Tap GET to download and install it.

2. If you start with a blank library of courses, tap the button at the bottom to enter the Featured courses screen.

3. Tap the More button for a complete list of categories.

4. Tap in the search field to search the catalog for a course.

5. Tap a course to view more information.

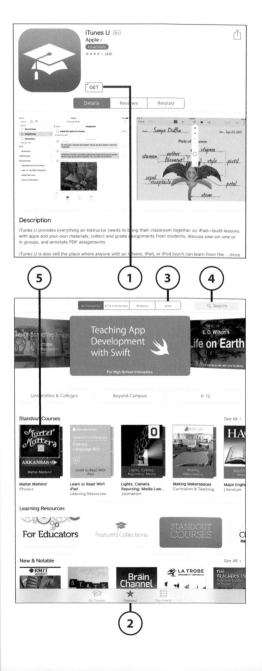

6. Read the description of the course.

7. Swipe up the page to move down and see all the course materials. Icons to the right of the names indicate what type of material: audio, document, video, and so on.

8. You can tap to download an individual item.

9. You can subscribe to the whole course, which will put it in your library and take you to your library screen.

10. To return to My Courses, tap the My Courses button at the bottom of the screen. Then, tap the course in your library.

11. When viewing the course, tap Materials to see a chronological list of the course materials.

12. Tap an item to view or listen to it.

13. You can download and listen/ read/view the item later.

Is It Really Free?

Yes, for the most part. Many major universities provide these courses for free. However, just like with a real course, you sometimes need to purchase extra materials to follow along. For instance, there may be a book, app, or other item listed. Sometimes you can purchase the item right on your iPad, such as a book in the iBookstore.

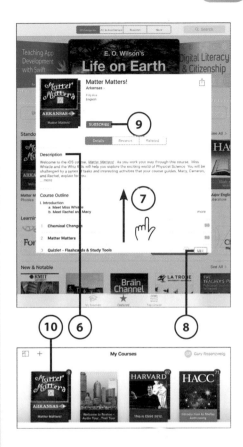

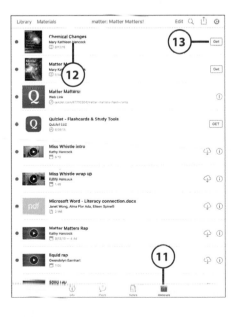

>>>*Go Further*

MORE EDUCATIONAL APPS

 Craftsy: You can purchase video courses for things like crochet, kitting, quilting, baking, weaving, and other crafts. You browse their catalog and buy the course with an in-app purchase. Then you follow along with video tutorials. You can also take notes and ask questions of your instructor.

 TED: This app gives you access to thousands of educational and inspirational videos from TED conferences around the world.

If you search the App Store, you can find apps that teach you just about anything. Want to learn to play guitar? How to bowl? How to repair your car? There are all sorts of apps for these. And when you can't find an app, you can use the YouTube app to search for tutorial videos.

Other Useful Apps

So many useful apps are in the store that it is impossible to cover them all in a book. Here are some quick mentions of others you can check out. Some are free, others you have to pay for.

 1Password: Mac users already know about the popular 1Password for Mac, which gives you a place to securely store passwords and other important information and conveniently access them through Safari.

 MindNode: If you use mind mapping software to organize your ideas and plan projects, then you'll be happy to know there is a pretty advanced tool that lets you do this on the iPad.

 WordPress: The official WordPress app lets you write, edit, and maintain your blog posts. It works for the WordPress.com blogging service and for WordPress blogs set up on independent sites. **Blogsy** is an app that also lets you work with your WordPress blog, as well as many other popular blogging platforms.

Day One: For those who like to keep journals, your iPad can replace physical paper ones with apps like Day One. You can include photos and keep it completely private with a password. **Momento** is another journaling app to check out. And **Heyday** is one with a focus on keeping travel journals.

 StarWalk 2: This is a must-have app for anyone even vaguely interested in astronomy. Even if you aren't, the beautiful, up-to-the-minute renderings of the night sky on your iPad will impress your friends. You can see what the sky looks like right now, right where you are, and use it as a guide to identifying what you see.

 Wolfram Alpha: Want to compare two stocks, see the molecular structure of sulfuric acid, or calculate the amount of sodium in your breakfast? Would you believe that one app does all three and has hundreds of other interesting answers to all sorts of questions? It is also the answer engine behind a lot of what the iPhone's Siri feature does, so you get a little bit of Siri on your iPad.

 Bloomberg: The iPhone comes with a Weather app, a calculator app, and a stocks app. The first two have good alternatives mentioned earlier in this chapter. For the last one, you also have good options. The Bloomberg app lets you track your stocks and keep up with financial news. **Yahoo Finance** is a decent alternative, as well. If you use an online broker, search for their app—most of them produce one.

 VNC Viewer: You can use your iPad to share your computer's screen. With VNC viewer, or any similar tool such as **iTeleport** or **Mocha VNC Lite**, you connect to a Mac using OS X's screen sharing or a PC using a VNC server. Then you not only can see what is on your computer's screen, but you can tap and type to control it.

Compose
music.

Stream movies
and television.

Track your
best scores
and challenge
friends.

Play
games.

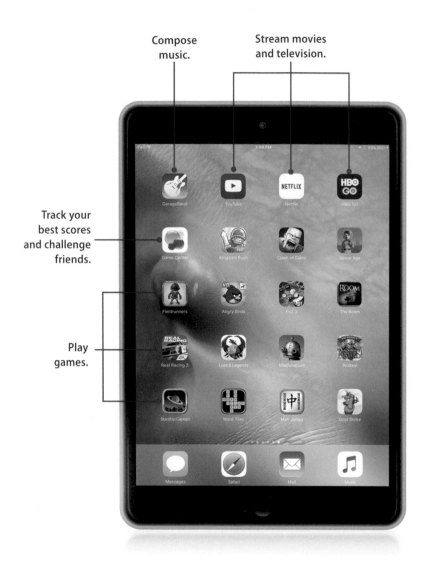

In this chapter, we look at apps that exist for entertainment purposes such as viewing movies, reading comics, listening to music, or playing games.

→ Composing Music with GarageBand
→ Watching Videos with YouTube
→ Watching Movies and TV Shows with Netflix
→ Using Game Center
→ iPad Games and Entertainment

Games and Entertainment

You can view a lot of information and get a lot of work done on the iPad, but it is still a great device for entertainment. The majority of entertainment apps out there are games, but there are also some general entertainment apps that we can take a look at.

Composing Music with GarageBand

It is hard to sum up GarageBand in just a few pages. This brother to the Mac GarageBand application is a very big app. It could almost deserve a book all to itself. Let's look at how to create a simple song.

1. Download and install GarageBand from the App Store. If you already have it, launch it from the home screen. See "Purchasing an App" in Chapter 15 for instructions on how to find and download apps.

2. If this is the first time you are using GarageBand, you can skip to step 3. Otherwise, you will see a list of songs you have created. Tap the + button and then New Song.

3. Now you can choose an instrument to start. Select the keyboard.

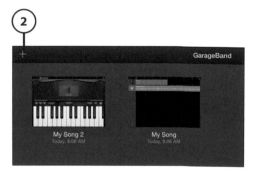

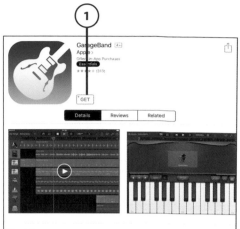

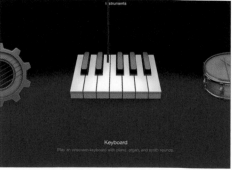

4. Tap the keys to play notes. The force at which you hit the keys and the spot on the key determines the exact sound it produces.

5. Tap the instrument button and swipe left or right to change from Grand Piano to one of dozens of other instruments.

6. Tap the record button to record what you are playing. A metronome will count down, so wait one measure before starting. Try just a few notes, a handful of measures.

7. Tap the Stop button, which appears instead of the Rewind button in this location, when you are done recording.

8. Tap the Undo button if you didn't quite get the notes right. Then try again.

9. After you have recorded a bit of music, the View button appears. You can use that to switch to the Tracks view.

10. In Tracks view, you see the bit of music you recorded. Tap on it once to select it. Tap again to bring up a menu that includes Cut, Copy, Delete, Loop, Split, and Edit. Tap Loop.

11. The music you recorded is now set to loop for the entire section of the song. Tap the Play button to test it.

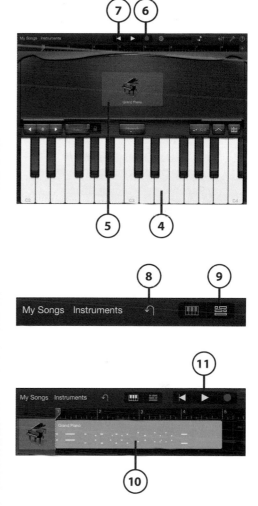

12. Tap the Loop button to view pre-made loops that you can add to your song. Make sure Apple Loops is selected at the top.

13. Tap Instrument to select the type of loop you want to add.

14. Tap an Instrument.

15. Select a loop to test it. You can even have your loop playing at the same time by tapping the Play button at the top and then tapping a loop from the Apple Loops menu to see how they sound together.

16. Drag a loop from the list to the area right under the loop you created.

17. Now you have your original loop and a bass loop. Tap play to hear them together.

You can continue to add loops. Add a bass line and maybe some guitar. You can also double-tap on the left side of each track where you see the image of the instrument, to return to the instrument view and switch instruments or record more notes.

Besides the piano, you can also play guitar, bass, or drums. And each instrument has several variations. Plus, there are smart instruments, such as the smart guitar, that only allow you to play notes and chords that fit well together.

See http://macmost.com/ipadguide/ for more tutorials on using Garage-Band for iPad.

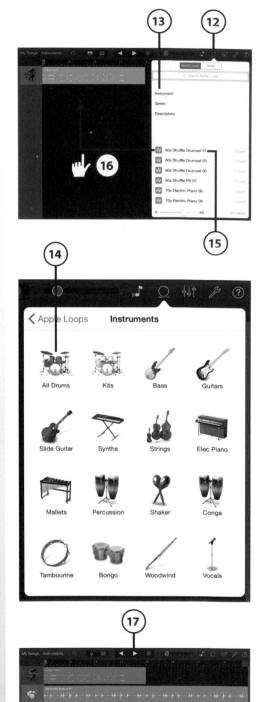

Watching Videos with YouTube

Although you can watch YouTube videos by browsing YouTube.com with Safari, the official YouTube app from Google gives you a dedicated video player for the millions of user-created videos on the service.

1. Search the App Store for the YouTube app for iPad. Tap GET to download and install it.

2. To see more options on YouTube on the same screen, make sure you are in horizontal mode. If you have a Google (Gmail) account, log in to access your playlists and comment on videos. To simply search and view videos, you do not need an account.

3. You see a list of videos recommended by YouTube. Tap the Popular on YouTube button, or any category on the left to see different featured lists.

4. You can tap here to dig down into more YouTube categories.

5. Use the search tool to search for any video on YouTube.

6. Tap a video to view it.

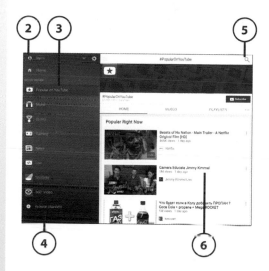

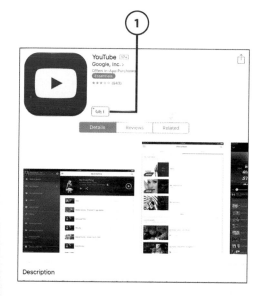

7. As the video plays, tap the middle of the video at any time to bring up playback controls.

8. Use the pause/play button to pause and resume the video.

9. You can tap and drag the circle left and right to move back and forth in the video.

10. Tap the expand button to expand the video to full screen. Then turn your iPad so it is in horizontal orientation to see the video fill the screen.

11. You can add a video to Playlist, Favorites, or the Watch Later list. You need to be signed in to your YouTube account to see this button. You can also share it with friends using email, messages, or social networks.

12. Tap the back button to return to the list, or search results you were looking at before choosing this particular video.

13. You can tap any related video to just go right to it.

14. If you are signed in, you can comment or give a thumbs up or down to the video.

15. Tap Subscribe if you are signed in to add the channel to your subscription list and receive notifications when new videos are added.

>>>Go Further
WHAT ELSE CAN I DO?

Want to contribute? Another app from Google called YouTube Capture lets you record video with your iPad's camera and upload it to YouTube. You can also share your videos from the Photos app or iMovie to YouTube with the Share buttons in those apps. Get ready for your 15 minutes of fame!

Watching Movies and TV Shows with Netflix

Netflix started as a DVD rental service using home delivery by mail rather than retail stores, but it is quickly changing into an online video rental service. One of the first acclaimed apps for the iPad was the Netflix app. Netflix subscribers can use it to rent and watch movies right on their iPads.

1. Search the App Store for the Netflix app. Tap GET to download and install it.

2. After installing Netflix from the App Store, run it and enter your email address and password, and then tap Sign In. If you don't have an account, you can actually sign up for a trial account right on your iPad.

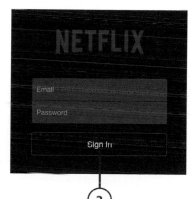

3. If you have an established Netflix account with multiple users, you might get asked which user you are. Select your name. Otherwise, you go right to the main Netflix screen with a list of movies and TV shows. Tap here to see a list of genres.

4. You can also use the Search function to find movies and TV shows.

5. If you are in the middle of watching videos, whether on your iPad or another device where you use Netflix, you have the ability to jump right in and continue watching.

6. When you choose a new video, whether from the front screen or through a search, you are first taken to an information screen. Read information to find out more about it.

7. In this case, the item is actually a TV series, you can scroll down to see a list of episodes. Tap the play button next to an episode to watch it.

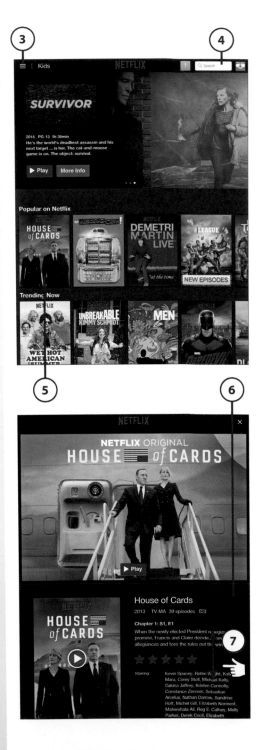

8. The video should start after a few seconds. It plays in horizontal orientation, so you need to turn your iPad on its side. There are Play and Pause controls at the bottom of the screen.

9. After the video starts playing, the controls disappear. To bring up the controls again, tap in the center of the screen. You can double-tap in the center of the screen to enlarge the video, or just turn your iPad sideways for a better view.

10. Use the large slider at the bottom to jump around in the video.

11. Tap the back button to return to the previous screen.

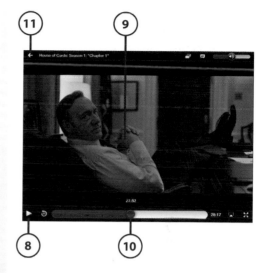

Connection Required

Although watching movies in the Netflix app is unlimited, you can't download and store the movie for later viewing. You need to be online to watch. iTunes rentals, on the other hand, can be stored and watched while offline, like on an airplane flight.

>>>Go Further

MORE STREAMING VIDEO

Netflix is not the only main choice for streaming video. Another app called Amazon Instant Video gives you access to similar content with lots of movies and TV shows. Instead of subscribing to Netflix, you can subscribe to Amazon's service through your Amazon Prime account.

Hulu, another service that streams TV shows and movies, also has an iPad app called Hulu Plus. It works with the same Hulu account that you may already be using to view shows on the Hulu website.

In addition, many TV networks provide their own app that lets you watch videos provided you get that channel through your local cable network or satellite provider. For instance, the app HBO Go lets you watch HBO shows on your iPad after you have proven that you get HBO at home. The separate HBO Now app lets you pay for access to HBO's programming if you don't get HBO at home.

Using Game Center

Apple has created a single unified system for high scores, achievements, and multiplayer gameplay. A large portion of the best games in the App Store have adopted this system, called Game Center.

Your game center account is the same one you use to purchase apps in the App Store. After you use the Game Center app to log in, you won't have to log in directly in any of the games. It all works seamlessly.

1. Tap the Game Center app to launch it. The app comes with your iPad.

2. Enter your Apple ID and password and Sign In.

Game Center

Game Center

Start using Game Center with your Apple ID to play games online with your friends, wherever they are.

Apple ID	name@example.com
Password	Required

3. You see the number of games you have that connect to Game Center. You can also see how many friends you have connected to, how many pending friend requests, and how many challenges your friends have made to you.

4. Tap Friends to see a list of people you have connected with in Game Center. You can challenge them to play a game.

5. Tap Games to see your scores and achievements for each game.

6. In the list of games, you can see your high scores. Tap a game to get more details. At the top of the screen, you see some recommended games based on ones you have played.

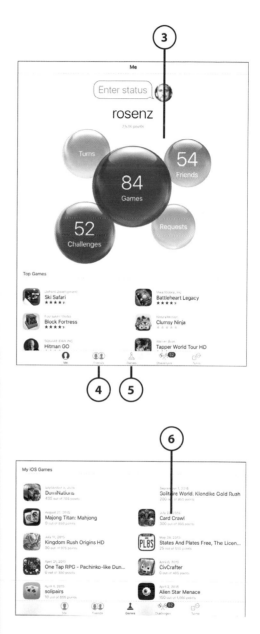

7. You can view a list of the world's best scores and see how you compare. Note that when you appear in the high scores list, you will be listed as "me." Others looking on their iPads see your name.

You can often also see high scores and achievements inside the games themselves, even though they are stored in the Game Center system. You can challenge friends to games or to beat your scores from inside some games.

What's in a Name?

You don't need to use your real name in Game Center. If you go into the Settings app and select Game Center on the left, you can examine your Game Center Profile settings. You can pick any nickname you want, and that will be used in the Game Center high score lists. You can choose to have your real name visible or private in your Game Center profile.

iPad Games and Entertainment

Even if you purchased your iPad to stay connected, get work done, or watch videos, you might want to check out the rich and wonderful world of games.

With the touch screen and accelerometer control, the iPhone and iPod touch turned out to be fertile ground for game developers. Add to that the large screen and fast processor of the iPad and you have a powerful and unique gaming device.

Let's take a look at some of the best games for the iPad.

Kingdom Rush

A major genre of touch device gaming is tower defense. In these games, you build defensive structures to stand up against a never-ending onslaught of enemy troops. The most popular in this group right now is Kingdom Rush.

The enemies come down the road and head for your kingdom. You place towers of various sorts on the road to stop them. You are fighting orcs, goblins, trolls, wizards, and demons with your archers, sorcerers, and cannons. Also check out **Field Runners** and **GeoDefense**.

Blockheads

Another type of game that is picking up steam recently is the sandbox game. This is where you explore and build a randomly generated world of blocks. The genre got its start with Minecraft, but 2D games like Blockheads appeal to a wider audience and work very well on a touch screen.

In Blockheads, you mine deep into the ground and explore the vast surface of a colorful world. The materials you collect can be used to build tools and houses. You can play on your own or with friends online. Also check out **Terraria** for similar game with a more sci-fi feel.

Machinarium

There are many adventure games for the iPad. Some feature gorgeous graphics and challenging gameplay like Machinarium. You move from screen to screen, solving puzzles. A story slowly reveals itself.

Also look for other popular adventure games like **Monkey Island 2 Special Edition, Superbrothers: Sword & Sworcery, The Bard's Tale**, and **Broken Sword: Director's Cut**.

Where's My Water

Some of the best iPad games have premises that are a little bizarre. For instance, Disney's Where's My Water game has you digging in the dirt to let water flow down to some pipes so an alligator can take a bath. Yes, that's the game.

But what makes this crazy game so good is the realism—at least how realistically the water flows as you swipe through the environment. Each level presents a more difficult challenge. You can buy new packs of levels that tell stories as in-app purchases.

Cut the Rope

Another strange premise is needing to cut ropes to swing candy into a monster's mouth. This time the physics puzzle is about the way the ropes react as you cut them. Not only do you need to break the ropes in the right places, but you need to be quick so you do it at the right time.

Cut the Rope has a free version with ads and a paid version without. Each level presents new challenges, such as puffs of air and spiders that crawl on the ropes.

Harbor Master HD

One of the new game genres that appeared on the iPhone was the draw-to-direct type of game. It first appeared with a game called Flight Control, which is also available on the iPad.

Harbor Master HD takes the genre a little further. The idea is you direct ships into docks by drawing with your finger. Simply draw a line from the ship to the dock and the ship follows the path.

The game gets harder as you go along, with more and more ships unloading cargo and then sailing away. You have to make sure the ships find a dock and that they never collide.

Angry Birds HD

Many people purchase games to play on an iPad. But some people buy an iPad to play a game. When that is the case, the game responsible is usually Angry Birds HD.

In this game, you shoot birds at a structure using a slingshot. Your goal is to destroy the pigs living in the building. Sounds a bit strange, but behind the premise is a good physics simulation that presents challenges with every level. And it has also spawned some sequels, like **Angry Birds Seasons HD**, **Angry Birds Rio**, **Angry Birds Space HD**, and **Angry Birds Star Wars HD**.

Plants vs. Zombies HD

Zombies are attacking your house, and you need to defend it. So, what do you use? Strange mutant fighting plants, of course.

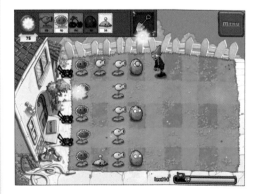

It sounds weird, and it is. But as a fun strategy game, it works. It plays like a tower-defense style game but with fun elements that you find in those $20 PC game downloads. Plus, if you like it, there is a sequel: **Plants vs. Zombies 2**.

Scrabble for iPad

There are thousands of word games for the iPad, and one of the best is one of the original word board games, Scrabble. Not only can you play against a tough computer opponent, a friend on Facebook, or your local network, but you can also play against a friend in the same room, using your iPhones.

You just both download the Tile Rack app for the iPhone and then use the iPad as the main game board; your tiles appear only on your iPhones. Another popular word game to check out is **Words With Friends**.

Temple Run 2

The original Temple Run spawned an entire genre of iOS apps called "endless runners." The character you control in the game runs forward at full speed. All you do is control whether the character jumps, slides, turns left, or turns right.

It sounds pretty simple, and when you start you only last for a few seconds. This leads to wanting to try it again and again to improve your score. Before you know it, you'll be making impossibly long runs and challenging your friends on Game Center. There are some other variations you can search for, such as **Temple Run: Brave** and **Temple Run: Oz**. An excellent game in the same basic genre is **Pitfall!**

The Room

Here's a mystery puzzle game with beautiful graphics. You manipulate objects in a room using natural gestures to solve puzzles. As you progress, a story unfolds.

You need to explore the small 3D game environment in order to notice tiny clues and interpret messages. It is a slow-paced game for those who like to think instead of furiously tap and swipe. Anyone who is a fan of old-style games like Myst will like this game.

Gold Strike

I'll go ahead and mention two of my own games here. Gold Strike was first a web-based game, then a PC game, and then an iPhone game. Once you try it, you'll see that it was really an iPad game all along, just waiting for the iPad to come along.

You tap groups of blocks to remove them before the mine fills up. Gold blocks give you points, and the larger the group, the more points you get. The iPad version also includes some game variations for extended play.

Just Mah Jongg Solitaire

Tile-matching games have been around for a while, but they seem to have been made for the iPad. The combination of touch and a large, bright screen make it perfect for these games.

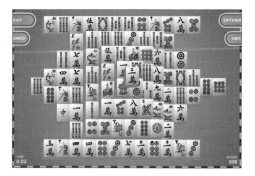

Just Mah Jongg Solitaire includes different tiles sets and layouts. You can play the standard Mah Jongg matching game, or use a set like Halloween or Egyptian Nile tiles for variety. One key feature of the game is that it creates solvable arrangements. Although ultimately solving a layout is up to you and the choices you make while playing, every game you play has at least one solution.

You can check out all of the author's iPad games at http://clevermedia.com/ipadgames/.

**Extend your iPad with printers,
cases, connectors, and keyboards.**

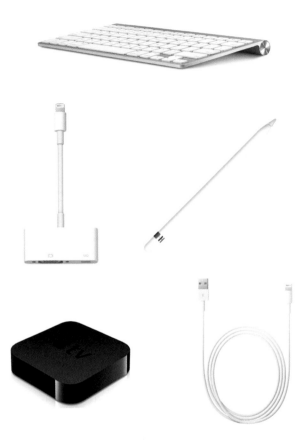

In this chapter, we look at some optional accessories like printers, video adapters, keyboards, headphones, and cases.

→ Printing from Your iPad

→ AirPlay Mirroring with Apple TV

→ Video Output Adapters

→ Using Wireless Keyboards

→ Importing Photos with SD Card and USB Adapters

→ Charging Your iPad with Power Accessories

→ Listening with EarPods

→ Protecting Your iPad

→ iPad Pro Accessories

iPad Accessories

Many accessories available for your iPad perform a variety of tasks, protect it, or just make it look pretty.

You might already have some things that work with your iPad— printers and wireless keyboards, for instance. Let's look at a variety of accessories to see how to use them.

Printing from Your iPad

You can print from your iPad without connecting any cables. Apple calls this function AirPrint. You can print a web page or document directly from your iPad over your wireless network.

The one catch? It works only with printers that support AirPrint. Fortunately, the list is growing fast and now includes printers by many companies. You can find an updated list of AirPrint printers at http://support.apple.com/kb/HT4356.

Printing from the Notes App

Assuming you have one of these printers and have set it up on your local network, here's how you print, using the Notes app as an example.

1. In the Notes app, with the note you want to print open, tap the Share button.

2. Tap Print.

3. Listed next to Printer you will see the name of the last printer you used, as long as the iPad is still connected through the network to this printer. But if you have never printed before, or the printers available have changed, you need to tap Select Printer.

4. If the printer is on and has been configured to your network, it should appear in a list. Tap it to select it.

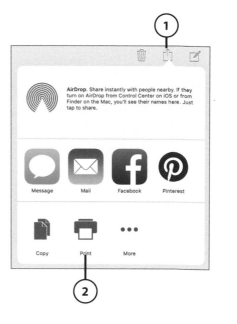

5. The printer name will now appear. You can tap its name again to select a different printer.

6. If there are any options to select, you will see them listed. If there is more than one, you may simply see an Options button—if you tap that, it expands to show all the options. In this case, there is more than one page, so a range of pages can be chosen. Plus, the printer can be switched between color and black and white.

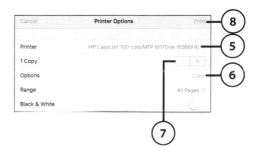

7. Tap the -/+ buttons to set the number of copies to print, or leave it at 1 Copy.

8. Tap the Print button to send to the printer.

   At this point, your iPad will launch a special Printer Center app. You may not notice it unless you quickly double-press the Home button to bring up the list of apps. You will then see this Print Center app running as the left-most app in the list. If your document is small and your printer is fast, it may print so quickly that you will never catch the Print Center app running.

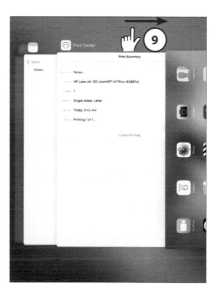

9. Double-press the Home button to bring up the list of apps currently running on your iPad. Swipe to look through the apps. You should see a Print Center app. If you are just printing one page and your network and printer are fast, it could appear and disappear before you even get a chance to see or select it.

10. Tap the Print Center icon.

11. You can see the status of the printing process and other information.

12. Tap Cancel Printing to stop printing.

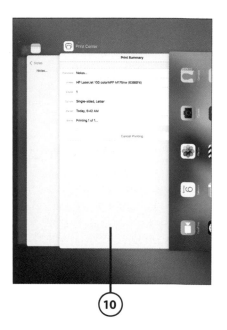

	Print Summary
Document	Notes...
Printer	HP LaserJet 100 colorMFP M175nw (63B6F4)
Copies	1
Options	Single-sided, Letter
Finished	Today, 6:43 AM
Status	Finished
	Cancel Printing

Different for Other Apps

How you initiate printing differs from app to app. Using Pages, for example, you go to the Tools button at the top of the screen and select Share and Print. You see Print as one of the options. But for most apps, you initiate printing by looking for a Print option in the Share button that looks like a box with an arrow pointing up.

Printing When You Can't Print

Not all apps include the ability to print. But that doesn't mean you can't print what you see on the screen. Just capture the screen by pressing the sleep/wake button and home button simultaneously (see "Capturing the Screen" in Chapter 9). Then, go to the Photos app and look in your Camera Roll for the new image. You can print that image using the Share button in the Photos app.

Bypassing Apple's AirPrint

Although not all Wi-Fi printers support AirPrint, there is a way to cheat. Some enterprising third-party developers have come up with software for desktop computers that sets up a printer connected to the computer as an AirPrint printer. You aren't really printing directly to a printer—you are going through the computer. Still, it may be a good option for some. Search on the web for the Printopia (Mac), handyPrint (Mac), or Presto (PC).

AirPlay Mirroring with Apple TV

The Apple TV may be the best iPad accessory of them all. It enables you to display the screen of the iPad on a high definition television. And it does this wirelessly, using the local Wi-Fi network and something called AirPlay mirroring.

Setting Up AirPlay

You need to make sure several things are in place before you can use Air-Play Mirroring.

1. Make sure that both your iPad and Apple TV are connected to the same local network.

2. Make sure both your iPad and Apple TV are up-to-date. Using older or mismatched versions of software on the devices could prevent AirPlay from working.

3. Turn on AirPlay on your Apple TV. To do this, go into Settings, AirPlay, and turn it on.

Apple TV

4. On your iPad, swipe from the bottom of the screen up to bring up the Control Center. See "Using Control Center" in Chapter 1.

5. Tap the AirPlay button. Note that it will only appear if you have at least one AirPlay device, such as an Apple TV, connected to your network and enabled.

6. Select which Apple TV you want to mirror the iPad's screen.

7. When you want to stop mirroring, repeat steps 4 and 5, but select iPad to turn off AirPlay mirroring.

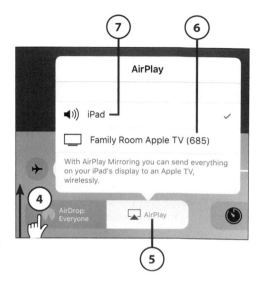

The Apple TV is a worthwhile device to have just for the ability to use AirPlay to show your iPad on a TV screen. However, you also get many other great features such as iTunes movie rentals, YouTube, Netflix, and many other video and gaming apps, depending on your specific Apple TV model.

The Mirror Crack'd

Some apps won't mirror to Apple TV at all. Certain video streaming apps have purposely restricted mirroring due to licensing issues and other reasons. So you might not be able to mirror when using apps from certain cable networks.

>>>Go Further
MORE ABOUT AIRPLAY

Mirroring your iPad's screen through an Apple TV is just one of many functions of AirPlay. You can also find AirPlay buttons in other apps, such as the Music app and other third-party audio apps. You can send just the audio stream from these apps to Apple TV to play music through your TV or home theater system.

You can also get audio-only AirPlay devices, such as Apple's own Airport Express base station and many small speaker systems and home theater attachments. These devices will appear when you try to use AirPlay from an audio app.

You can also use the Bluetooth ability of your iPad to send audio from some apps to wireless speakers. Check out http://store.apple.com/us/ipad/ipad-accessories/speakers for Apple's list of audio devices that use either AirPlay or Bluetooth to connect to your iPad.

Video Output Adapters

In addition to using an Apple TV to wirelessly mirror your iPad's screen to a TV or projector, you can also use one of two cables to directly connect your iPad to a screen.

There are two models. One is for VGA connections, such as you may find on many boardroom and classroom projectors. The other is an HDMI connector, which works for most HD televisions produced in the last few years. However, you will find televisions with VGA connectors and projectors with HDMI connectors. Check your device first before purchasing one of the two adapters. If you have both types of connections, get the adapter for the more modern and versatile HDMI connection.

Apple's Lightning Digital AV Adapter   **Apple's Lightning to VGA Adapter**

Both adapters have a Lightning connector on the one end that plugs into the bottom of your iPad. The other end has either the HDMI or VGA connector, plus a port to connect a Lightning cable. This is for connecting your iPad's power adapter so your iPad is receiving power at the same time it is sending the video signal to the TV or projector.

You don't need to use this Lightning port—you can run your iPad on its battery while connected to the screen. However, connecting your iPad to AC power prevents your battery from draining and your iPad from running out of power while you are presenting. Wouldn't want to have to stop your presentation just before the slide where you ask the board members for money, would you?

1. Connect the adapter to the dock port on your iPad.

2. Connect the other end of the adapter to a standard HDMI or VGA cable. You cannot hook the adapters directly to a TV or projector because they have female connectors. A male-to-male connector bridges the gap between the adapter and the TV or projector, just like it would if you were connecting to a laptop computer.

3. Connect the other end of the cable to a monitor or projector that accepts either HDMI or VGA.

4. If you are using the VGA adapter and also want audio, then use an audio mini jack to connect the headphone port of the iPad to the line in the projector. The exact type of cable you need depends on what audio input the projector takes.

5. At this point, the video on the projector or monitor should mirror that of the iPad. Some apps may show different things on the iPad's screen and the external display. For example, Keynote will show the presentation on the external display, while you have the presentation plus controls on the iPad's screen.

TV Compatibility

The video coming from the iPad is compatible with both 720p and 1080p HD televisions and video devices. It also includes audio over the HDMI cable. Many televisions support only 1080i, not 1080p. In that case, the video may be shown in 720p instead.

No Lightning?

If you are using a first-, second-, or third-generation iPad, you have a 30-pin dock connector at the bottom instead of a Lightning connector. These two adapters won't work with your older iPad, but you can still find the old 30-pin versions of these adapters if you search online retailers.

Using Wireless Keyboards

If you have a lot of typing to do and are sitting at a desk anyway, you can use Apple's wireless keyboard with your iPad. This is the same wireless keyboard that you would use with a Mac. You can also use just about any other Bluetooth-compatible wireless keyboard.

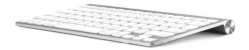

Apple Wireless Keyboard

Choosing the Right Wireless Keyboard

If you have an older Apple wireless keyboard, it might not work with your iPad. The Apple Store warns that only "newer" keyboards can successfully connect to the iPad. Reports from people with older wireless keyboards indicate that this is true. However, you don't need to stick with Apple's wireless keyboard. Most Bluetooth keyboards work fine with the iPad. Search your favorite online store for all kinds of compact wireless Bluetooth keyboards. Check reviews to see if anyone has mentioned trying the model with an iPad. If you are having trouble connecting to a keyboard or any Bluetooth wireless device, Apple has some troubleshooting tips at http://support.apple.com/kb/TS4562.

1. To connect to the Apple Wireless Keyboard, first make sure you have good batteries in it (not shown).

2. Tap the Settings app on your iPad and tap Bluetooth.

3. In the Bluetooth settings screen, make sure Bluetooth is turned on. Switch it on if not.

4. Turn on your Apple Wireless Keyboard by pressing the button on its right side. You should see a small green light turn on at the upper-right corner of the main face of the keyboard.

5. After a second or two, the keyboard should appear on your iPad screen. Tap where you see Not Paired on the iPad screen.

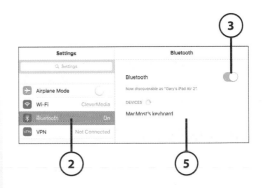

6. Look for a 4-digit number in the message displayed. Type that on your keyboard. Then press the Return key.

7. After the connection is established, you should see Connected next to the name of your keyboard.

8. After you connect, the iPad automatically uses the physical keyboard by default, rather than bringing up the on-screen keyboard (not shown). To use the on-screen keyboard again, you can either disconnect or power off your Apple Wireless Keyboard, or you can press the Eject button at the upper-right corner of the keyboard to switch to the on-screen keyboard at any time.

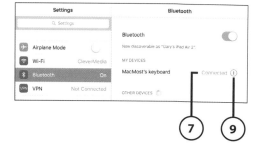

9. If you want to disconnect the keyboard so it is no longer paired with your iPad, tap the i button, and then tap Forget this Device.

>>>Go Further
SPECIAL KEYS

The Apple wireless keyboard was not made for the iPad—it existed first. But the iPad recognizes many special keys on it and uses those keys in various ways.

- **Brightness (F1 and F2):** Changes the brightness of the iPad screen.

- **Volume (F10, F11, and F12):** Mutes, lowers, and raises the volume.

- **Eject (to the right of F12):** Brings up or dismisses the on-screen keyboard.

- **Arrows:** Navigates around in editable text.

- **Arrows+Shift:** Selects editable text.

- **Command:** Can be used with X, C, and V for cut, copy, and paste inside editable text.

- **Command+Z:** In many writing apps, you can use this to undo, just like when typing on a desktop computer.

- **Audio Playback Keys (F7, F8, and F9):** Goes to previous track, play/pause, and next track.

- **Command+Space:** Starts a Spotlight search, just as if you were on the Home screen and swiped down from the middle of the screen.

Importing Photos with an SD Card and USB Adapters

Apple sells two adapters that can be used to connect your camera to your iPad. The first is a Lightning to SD Card Camera Reader that lets you take an SD card and connect it to your iPad. The second is the Lightning to USB Camera Adapter that lets you plug your camera and other devices directly into your iPad. If you have a 3rd generation or older iPad, you need to get the old Apple iPad Camera Connection Kit which includes both of these adapters, but designed for the 30-pin dock connector, not the Lightning connector.

Here is how to import photos directly from your camera or SD card.

1. Connect either the camera connector or the SD card reader to your iPad's dock port (not shown). Connect your camera using the USB cable that came with it, or slide the SD card into the card reader. If you are connecting a camera, you will most likely need to switch the camera on and into the same mode you use to transfer pictures to a computer.

**Apple Lightning to SD
Card Camera Reader**

2. After a slight delay, the Photos app should launch and images on the camera or card should appear on your iPad's screen. You may need to tap the Import button at the bottom of the screen to see the photos.

3. Tap Import All to import all the photos on the card.

4. Tap the Delete All button if you want to delete the images without ever importing them into your iPad.

5. If you don't want to import or delete all of the images, tap one or more images to select them.

6. Tap Import.

7. Tap Import Selected to bring in only the selected photos.

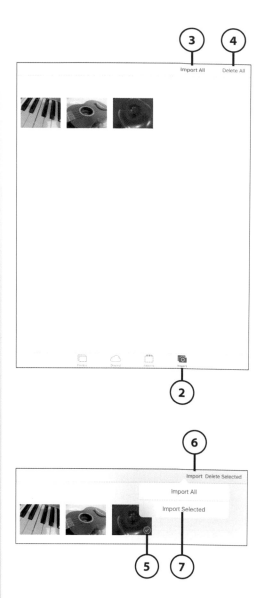

8. After importing the photos, you are given the chance to delete them from the camera or card. Tap Delete to remove them.

9. Tap Keep to leave the images on the camera or card.

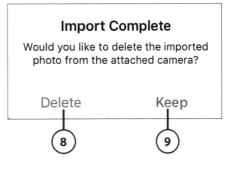

Wirelessly Transfer from Camera to iPad

With the Eye-Fi card (www.eye.fi), you can take pictures with your digital camera and wirelessly transfer them from your camera to your iPad. You can even do this while you are taking more pictures. The card is something you install in your camera that acts like a regular SD card, but it also contains a tiny wireless transmitter. Then you use a free iPad app to connect the card to your iPad. Snap a picture and it appears on your iPad.

Charging Your iPad with Power Accessories

A power user of any gadget usually acquires additional power chargers and cables. For instance, you might want to charge your iPad at home and at work, or even while traveling. Here are some suggestions for accessories that will keep your iPad charged. All of these are available in Apple Stores, the Apple online store, other online retailers, and many computer and electronics stores.

If you travel between two locations, such as home and work, or home and school, then carrying your one and only power adapter with you may be a problem. It is too easy to forget to bring it along.

You can buy a second charger and dock cable from Apple that is the equivalent of the one that came with your iPad. Alternatively, the iPad Dock from Apple enables you to stand the iPad up vertically while it's either plugged in to a power outlet or docked with your computer. You can also use the iPad in this position and even pipe the audio into external speakers through the dock.

Here is a list of items you might want to consider:

- **Apple Lightning to USB cable**: An extra dock cable to plug your iPad into a Mac or PC for syncing and slow charging. Many cars and some public places like airports now have USB outlets that you can use with this cable or the one that came with your iPad. It is always good to have a spare cable, as losing your only one means you can't charge your iPad. If you have a 3rd generation or older iPad, you need the old 30-pin dock connector instead of this Lightning cable.

- **Apple iPad 12W USB power adapter**: A 12-watt adapter that charges the iPad at full speed, faster than a standard USB port. This doesn't come with a cable, so if the plan is to have a complete set of power adapters and cables in two locations, make sure you pick up the aforementioned USB cable too.

**Apple iPad 12W
USB power adapter**

- **Car Charger**: You can find car USB phone chargers very cheap at superstores and online, and then use your own Lightning cable to connect your iPad. Make sure that the device outputs at least 10 watts of power, or it will charge your iPad slowly or not at all. Apple doesn't have an official car charger, but it sells several third-party brands in the Apple Store.

Incase High Speed Mini Car Charger

- **External Battery**: If your needs are extreme, and the 10+ hour normal battery life of your iPad isn't enough, you can shop for an external battery pack. They all work by charging them up before you leave home, and then you plug your iPad into them with your Lightning cable. The iPad thinks it is getting power from a wall charger—it doesn't care that it is a battery pack instead. Apple sells some in its store that can add a few more hours, or even as much as a full charge, to your iPad.

Not All Power Is the Same

Your iPad requires extra power to charge properly. With the power supply that came with your iPad, a 10- or 12-watt model, it should charge fully after about 4 hours. But with a smaller 5-watt iPhone power supply, or while hooked up to a standard 6-watt USB port on a computer, it takes twice that amount of time. Some low-power USB ports on computers won't charge the iPad at all.

Listening with EarPods

Although you can use any standard earphones with your iPad, the official Apple EarPods headphones come with a controller on the cord that gives you additional functionality.

You don't get a set of EarPods when you buy an iPad, but you do get a set when you buy a new iPhone or iPod, so you may already have these. You can also purchase them separately from Apple in Apple Stores and online.

In addition to the controls, the EarPods have a microphone that usually gives you better quality recording than using the one on the body of the iPad, which is typically farther from your mouth. It is a good idea to use the EarPods mic when making FaceTime or Skype calls, or recording using audio apps.

Here's what you can do with the controller on the EarPods while you have music playing with the Music app. These also work in many third-party music apps and even audiobook players. You don't need to have the audio app on the screen, or even your iPad unlocked to use these. The audio just needs to be playing.

1. Press the + button to raise the volume.

2. Press the – button to lower the volume.

3. Press the center button once quickly to pause the music. Press again to resume.

4. Press the center button twice quickly to skip to the next song. If you hold the second press, the current song will fast-forward until you release.

5. Press the center button three times quickly to go to the previous song. If you hold the third press, the current song will rewind until you release.

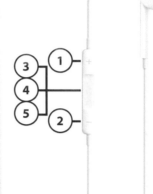

Apple EarPods with Remote and Mic

EarPod Alternatives

The EarPods are not only inexpensive, but regarded as pretty high quality. However, if you do prefer other headphones, note that they usually do not come with controls on the cord. Sometimes you will find only the volume controls, and other times you will find all three buttons—but the center button only serves to pause music and won't perform other actions.

>>>*Go Further*

MORE FUN WITH EARPODS

FaceTime: If you get an incoming FaceTime call while the EarPods are connected, you can press the center button to answer the call. To decline the call, hold the button down for a few seconds.

Siri: You can also use the center button to activate Siri. Just press and hold the center button for a few seconds until Siri appears. Then the microphone on the EarPods comes in handy so you can talk to Siri through it as well.

Camera: What? There's a camera in your EarPods headphones? No. But you can use the + button on the cord to trigger taking a photo with the Photos app. It works just like the onscreen camera button. You can also use the volume up button on the side of the iPad. This allows you to take a photo while not physically holding your iPad.

Protecting Your iPad

Most iPad users buy something to protect their iPad. Protection ranges from large impact- and weather-resistant cases to thin screen coverings. Some users even buy multiple cases to use in different situations.

iPad Smart Cover and Smart Case

A cover is just a cover, right? But Apple didn't make "just a cover" for the iPad. They made a "smart cover." By using magnets, this cover sticks to the front of the iPad without hiding the rest of the iPad's design. And it is highly functional, acting as a stand as well. It does not, however, work with the original iPad.

Compatibility

The covers discussed here also do not work with the iPad Pro. I cover the iPad Pro in the later section, "iPad Pro Accessories."

The Smart Cover also performs two other functions. First, your iPad can detect when it is closed or opened. You can turn this option on or off by going to the Settings app, under General settings, and looking for the Lock/Unlock option.

Another function your Smart Cover performs is to clean the screen. The material on the inside of the cover gently wipes the screen each time you open and close the cover. Your screen might still need a good wipe-down with a soft cloth every once in a while, but the Smart Cover does keep it a little neater.

The Smart Case is basically the same as the Smart Cover, but it includes a cover for the back of the iPad as well and only fits the full-size iPad. You can get the Smart Cover in several colors made from either polyurethane or leather material.

The iPad Air Smart Case

Protective Covers

Instead of the Smart Cover, or in addition to it, you may want to get a protective cover for your iPad. The problem here is not finding one, but choosing from the hundreds of models already available.

Some covers cover only the back and sides of the iPad, leaving the screen open. Often these covers work in conjunction with an Apple Smart Cover, allowing you to use both at the same time.

The advantage of a cover over a case is that the cover stays on the iPad while you use it. So if you drop your iPad while trying to use it, the cover provides some protection.

Protective Cases

A case or sleeve, on the other hand, is something you would put your iPad inside of in order to protect it while not using the iPad. Then you would take the iPad out to use it.

Some cases fit loosely enough to allow you to also put a cover on the iPad, giving double the protection. There are also many products that are between a cover and a case, offering the protection of a case, but allowing you to still use the iPad without taking it out—at least to a certain extent. Some manufacturers use the terms "cover" and "case" interchangeably.

When looking for a case, there are many things to consider. Don't just look in a local Apple Store—it stocks only a few cases. Look online to discover a wide variety. Pick one that fits your needs and style.

Size Matters

Remember that each version of the iPad is physically different. They are slightly different dimensions and thicknesses. The port on the bottom and the locations of the buttons are different as well, which means some cases may not have a properly sized or aligned opening. Check the product carefully to make sure you are getting one that fits your device.

A Keyboard and a Cover

Some covers and cases combine protection with a keyboard. They allow you to unfold the cover so the iPad, and a keyboard built into the case, resemble a small laptop computer. If you like using an external keyboard, and want to carry the keyboard around with your iPad, this may be the best setup.

iPad Pro Accessories New!

The iPad Pro has two unique accessories that you can get from Apple that help you interact with the iPad. These currently don't work on other iPads, but in the future Apple may come out with variations for future iPads with smaller screens.

Apple Pencil

The Apple Pencil for the iPad Pro

The Apple Pencil is a stylus for the iPad Pro. It allows artists to use the iPad Pro as a canvas. You can draw using Apple's tools, such as the drawing tools in Pages. You can also draw using third-party apps like Paper by FiftyThree, mentioned in Chapter 16.

The Pencil senses where the tip of the pencil hits the iPad's touch screen. It also knows the amount of force you are applying and the angle you are holding the Pencil.

Although it is easy to see why an artist may want to use an Apple Pencil, it can also be useful for non-artists. For instance, you can use it with Microsoft Office apps to mark up a document with notes and symbols.

Smart Keyboard

Apple's Smart Keyboard for the iPad Pro

What makes the Smart Keyboard from Apple different from other keyboards for the iPad is the use of a special surface port on the iPad's side. When you magnetically attach the Smart Keyboard to the iPad Pro, it not only connects to the main body firmly, but it also transfers data and a small amount of power through the surface.

This means that the Smart Keyboard doesn't need to be connected via Bluetooth like other keyboards. It also means it doesn't need a battery because it gets its power from the iPad.

Typing on the Smart Keyboard may also feel better for you than on most other keyboards that work with the iPad. This is because Apple uses the same hardware found in the most recent MacBook.

Keep your apps
up-to-date.

Get tips about
how to use
your iPad.

Find your iPad
if it is lost.

Keep your iPad's
operating system
up-to-date.

As you continue to use your iPad, you might have questions about how to do things and face problems you can't solve. There are many ways to seek advice and help. You should also take steps to secure your iPad against theft.

→ Getting Help on Your iPad

→ Getting Help from Apple

→ Keeping Your iPad Up-To-Date

→ Securing Your iPad

Maintaining Your iPad and Solving Problems

Apple provides excellent support for their products. You can visit one of the Apple Stores for direct hands-on help. Apple also has a place on their website where you can seek out information and communicate with other iPad users. Additionally, there are often ways to get help from inside some apps and buy using the iOS Tips app included on your iPad.

Getting Help on Your iPad

The Tips app offers general advice on using your iPad. Some apps include extensive help information inside the app.

Using the Tips App

The Tips app offers bits of useful advice about using your iPad. It does this by presenting a single tip on a screen, along with a graphic or animation.

Tips

1. Tap the Tips app icon on your home screen.

2. The first time you use it, you need to tap Start Learning to begin.

3. Each screen has a single tip.

4. Tap the list button to see a table of contents.

5. Swipe to the left to go to the next tip.

6. You can share the tips by sending a link to the tip view Messages or email. Each link goes to the same tip at Apple's http://tips.apple.com website.

Updates

Apple should be updating the Tips app with new tips on a regular basis. So check back every so often to see what is there and learn something new. You might also get notifications from Apple when new items appear in the Tips app.

Tips

Get the most from iOS 9 with these tips from Apple.

Start Learning

Ask Siri to find those vacation photos

You can ask Siri to find photos taken at a certain time or location.

Like

1 of 4

Getting Help Inside Apps

Many third-party apps have how-to and help information inside them. Where to find it and how to use it depends on how the app developer designed the app. Pay careful attention to the buttons and navigation toolbars inside of apps to look for this information.

For instance, let's take a look at Pages. It has both a help overlay system, which gives useful labels to buttons, and extensive documentation.

Pages

1. Tap the Pages icon to open it. Then, open an existing document or start a new one. See Chapter 11, "Writing with Pages," to learn how to start a new document.

2. Tap the ? button at the top right.

3. Help overlays, called "coaching tips," are turned on. The yellow labels appear, pointing to buttons and explaining their use with a few words.

4. A button at the bottom left appears that takes you to the documentation. Tap it.

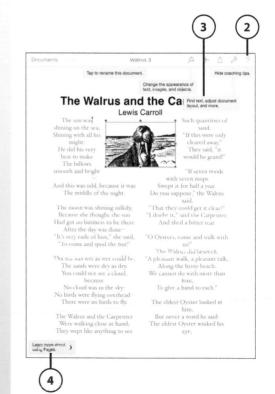

5. Tap a subject to see a list of subtopics.

6. Tap a subtopic to see documentation about it.

7. You can read about the particular subtopic.

8. Tap the list button to return to the table of contents.

9. Tap the search button to search for keywords in the documentation.

10. Tap Done to close the documentation window.

External Documentation

Many app developers put documentation on their websites. Be sure to look for links to this inside the app, but also use the App Store to find the name of the developer and search for his or her website. Sometimes the App Store listing includes a direct link to the website. Developers may not include documentation, but may instead have instructional videos or support forums that may help.

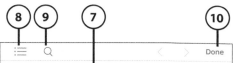

Getting Help from Apple

Apple offers various support options. You can visit an Apple Store, or ask a question online. Your iPad comes with a warranty, which you can extend for up to two years.

Visiting the Genius Bar

One of the most straightforward and easy ways to get help from Apple is to use the Genius Bar. This is an area inside every retail Apple Store. If you have an Apple Store at a nearby mall, then you have a Genius Bar there, too.

Although you can walk into the store and ask for an appointment, you usually have to wait a while, or come back later. It is easier to make an appointment online at Apple's site, and then show up at the appointed time.

Appointments at the Genius Bar are free. You don't need to be covered by a warranty or even have bought your iPad at that store. All you need is to have a question about an Apple product. If you have a question about your iPad, whether if it's about how to do something or if you think it is broken, you should bring your iPad with you.

Note that the process for making an appointment at the Genius Bar has changed many times in the last few years. The following steps may vary somewhat if Apple changes them again.

Making Appointments

If the nearest Apple Store is too far away to make a drop-by visit practical, you're best off using Apple's online troubleshooting; if it doesn't work, make an appointment in advance. Start by going to http://www.apple.com/support/ipad/contact/.

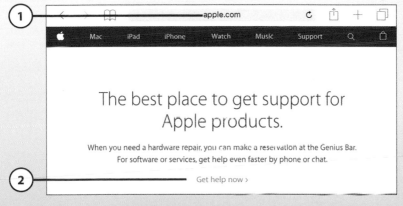

1. Go to http://www.apple.com/retail/geniusbar/to start making your appointment. You can do this on your iPad, computer, or anything with a web browser.

2. Tap on the Get Help Now link. Apple takes you through a series of screens to see if your problem can be solved without a Genius Bar visit before you can make a reservation.

3. Select the product you are concerned about, in this case your iPad.

4. Select the appropriate category. For instance, if your iPad's screen has cracked, tap Service Requests & Troubleshooting.

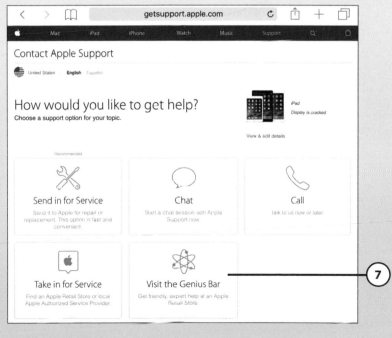

5. You can enter your phone number or email address here, and Apple might try to help you via text message or email. If you know you want to go to the Genius Bar, you can skip this step.

6. Tap No thanks, Continue.

7. Tap Visit the Genius Bar.

8. Tap here to enter your location, or leave it at "Current location." This address is used to find your closest Apple Store.

9. Tap here to select your specific iPad model.

10. Tap Go.

11. Select an Apple Store from the list.

12. Tap Choose Store.

13. Tap the block of time when you want to make the appointment.

14. Tap Continue.

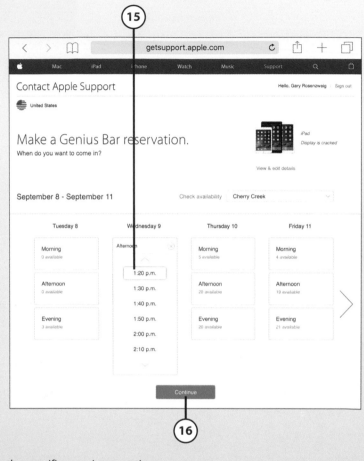

15. Tap the specific appointment time you want.

16. Tap Continue.

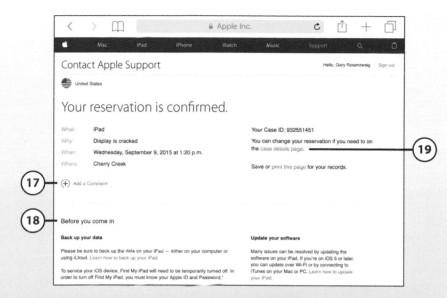

17. You can add a comment to your reservation, such as a short description of what you will be asking about. This isn't required, however.

18. Pay careful attention to the instructions. In particular, note that it asks you to back up your device. In the event that something is wrong with your iPad, you may have to turn it in for repairs or possibly be given a replacement. If so, all your data may be lost. But if you back up your iPad to your computer using iTunes, you can use iTunes to restore your device to its previous state. See "Back It Up!" in Chapter 3.

19. You can view your appointment by tapping "case details page." This gives you the option to reschedule or cancel an appointment.

What if My iPad Is Broken?

If your iPad has stopped working or isn't functioning properly and you think it might need to be replaced, the Genius Bar should be your first stop. If they determine it needs to be replaced or repaired, they can start that process for you. Although the initial appointment at the Genius Bar is free, repairs may cost you, depending on whether you are still covered by Apple's warranty. See "Extending Your Apple Warranty," later in this chapter.

Asking a Question Online

What if your question isn't critical or urgent? You can always tap into the huge community of iPad users by asking a question on Apple's discussion forums.

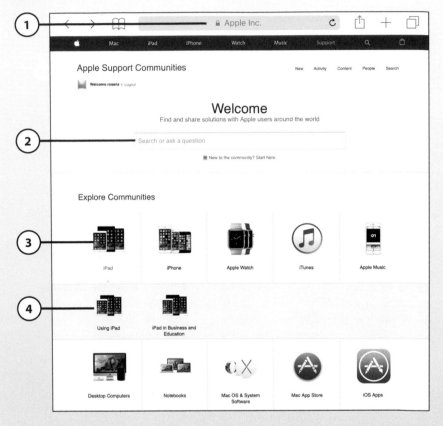

1. Using the web browser on your iPad, or any computing device, go to http://discussions.apple.com. The first time you are there, you are asked to create a user name. This is displayed on any questions you ask or comments you make.

2. You can jump right in and search.

3. However, you can find iPad-related answers more easily if you tap iPad first.

4. Then, tap Using iPad, unless your question has to do with business or educational uses for the iPad, in which case tap iPad in Business and Education. You can go directly to this page with the URL https://discussions.apple.com/community/ipad/using_ipad.

5. You see a list of recently asked questions. Tap any to view the question and replies others have left.

6. Type some keywords to search the questions asked to see if someone else had the same question you do.

7. You can see a complete list of all matching questions. You should check here first before asking the question yourself.

8. If you do want to ask the question, tap the Submit button to fill out a form with more details.

It's Not All Good

No One from Apple Is Here

The Apple discussion boards are all about users helping users. There are no Apple support personnel answering questions there. It is just other users like yourself, though some may have more experience than you and be able to help.

Another mistake people often make in the discussion boards is to make suggestions or give feedback. There's no guarantee that Apple will see it in the discussion boards. However, there is a place where you can leave suggestions. Go to https://www.apple.com/feedback/ipad.html and fill out the form there. You most likely will not get a response, but someone from Apple will see your feedback; and if others also feel the same way, you just might see a new feature in an upcoming version of iOS or the next iPad.

>>>Go Further

EXTENDING YOUR APPLE WARRANTY

Apple calls their warranty AppleCare. When you buy a new iPad from Apple or an authorized retailer, you get one year of AppleCare, plus 90 days of phone support. You can see the details at http://www.apple.com/support/products/ipad.html.

You can extend your warranty by buying AppleCare+. This gives you two years of AppleCare and two years of phone support. Prices may change, but in 2014 in the U.S., AppleCare+ costs $99. You don't need to buy AppleCare at the same time as your iPad. Currently, you can purchase it any time up to 60 days later.

Typically, you might think that a warranty covers defects, but not accidents. If your iPad stops working through no fault of your own, Apple will replace it. But, what about if you drop it? Then you are out of luck, right?

Actually, AppleCare+ comes with some amount of accident coverage. If you break your iPad, you can get it repaired or replaced for a small fee—currently just $49. Prices and conditions can change, so be sure to check the latest details before you buy AppleCare+.

Keeping Your iPad Up-To-Date

One of the most important things you need to do to keep your iPad running smoothly is to make sure it gets all the latest software updates.

Updating iOS

Apple comes out with regular free updates to iOS. Some are minor updates that fix problems and make your iPad more secure. Others include new features.

Settings

1. Tap the Settings icon on your home screen to open it.

2. Tap General.

3. Tap Software Update.

4. In this space, you should see a message telling you that your version of iOS is up-to-date. Otherwise, you might see a Download and Install button and some instructions that allow you to perform an update.

Your iPad should alert you when an update is available. But it is a good idea to periodically check the Settings app to make sure you didn't miss it.

Updating Apps

You should keep your apps updated as well. Just as with iOS, minor updates will fix problems, and major updates often introduce new features.

1. Tap the App Store icon on your home screen to open it. Note that the number in the red circle indicates that you have some apps that need updating. But even if that red circle is not there, you might want to check anyway—it would force the App Store app to see if there are any updates.

App Store

2. Along the bottom of the screen, look for and tap the Update button.

3. Look for Available Updates. If you don't see it, that means all of your apps are up-to-date.

4. You can tap the Update button to immediately update a single app. If you have a lot of updates but are short on time, you might want to update the apps you know you use right now, and then save the others for a more convenient time.

5. Or, you can update all of the apps using the Update All button.

6. You can also read about apps that have recently been updated. Each update entry includes information from the developer about what is new.

Securing Your iPad

Not only is your iPad valuable, but the information you have on it is valuable as well. If your iPad is lost or stolen, you want to make sure no one gets your information, and that you have a chance of getting your iPad back.

Basic Security Measures

There are four main actions you need to take to secure your iPad and your information.

1. **Set a passcode.** This is covered in "Password Protecting Your iPad" in Chapter 2.

2. **Secure your Apple ID and iCloud account with a strong password.** A strong password means you should not use a word that appears in the dictionary, a name, or a date in any format. Even a combination of those will make it easier for a malicious hacker to break into your iCloud account. Choose a password with random letters and digits, even mixing the case of the letters.

3. **Make sure Find My iPad is turned on, and you know how to use it.** We'll cover that in the next section.

4. **Back up your iPad often.** See "Back It Up!" in Chapter 3. You can back up your iPad to a computer using iTunes. You can also turn on iCloud backups by opening the Settings app, tapping iCloud, and then tapping Backup. There's no reason you can't do both. These options help you restore your documents and settings to a new iPad if the need arises. Of course, using iCloud to store your data, such as with Pages, Numbers, and Keynote, also means that all your documents would be in your iCloud account and accessible to your other devices.

The Apple Two-Step

In addition to setting a strong password for your Apple ID, you want to use Apple's two-step verification system to make it even harder for someone to access your data. See http://support.apple.com/HT204152 to get started.

Using Find My iPad

So what happens if your iPad is missing? Your main tool in dealing with that is the Find My iPad feature built into iOS. It does more than its name suggests: not only can you locate your missing iPad, but you can also remotely wipe all your personal information from it.

Setting Up Find My iPad

Find My iPad should be on by default when you set up your new iPad and sign in with your Apple ID. To check, we'll use the Settings app.

1. Launch Settings.

2. Select iCloud on the left.

3. Check to make sure Find My iPad is turned on. If it isn't, tap it to switch it on. You'll go to a simple screen with an on/off switch to turn it on.

That's it. That is all it takes to add a huge security feature to your iPad. Now let's learn what to do if your iPad is missing.

Settings

Locating a Lost iPad

Now your iPad is missing, and it is time to take action. You can log on to iCloud on any computer, another iPad, or pretty much any device with a browser. In fact, you can use a special Find My iPhone app you can download from Apple in the App Store. It is called Find My iPhone, but it works for iPads and even Macs. If you have an iPhone, or a second iPad, it is worth having this app on both devices so you can use it in case the other goes missing.

In this example, we'll use a computer to log in to iCloud.com.

1. Run the Find My iPhone app, or go to http://icloud.com in a web browser.

2. Sign in with your Apple ID and password.

3. Select Find My iPhone.

4. This is where you keep your fingers crossed. If your iPad has been turned off, wiped by an evil genius, or destroyed in some way, then you might not be able to locate it. But give it a few minutes to try.

5. Whew! None of those happened. There's your iPad on a map. You can zoom in and figure out where the iPad is before going any further. Perhaps you simply left it at a friend's house, in your car, or it fell behind the sofa. Best to be sure.

6. If you tap on the green dot, you get some information in a bubble. You see the name of your iPad and the last time a signal from it was received.

7. Note that you might have more than one device registered with Find My iPhone/iPad/Mac. Select the pull-down menu to focus on only one.

8. Tap the i button to bring up a set of commands.

9. Your first option is to have your iPad play a sound. Even if the volume has been turned down and muted, a sound will play at full volume. Use this if you see that your iPad is somewhere nearby, and you have simply misplaced it.

10. Your second option is to put your iPad into "Lost Mode." This locks it. Since you would have already set a passcode for your iPad, this should be redundant. But you can also use this to display a message on your iPad's screen. This can be useful if you have simply forgotten your iPad in a friendly location, and you want to see if someone has found it and is willing to help you by contacting you.

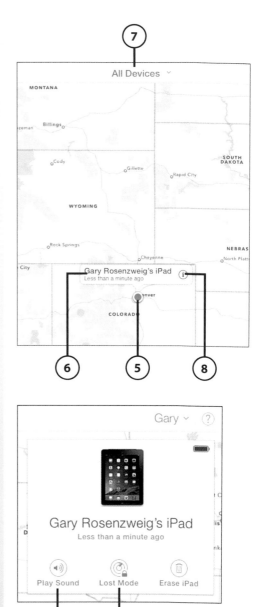

11. The nuclear option is to use Erase iPad. This wipes the memory of your iPad, clearing all your personal information. The downside is that you can no longer track your iPad using Find My iPad. So it is the option to use when you have given up finding it and simply want to secure your information.

Gary's iPad
3 minutes ago

Play Sound   Lost Mode   Erase iPad

(11)

>>>Go Further

YOUR SECRET WEAPON: ACTIVATION LOCK

When you turn on Find My iPad, you are also turning on Activation Lock. This is an iOS feature that prevents anyone else from erasing your iPad and reactivating it with a new Apple ID. You also can't turn off Find My iPad, and thus can't turn off Activation Lock, without your Apple ID and password.

This basically makes your iPad useless to anyone who steals it. They can't unlock it because you have a passcode. They can't wipe it because they don't know your Apple ID and password.

Activation Lock continues to work even after you have used the Erase iPad option of Find My iPad. It is still useless to anyone else without your Apple ID and password. So you get the last laugh, sorta.

It's Not All Good

So Why Would Anyone Steal an iPad?

With Activation Lock, a thief can't use your iPad. So why steal it? There are still reasons why someone would swipe an iPad. First, some people don't turn on Find My iPad or set a passcode. So some thieves might find it worthwhile to steal an iPad, hoping this is true. And even if the iPad is locked, there may still be a way to make a buck from it by selling it for parts.

It's Not All Good

I Found It...Now What?

Say that your iPad was stolen and you've located it. It is probably not a good idea to confront a potential criminal on your own. Call the police. Be sure to tell them that you are able to track the iPad and know exactly where it is. Stories of people doing this are all over the web. Sometimes the police are very helpful, and sometimes a small theft isn't enough to take their attention from larger matters. Most stories seem to end with the police happy to help in a straightforward case of recovering stolen property.

Index

B

E

F

N

O

Q

R

W

X-Y

Z